MORE STUFF YOU CAN USE

Drumming from A to Z:

Written by: Rob Mitzner
Musical Notation: Rob Mitzner
Video Editing: Rob Mitzner
Drums Recorded at C-Room Studio, Brooklyn, NY
Audio Mixing: Charles Burst, Seaside Lounge Studios
Layout Design: Rob Mitzner
Graphic Designer: Ricky Hammerschmidt
Book Editor: Joe Bergamini
Front & Back Cover Photos: Thomas Mester

I0794314

Rob Mitzner is an artist endorser of Yamaha Drums, Vic Firth Sticks, Remo Drumheads, Paiste Cymbals and Low Boy Custom Beaters

YAMAHA

VIC FIRTH THE PERFECT PAIR

REMO

PAISTE

LOW BOY CUSTOM BEATERS

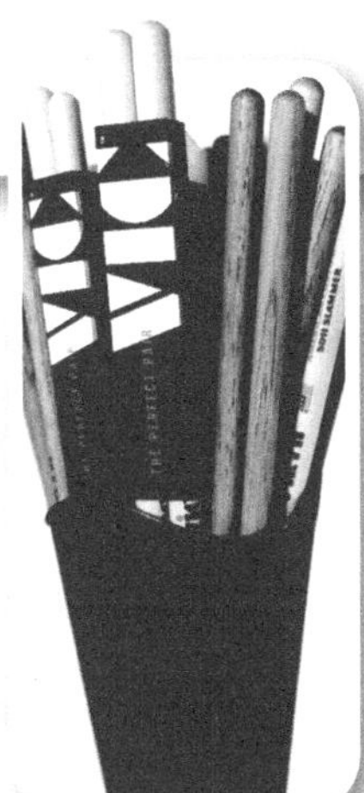

ABOUT THE AUDIO & VIDEO

The QR codes in this book link to the video lessons that go with each song. **Simply scan the codes to view each lesson.**

The audio files are stored in the link above. In this folder you can find four versions of each song: a full performance, minus drums with click, minus drums without click, and the click alone (in case you want to download and mix in your DAW).

To Download Audio and Video for this Book: Go to
halleonard.com/mylibrary
Enter Code: **8143-9785-1341-9172**

HUDSON MUSIC

Table of Contents

MORE!
STUFF YOU
CAN USE

Introduction

Did you ever sit down behind the drums at a rehearsal or gig and one of the other band members asked you to play a groove that you'd never even heard of? As a working musician in New York, this has definitely happened to me and it's not the most pleasant feeling! After the initial dread and angst wears off, you're left with only your own expertise and real-life musical experience to defend yourself. The more music you know, the more you'll be able to play.

However, I've found that it's not quite as simple as mechanically learning one groove in every style and parroting it out when someone asks. Every genre and subgenre of music has a rich history of artists who made bold choices and dared to do something different. Knowing where music came from, who did it first and why it's important can be just as valuable onstage as moving your hands. This is how a good drummer becomes a great musician. If you can back up your technique and feel with years of listening, you'll learn more than just the grooves. You'll learn the musical language.

No matter what style you're playing, you want your grooves and fills to be musically appropriate and not just a couple favorite licks that you cut and paste everywhere. Certain phrasing works fabulously over jazz, Latin or world music, but not as well over rock. Electronic music has its own drumming language, bred from programming. There are even differences within the styles themselves. R&B, soul and gospel drummers played a lot differently in 1960 then they do today and the musical language they use reflects that.

As a drummer, it's important to know all of this and use it to make appropriate musical decisions that reflect the situations you're in. Of course, we all have our favorite phrases and hand/foot combinations that we come back to a lot, but the key is making them sound authentic within the genre we're playing. This is easier said than done. Everyone sounds like themselves when they play, and that's ok! The idea is to diversify your knowledge base enough so that when someone asks for a groove, you have the experience and muscle memory to get the job done and make it believable.

In my first book, *DRUMMING IN A BAND: STUFF YOU CAN USE* (Hudson Music), I covered a variety of musical styles and how to apply them when you're playing in a band with other people. This book is loosely designed as a sequel, but with a slightly different format. I wanted to dive deeper into the history and musical language of each style and discuss bands, artists and drummers who played a pivotal role in creating and moving them forward.

I will admit that when I began writing this book, I was probably not a true "expert" in every one of these styles. There were many where I had a basic understanding of what to play, but not the full history behind them. So, I did my homework and the result has been absolutely thrilling. I feel so much more knowledgeable and prepared than before I started. I read academic works, watched documentaries and listened to more new music than I have since I was a teenager.

If you go through this material with the same voracious energy and thirst for musical growth, you can feel this way too. Learn where the music came from, then take that information, practice it and adapt it to whatever you're doing. **This is the real *Stuff You Can Use*!**

Rob Mitzner

The Rundown

There are 32 styles in this book organized alphabetically with fun and whimsical titles. Each begins with a "chalkboard" that lists the genre and where/when it originated. I've also ranked the difficulty level from 1 (easiest) to 10 (hardest). This number is totally subjective, but I hope it helps you pick and choose what to tackle. This book is designed primarily for intermediate and advanced players with at least two years of playing experience, however there are some grooves suitable for beginners too.

Each chalkboard also includes a list of relevant artists and influential drummers to check out. I highly recommend that you do this! Hearing these folks will give you an invaluable point of reference beyond the play-along tracks (more on those in a minute). Next, I've provided a brief historical recap of each style. This is not meant to be a complete rehashing of every single band, album or drummer that contributed. I'm sure I missed a bunch, and that's ok! I just want to provide a little context and some interesting anecdotes. It's merely a frame for the picture, not the whole painting. If you find a style that really hooks you, I encourage you to seek out more detailed sources and take a deeper dive.

I also made some intentionally unconventional choices in which styles I picked. I wanted to feature some less mainstream subgenres that I felt were musically important and fun to play (and of course, at least one groove for each letter of the alphabet). So, you might find some things you've never seen in a drum book before, and I think that's awesome! Some sections are primary musical genres, some are subgenres or offshoots, while others are simply homages to a drummer, artist or musical moment in time.

Once you dig in, you'll find the grooves themselves plus variations, fills and musical language. For the more technically challenging ones, I highly recommend practicing your limbs separately at first. Even I sometimes get impatient practicing this way and try to put everything together right away. Big mistake! Patience and discipline in your practice routine will go a long way towards learning more quickly. So, break it down slowly and save yourself a boatload of time.

Once you've checked out the basics, use the code on the inside of the first page to download or stream the play-along tracks. Each was created specifically for this project with the help of some of my favorite musicians and longtime collaborators. Dmitry Ishenko, who you may recognize from my first book holds down the bass and Elias Meister plays guitar. These guys are the best of the best. They can play almost any style, they've worked with some of the world's most talented artists and most importantly, they know a ton about music. If you really want to know what to play as a drummer, these guys are an unbelievably valuable resource. Therefore, I decided to interview them and include their quotes and tips for each groove. All 32 tracks feature this trio, with sax player Wes Maples joining us on 8 tunes. His horn arrangements played an integral role in making this music feel authentic and alive. Andrea Capozzoli (trumpet) also contributed to the horn arrangements and Lars Potteiger played organ on one selection. They're great too.

The tracks themselves, the video interviews and my explanations are designed to help you experience how this music lives and breathes in the real world. This is "how it is in the streets," with play-alongs that are more like album demos than static loops. When you work with them, you'll feel the section changes, the push-and-pull, the musical interaction and most of all, the emotion of a live band.

Each track has two measures of count-in and most are approximately three minutes long. Many go back and forth between two basic sections, but some just build on one idea for the duration. There are versions with and without drums, and the drummerless ones have a click and percussion loops to help you stay on track (I recorded all the percussion instruments myself, fully live with no looping).

My hope is that all these tools provide a wide-lens snapshot of each genre that helps you learn while having a total blast along the way. So, enjoy the ride, have a seat behind the kit and let's get started with letter "A"!

Drum Notation Key

Afrobeat It

Genres: Afrobeat

Difficulty Level (1-10): 6

Area of Origin: West Africa (Nigeria), late 1960s

Artists to Check Out: Fela Kuti (and son/grandson Femi and Seun), Kokolo Afrobeat Orchestra, Newen Afrobeat, Kokoroko, Antibalas, The Daktaris, Ebo Taylor, Dele Sosimi, Zongo Junction

Drummers to Check Out: Tony Allen, Charlie Ferguson, Jojo Kuo, Moses Boyd, Ayo Salawu

The History

Nigeria in the 1970s was rife with social inequalities, poverty and political corruption. It was also undergoing a musical transformation as native artists like Fela Kuti began traveling abroad and incorporating elements of American funk, soul and jazz into their music. After years of struggling to break through, Kuti found his true voice with the tight horn arrangements, infectious grooves and sharp vocal bursts of Afrobeat. This music gave voice to widespread social inequalities and served as a rallying cry for change.

At Kuti's side was legendary drummer Tony Allen, who is widely considered the godfather of Afrobeat drumming [1a]. His amazing musical legacy has influenced an entire generation of drummers. Allen didn't just come up with the Afrobeat groove, he was instrumental in actually creating the genre itself. He played with a loose feel and an impeccable groove. His drumming was melodic and interesting, serving as the perfect backdrop for Kuti's brilliant songwriting. Kuti himself said it best: "without Tony Allen, there would be no Afrobeat [1b]."

As this style spread throughout the world, a burgeoning Afrobeat scene sprung up in Brooklyn, NY in the 1990s. Bands like Antibalas, Kokolo Afrobeat Orchestra and The Daktaris rose to prominence, bringing this music to a whole new audience. It remains popular today with bands in Europe, America, Africa and beyond carrying on this rich Afrobeat legacy.

The Music

Afrobeat drumming is built on repeating parts that fit together perfectly to form the drum groove. The hi-hat drives the beat forward while the bass drum and snare are the meat and potatoes. The beauty of this groove is that it feels both loose and tight at the same time. There's quite a bit of freedom to vary the part as long as your snare and bass drum stay mostly the same. The first snare hit is on beat 2 while the other is displaced, which essentially chops the phrase into two parts. You can also reverse the phrase and put the displaced snare in the first part while playing the backbeat on beat 4. The feel should be relaxed and a little behind the beat, but still sharp and grooving. This one should make people want to dance!

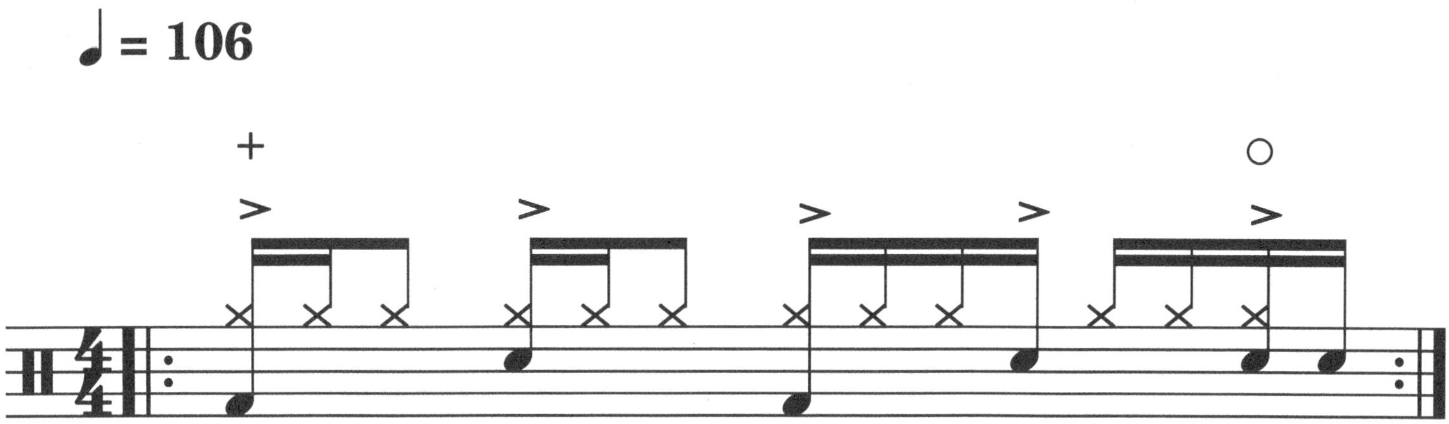

Variation #1

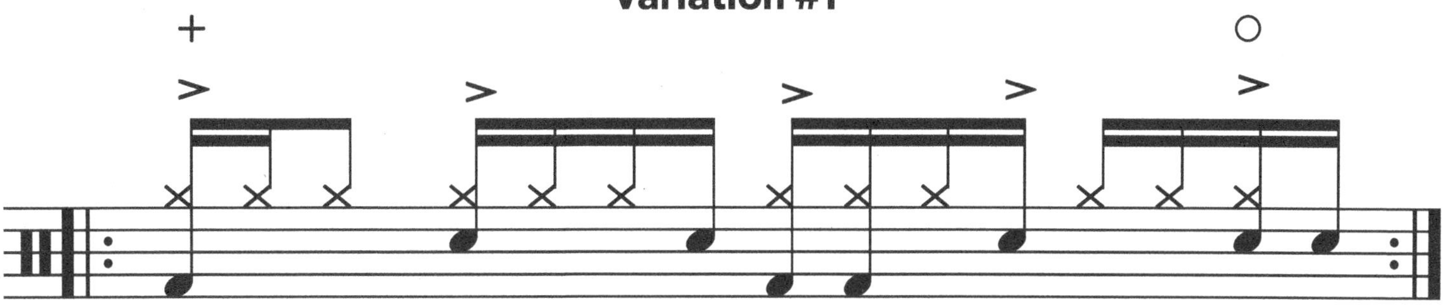

MORE Stuff You Can Use

It's good to add some short fills as long as they don't interrupt the flow of the groove (work on them with a metronome). It's also important to remember that Afrobeat songs tend to be very long and repetitious, so try to focus on maintaining stamina when you practice.

Fill #1

Fill #2

You can also switch to the bell of the ride on the B section to open things up.

Variation #2

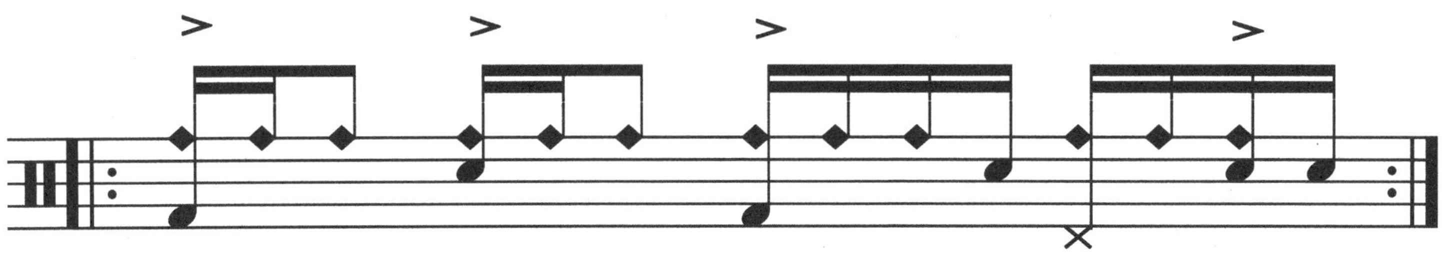

It's important to create a big volume difference between the accented and non-accented notes to give the pattern shape and definition. This is the "secret sauce" that will make it groove harder (this tip applies to almost everything in the book). Your first impulse might be to smack the accents harder, but remember that this groove should be bouncy and not too heavy. Try lowering the volume of the non-accented notes instead, which is called "ghosting." Volume is all relative, and your "louds" will seem louder if your "quiets" are quieter. Practice the limbs separately at first starting with your feet, which are the backbone of most grooves. Imagine your groove is a house. Start with a solid foundation and build your way up.

I've found this type of groove is useful and fun to work with even if you're not specifically playing in an Afrobeat band. This musical vocabulary will help you play funk, jazz and even pop music. Afrobeat has also become a huge influence in modern hip-hop. Have fun with this one!

The Band

Dmitry Ishenko (bass):

"The essence of an Afrobeat groove is a cross between American funk and soul and the looseness of African rhythms. American soul music had a huge influence on Fela Kuti, especially James Brown who had tight interlocking parts that are always repeating...but then you bring in the African element and get this multi-dimensional looseness to it. As a bass player, I'm playing the same line over and over like in a James Brown groove, but at the same time I'm pulling it back. That's where more of the African influence comes in since I'm trying to be on the back of the beat and make the groove very round."

Elias Meister (guitar):

"The feeling when we play an Afrobeat song is mixed because I definitely feel it being laid back. It's something I would call music from the hips, like you're feeling a dancing thing but you're also moving forward...but it's definitely relaxed. I'm thinking about people dancing for sure."

Wes Maples (sax):

"Afrobeat 101 for horn and rhythm section players is that there's a bar of straight rhythm and then a bar of syncopated rhythm. So, we're trying to pay respect to that overall pulse even throughout the bridge. The main thing I want [from the drums] is a textural change when it goes to the bridge which encourages a change for the horns as well. Maybe switching the pattern, going from a closed hat to an open hat, adding more cymbals or more sustained high frequencies. That encourages the horns to alter up the rhythm or change the texture but still keeps the same pulse of the overall song."

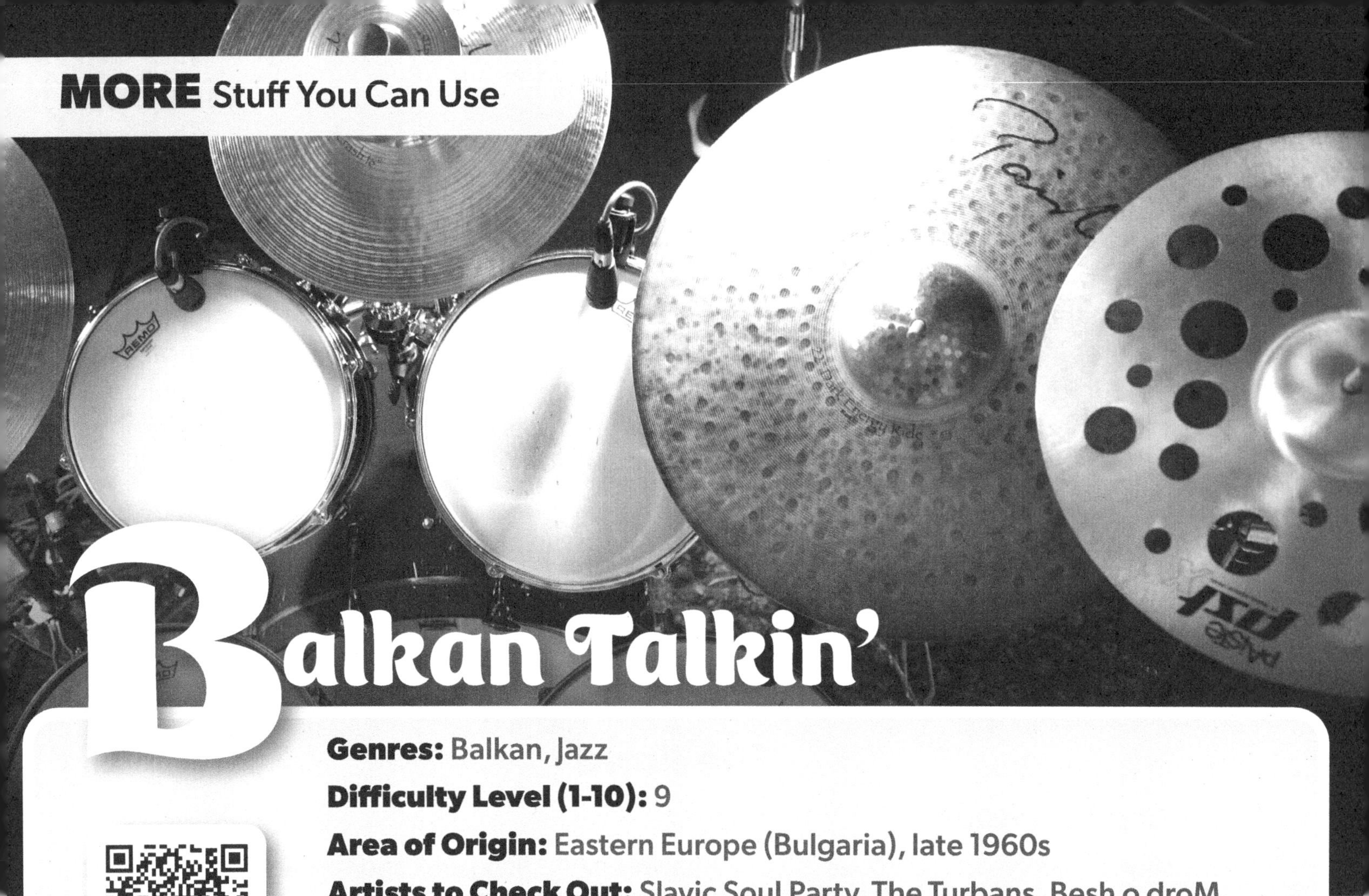

Balkan Talkin'

Genres: Balkan, Jazz

Difficulty Level (1-10): 9

Area of Origin: Eastern Europe (Bulgaria), late 1960s

Artists to Check Out: Slavic Soul Party, The Turbans, Besh o droM, Duško Gojković: *Swinging Macedonia,* Lala Kovačev Group: *Balkan Impressions Vol. 2,* Pachora

Drummers to Check Out: Stoyan Yankoulov, Cees See, Branislav Lala Kovačev, Garo Tavitjan

The History

As American jazz stretched around the world in the mid-20th century, artists began combining traditional folkloric dance rhythms from their home countries with this spirit of improvisation. In Eastern Europe, this cross-pollination was turbo-charged by the fall of Communism, spawning the new hybrid genre of Balkan jazz. A key early figure in this renaissance was Yugoslavian trumpeter Duško Gojković, who worked with Dizzy Gillespie, Miles Davis and Chet Baker [2a]. His 1966 album *Swinging Macedonia* featuring Dutch jazz drummer Cees See is considered one of the most important early works of Balkan jazz.

While most of this new music featured odd-meter rhythms juxtaposed with jazz soloing, each country or region had its own variations. The groove below is traditional folk dance from western Bulgaria called the Kopanitsa. As choreographer and folk-dance expert Richard Unciano aptly puts it, "Kopanitsas vary in speed from moderate to 'hang-on-to-your-hat' fast. It's enough to boggle the mind and fire up the feet! [2b]."

The inspiration for this play-along track came from Bulgarian drummer Stoyan Yankoulov, who is one of the true modern masters of this style. Others like Macedonian-born Garo Tavitjan and jazz drummer Jim Black continue to push the boundaries of musical invention in Balkan music.

The Music

Odd-meter grooves can be really daunting for drummers who don't have a lot of experience playing them, especially when they move beyond the more commonly used 5/4 and 7/4 time signatures. Unless you grew up listening to them, these rhythms can seem like a foreign language. I'll never forget the time I played with an Albanian orchestra and the entire concert hall was clapping the 3-2-2 subdivisions along with us. But just like any other style, once you become comfortable with the musical language, the drum part falls right into place.

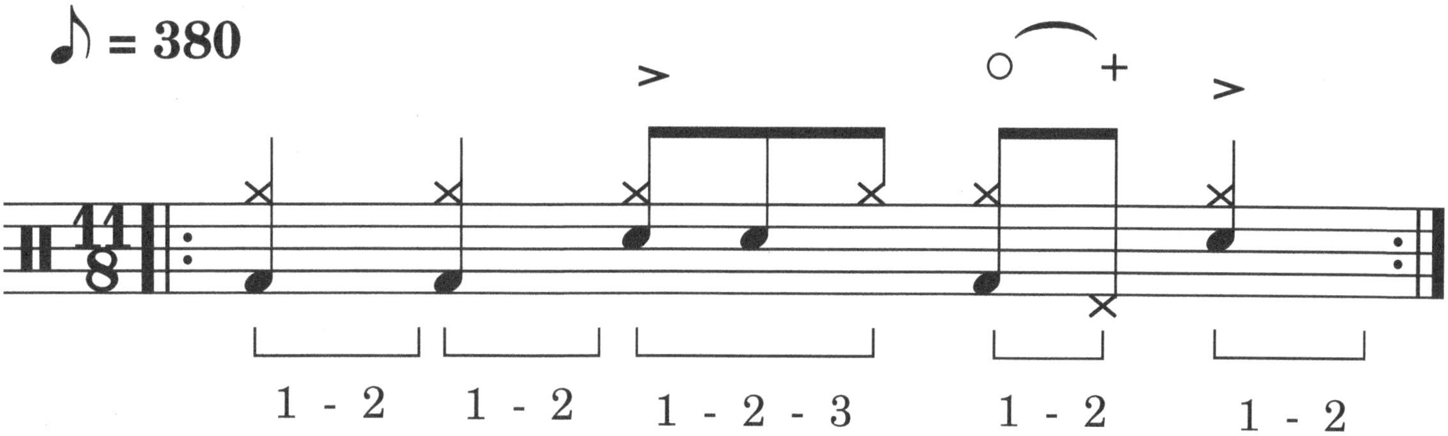

With this Kopanitsa, start by dividing the 11 into smaller chunks of 2-2-3-2-2. Try clapping and counting "**1**-2, **1**-2, **1**-2-3, **1**-2, **1**-2" slowly at first (clap only on the 1's). Then try it with the metronome. There's an isolated click track in the play-along folder which you can slow down using the library's built-in software.

Choreographer Unciano also suggests a helpful trick [2b]: "The best way to describe the 'feel' of the Kopanitsa rhythm within the 11 meter is to count from 1 to 5 with a quick hiccup on number 3. Timing or rhythm-wise, it would be quick-quick-slow-quick-quick, with two beats-per-quick and three per-slow or 2-2-3-2-2 = 11."

Once you start to feel it, jump behind the kit and play the kick and snare parts before you add the rest. As you get more fluid with the musical language, you can add some variations.

MORE Stuff You Can Use

Open the hi-hat slightly by lifting your toes inside your shoe, switch to the ride or work in some crashes.

Variation #1

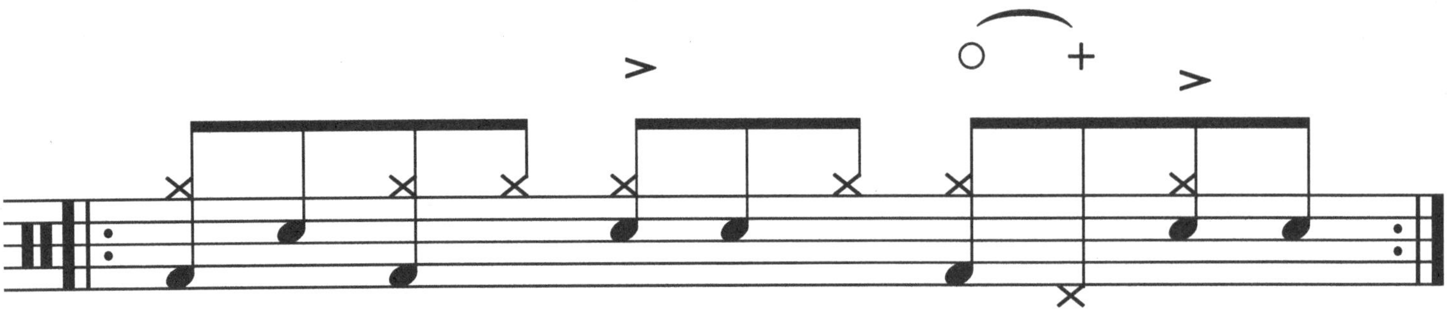

Variation #2

You can also add some rolls or beefy two-handed tom fills.

Fill #1

Fill #2

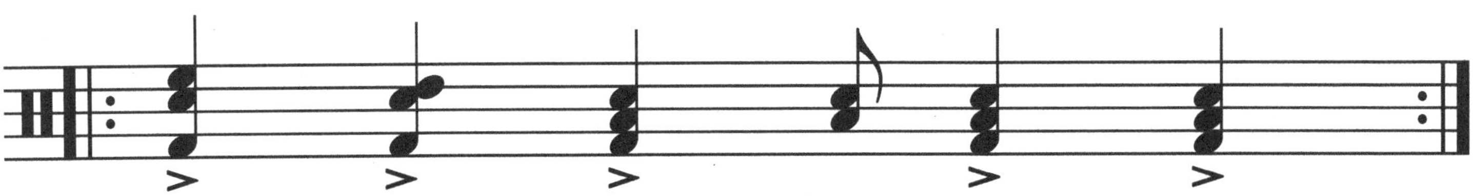

Balkan Talkin'

It's great to experiment when you're using the play-along track since it's ok if you get thrown off and have to regroup. However, if you're playing something like this with a band, keep it simple at first and be as clear as possible with the downbeats. The other musicians will thank you since it will make them more comfortable, which will ultimately make the music better. You can try out some more abstract stuff like filling over the bar line once everyone has it dialed in. This is exactly how it worked when we recorded it. Follow the form of the play-along by repeating back to Letter A each time.

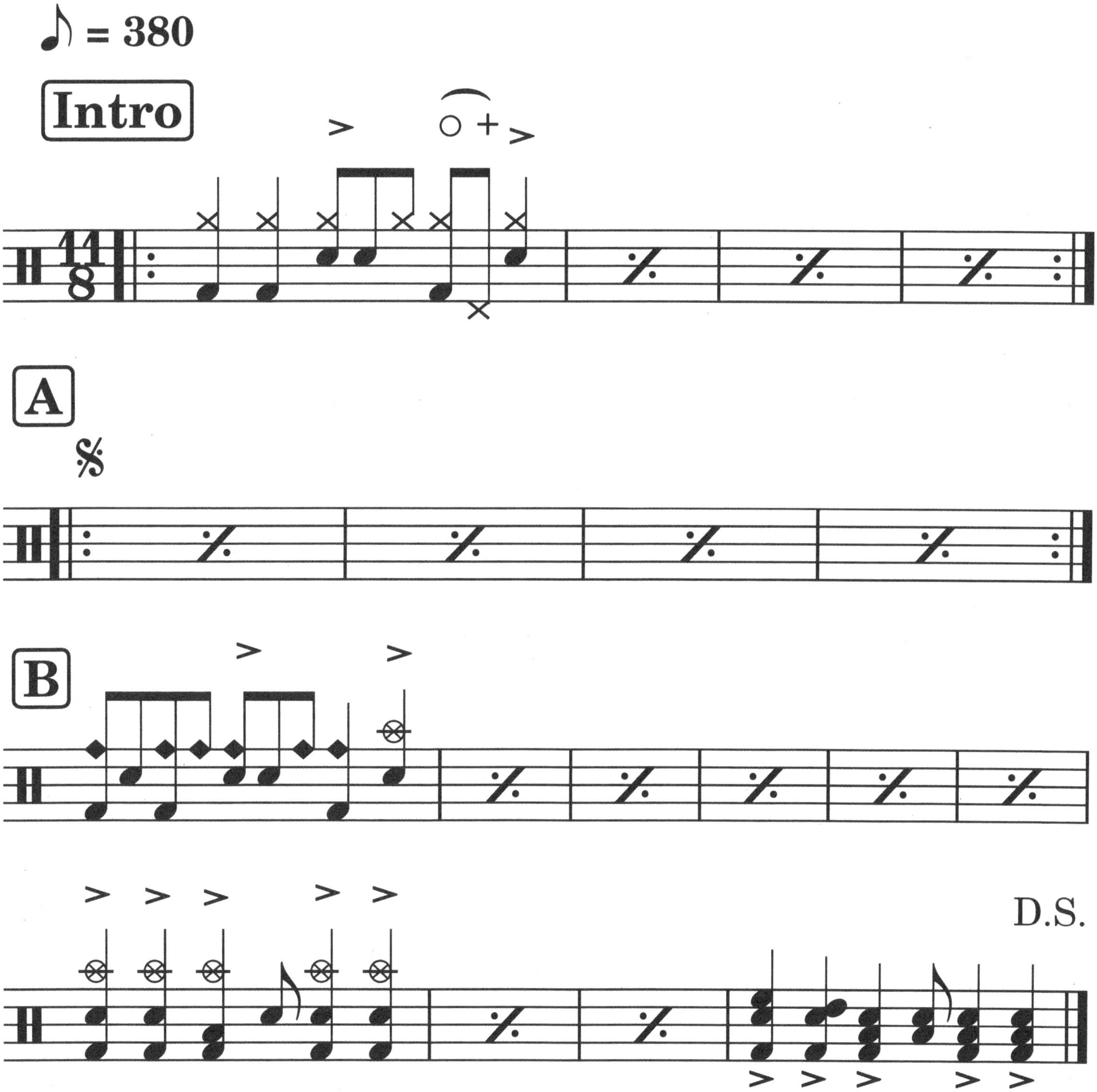

I've also included a lead sheet for this track. This is the most common type of chart you are likely to encounter on a gig, so it's important to get comfortable with it. Focus on the information that is relevant to your part such as the form, hits and melody.

Balkan Talkin'

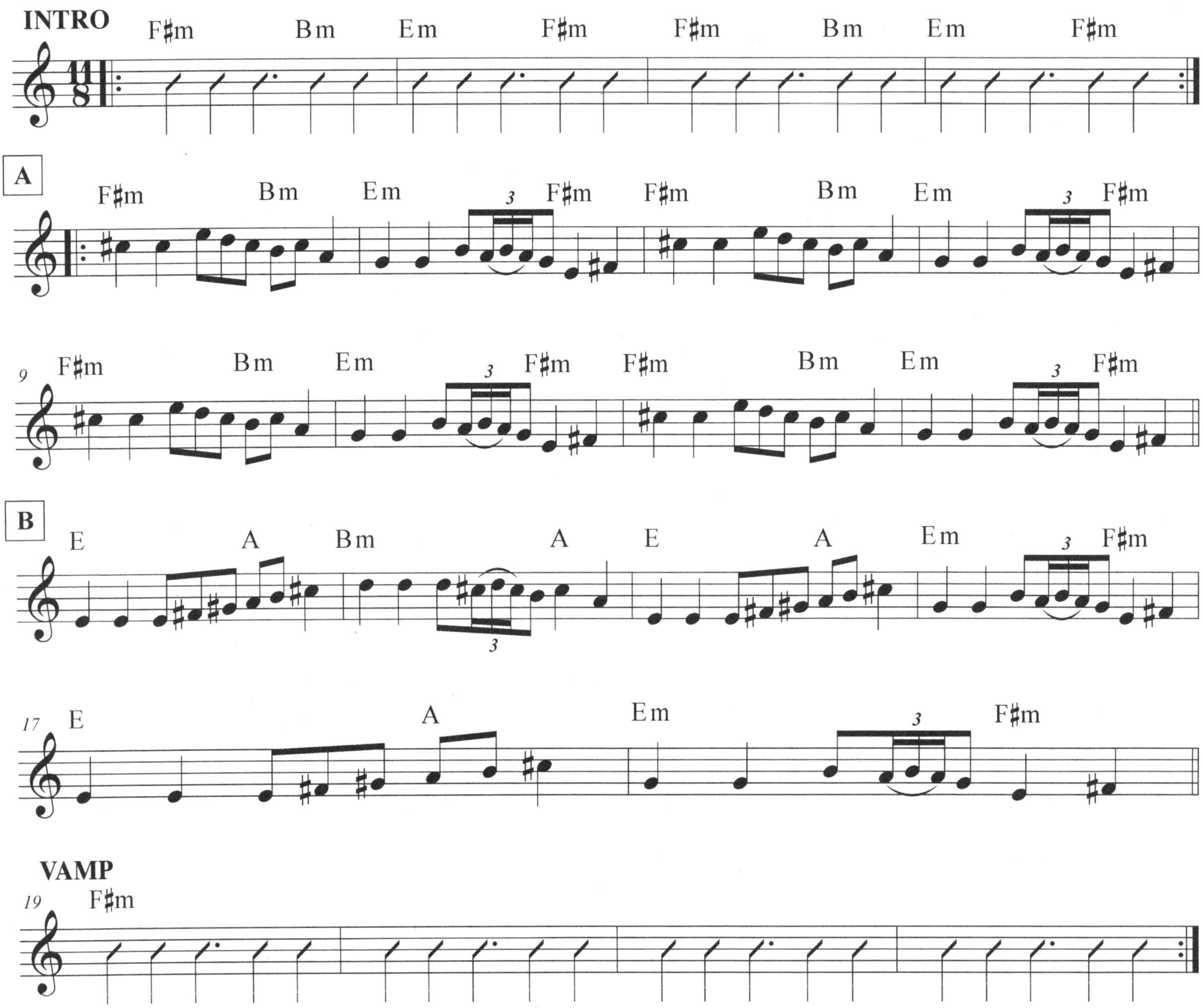

The Band

Dmitry Ishenko:

"With Balkan music, it's all about the combination of 2's and 3's. So, in this particular groove (11/8), we chose 2-2-3-2-2. It's really important to have a clear indication of where each of those little groupings land, and as a bass player I am outlining that. That's my main role. I don't really get too far away from just purely outlining what I call the clavé, which is the underlying rhythmic feel...and I expect the drums to do the same, especially the kick drum. For me, it's vital to connect to the kick drum when it's doing that same pattern over and over and propelling us forward.

"A while back somebody gave me an easy way to process this information by thinking of it in terms of "short" and "long." The 2's are short and the 3's are long. In this case, it's going to be short-short-long-short-short. That makes it easier because it's always grouping up the 2's and 3's."

Wes Maples:

"If you try to count the whole thing, it interrupts the flow and you get left behind. It's too much mental gymnastics. The trick is to spend enough time with the groove to internalize it so it becomes somewhat subconscious. I think that's how it's meant to be interpreted. I don't think the composers were thinking so much in terms of the numbers of the meter, it was more the feeling of it."

Elias Meister:

"I'm not counting any numbers when I play something like this, but it's definitely not something that's very easy for me. It took many years to get more comfortable with it. I think the key is to feel this uneven pulse inside your head. This meter is very hip, so there's not much need to obscure it or expand it. If you stick to the groove it will work just fine."

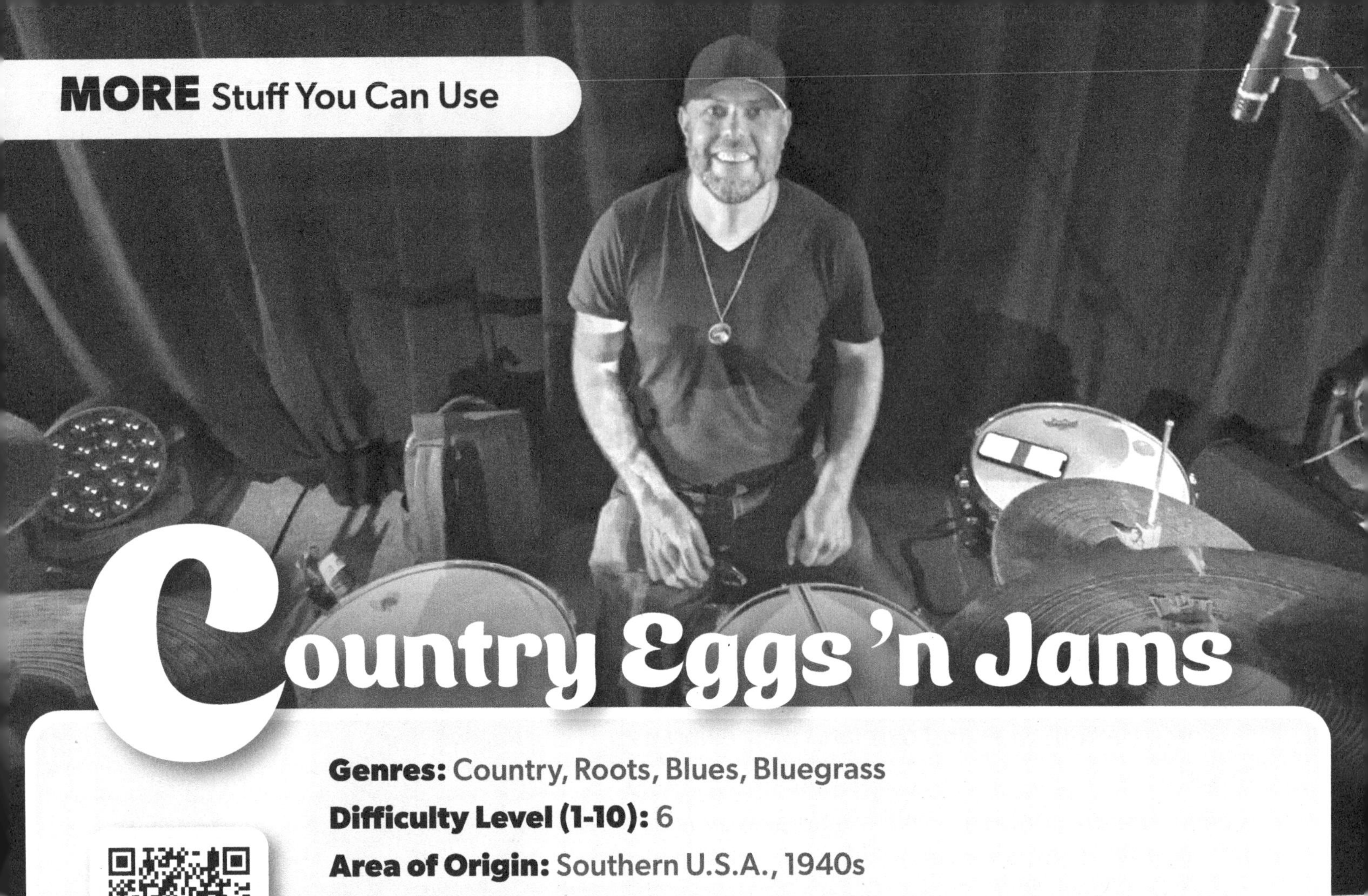

Country Eggs 'n Jams

Genres: Country, Roots, Blues, Bluegrass

Difficulty Level (1-10): 6

Area of Origin: Southern U.S.A., 1940s

Artists to Check Out: Dolly Parton, Patsy Cline, Johnny Cash, Hayes Carll, The Steel Wheels

Drummers to Check Out: Mike Meadows, W.S. "Fluke" Holland, Stanton Moore, Sonny Payne, Walter Martin, Buddy Harman, Kevin Garcia

The History

The historical roots of drum set players adding percussion to the kit stretch back deep into the 20th century, with Duke Ellington drummer Sonny Greer as an early pioneer. Recalling a stint at the legendary Cotton Club, author James Haskins describes Greer's rig: "He had an incredible battery of percussion equipment, everything from tom-toms to snare and kettle drums. And once he realized the band was at the club to stay a while, he brought in the really good stuff...he was even known to use timpani heads on his bass drum so the drum could be tuned to a precise pitch [3a]."

Blues drummer Walter Martin was another innovator, adding kettle drums to early Louis Jordan tunes "Barnacle Bill the Sailor" and "Sam Jones Done Snagged his Britches On [3b]." But don't worry, there won't be timpani required for this groove! However, adding elements like tambourine and shaker became even more commonplace among Chicago blues drummers in the '40s and '50s. Nowadays, this trend can be found in many different styles of music, including pop, country, blues and jazz. As the great New Orleans drummer Stanton Moore says in his book *TAKE IT TO THE STREET*, "incorporating the tambourine into the drum set can add an element that is both hip and texturally interesting [3c]."

The Music

This drums/percussion hybrid groove has a lot of moving parts that fit together to create a feeling of forward motion. It features a tambourine clipped to the rod of your hi-hat stand along with a shaker which replaces your right stick (I used a handful of egg shakers which I call the "3-egg omelet"). This type of setup is also useful in more stripped-down musical situations where you're looking to create a different vibe or feeling.

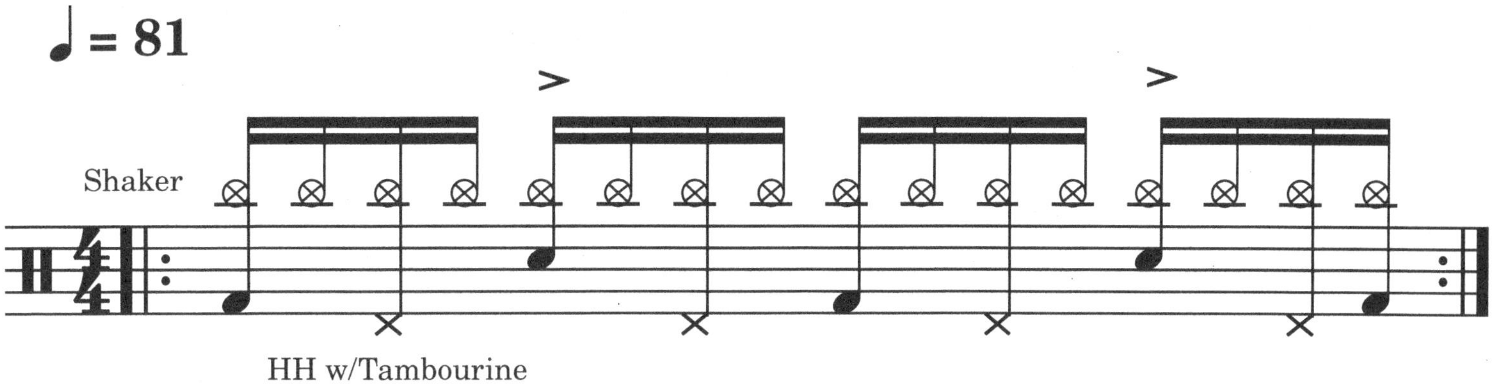

The upbeats on the hi-hat/tambourine sound almost like a train chugging down the tracks, while the shaker plays constant 16th notes. The bass drum and snare have the opposite effect, playing a simple backbeat. This reverse motion almost makes it feels like the kick and snare are playing in half-time. The trick is to make it all blend together smoothly. The feel should be loose and laid back but not sloppy. It's important to use proper wrist technique when you play the shaker or your arm will get tired quickly. Try adding some "e's" and "a's" on the kick drum and snare to make it even funkier.

Variation #1

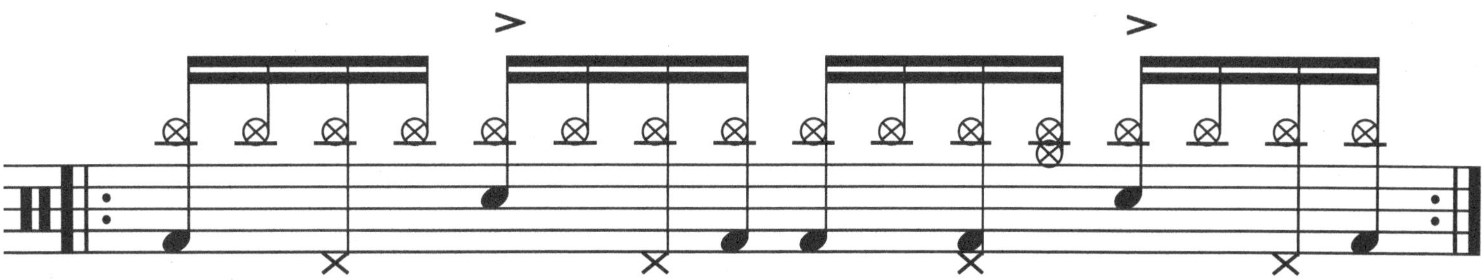

Variation #2

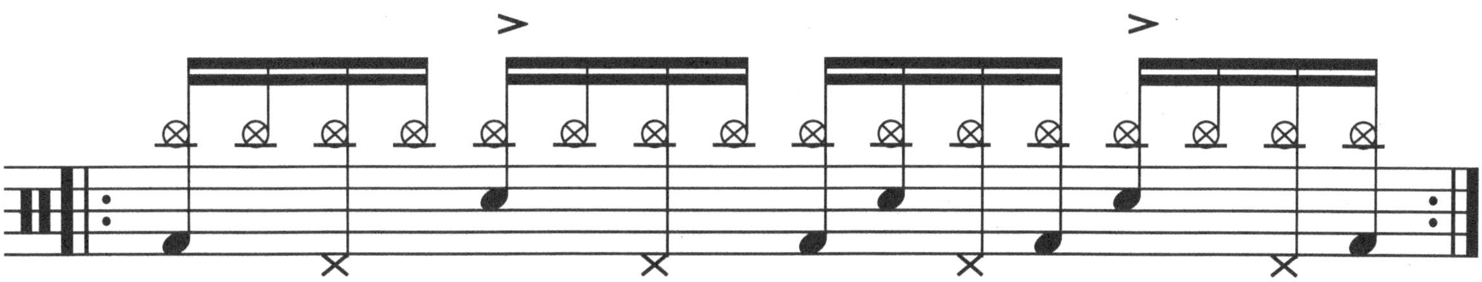

MORE Stuff You Can Use

This variation is a 2-bar phrase with a hit on the "and" of beat 2 of the second measure. Hit the crash with your left hand while your right continues scrambling the eggs.

Variation #3

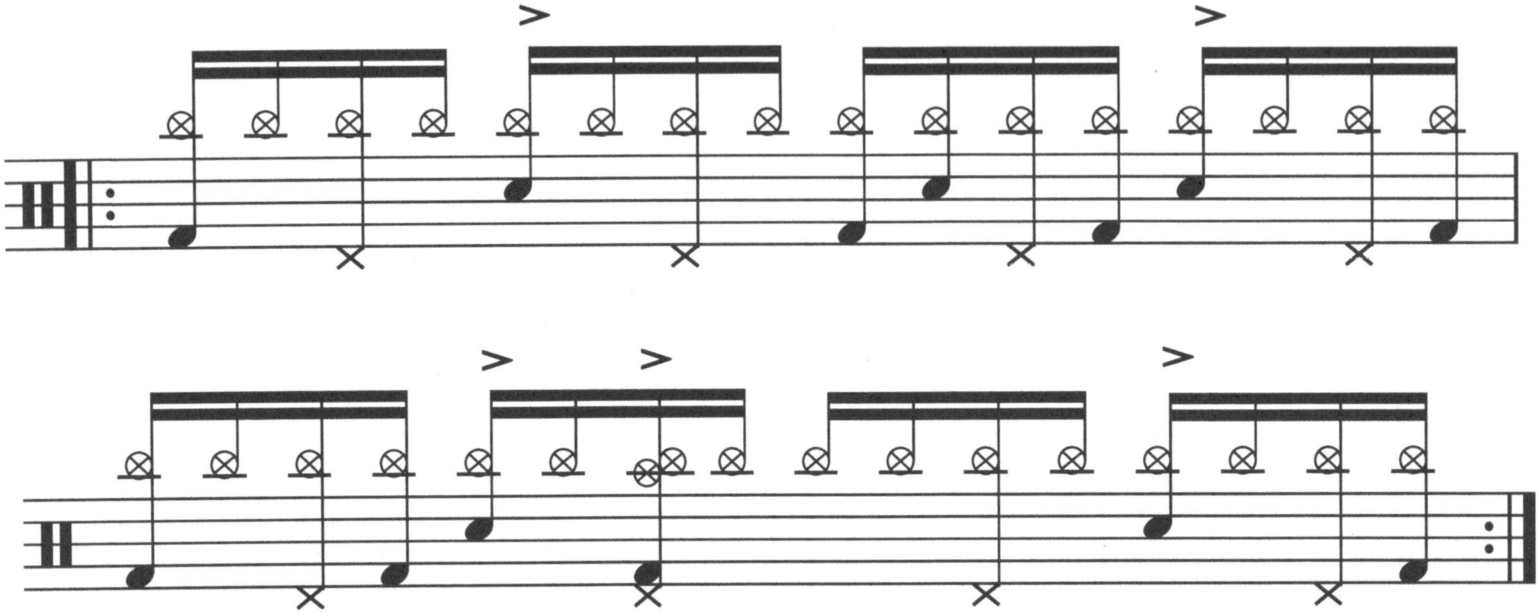

This one is all about getting the feel just right, and it can be tricky to get everything locked in together. I use variations of this beat all the time when I play gigs and sessions. It's groovy and accessible, but just different enough to be useful in country, blues and pop/singer-songwriter situations. This is definitely some Stuff You Can Use.

The Band

Dmitry Ishenko:

"It's a very simple bass line. I'm basically just playing quarter notes, and [harmonically] I'm only playing roots. I'm not playing fifths, so it's just four notes per bar. I make the notes short on purpose. It's a stylistic choice, maybe coming out of listening to Dolly Parton as a child. What I'm really listening for is the bass drum because we're locking in on the quarter notes. They have to be sort of laid back but propulsive at the same time."

Elias Meister:

"The best way to play drums on an old-school, slinky country beat is definitely simple. Nothing crazy, no big fills, nothing too busy...something that's feeling good in the pocket. It's nice to mark the top of the measures together with the drums and the bass, and the fills and the markings can be extremely simple. Even just hitting a cymbal on the one, that's already enough of a marking. It doesn't have to be a fill over the bar line or anything like that. I'm thinking a lot about hitting thirds on the guitar and really outlining the harmony, but in a very basic way."

Dr. John

Genres: New Orleans, Roots, Blues

Difficulty Level (1-10): 5

Area of Origin: New Orleans, 1970s

Artists to Check Out: Dr. John, Allen Toussaint, Professor Longhair, The Neville Brothers, The Meters, Leon Redbone, James Booker, Galactic

Drummers to Check Out: Zigaboo Modeliste, Fred Staehle, Johnny Vidacovich, Earl Palmer, Herman Ernest III, Herlin Riley, Stanton Moore

The History

The origin of New Orleans grooves or "street beats" goes back to the 1800s when drummers began combining European and Civil War marches with African/Caribbean music to play during jazz funerals [4a]. While these events included many different types of grooves (most famously the second-line pattern), they all had one thing in common: they were played for dancing, marching and celebrating life, death and everything in-between.

Acclaimed jazz drummer Herlin Riley traces the beginnings of this style back to the ragtime music of the late 19th/early 20th centuries explaining, "the older musicians would say to 'rag' something is to syncopate it. For elements of surprise, they would play breaks on the downbeats as well as on off-beats... and in playing rag, different parts of the drum set were used for playing time...I think it was just a matter of how they wanted to color the music at that particular spot by getting different nuances out of a certain part of the kit [4b]."

Pianist and songwriter Mac Rebennack, better known as Dr. John was one of the most influential artists in New Orleans music, with hits like "Iko Iko" (1972), "Right Place Wrong Time" (1973) and "Such A Night" (1973). The jaunty, syncopated groove on the play-along track was inspired by his late 1980s cover of the tune "Junko Partner," with the great Fred Staehle on drums.

Another important drummer from this period was Herman Ernest III, who joined Dr. John's band The Lower 911 in the late '70s and played on many of his albums over the course of 30 years. Known to friends as "Roscoe," he also worked with famed New Orleans artists like Allen Toussaint and The Neville Brothers (and played drums on Patti LaBelle's hit song "Lady Marmalade" in 1974). The Meters, with the legendary Zigaboo Modeliste on drums, were also pioneers in blending jazz and funk with traditional New Orleans grooves.

Today, this music continues to evolve with artists like Tank and the Bangas, Trombone Shorty and Galactic leading the parade.

The Music

New Orleans music is all about getting the feel just right, and this groove is no different. The bass drum plays on beats 1 and 3 throughout, while the snare answers with a relaxed marching-style pattern. It's almost like a 2-beat groove with a bunch of funky stuff in-between. This has to swing hard, so lay back on the beat and try to create a big difference between your accented and non-accented notes for shape and definition. It should feel...festive! But it also needs to be precise and not drag too far behind the beat (and the rest of the band). Keep it loose, but make sure to lock in your bass drum with the bass player. This will really tie the whole thing together.

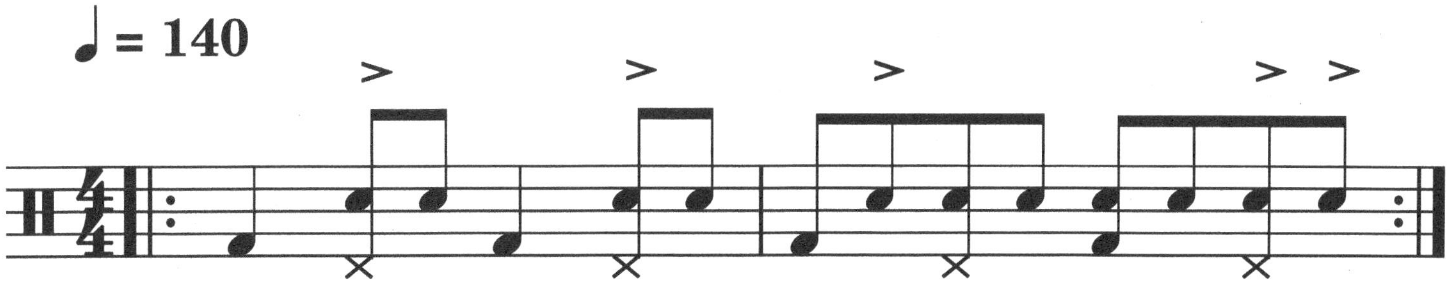

The bass drum is the taskmaster that keeps everything on track, while the snare brings the party vibes with drags, flams, rolls and rim shots. Add some strategically placed crashes, cymbal chokes and tom fills for more fun variations.

Variation #1

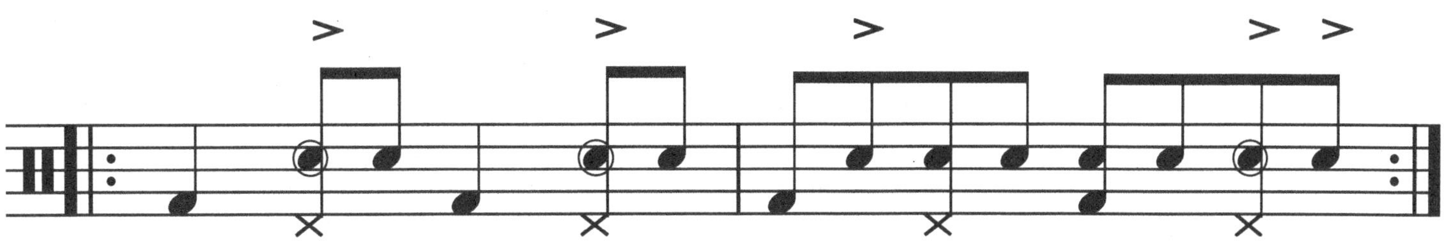

MORE Stuff You Can Use

Variation #2

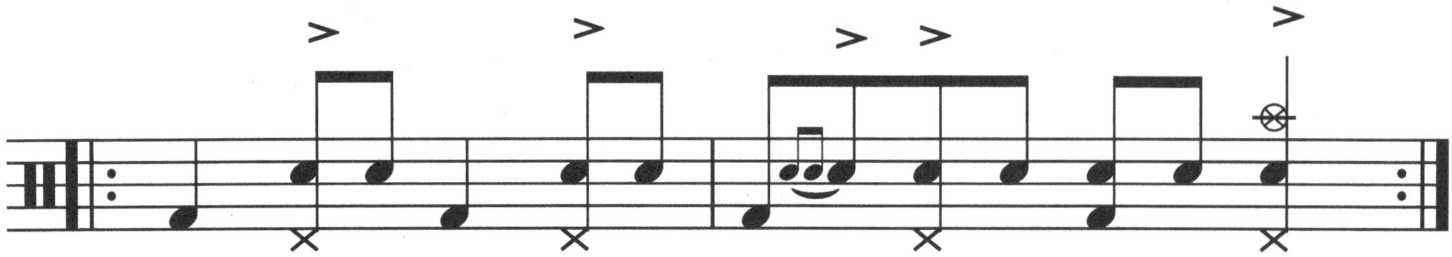

Variation #3

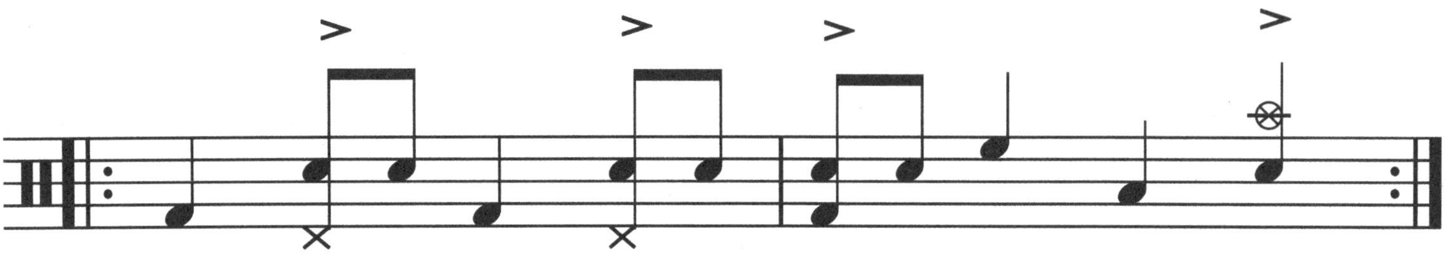

Fill #1

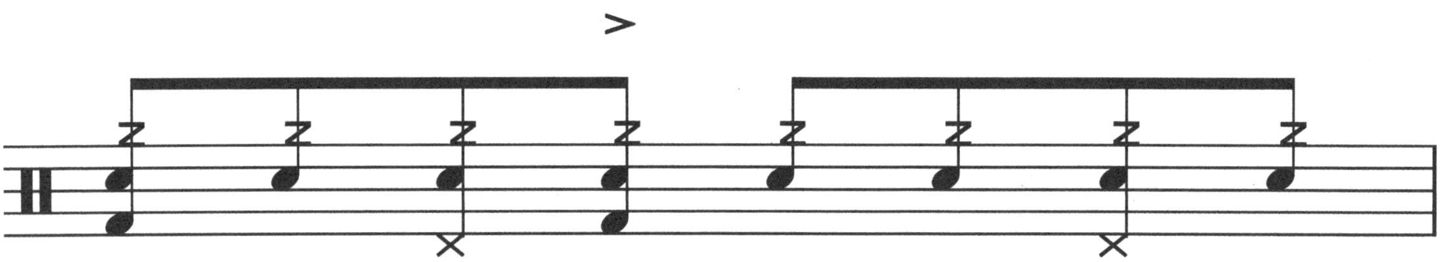

I sometimes like to put a crash on beat 4 at the end of a fill instead of on the downbeat just to mix it up. This is an important concept called creating "station points" which I learned from my teacher Bob Gullotti. Sometimes ending fills or phrases on beats other than one can make your drumming feel less square and predictable. Play around with it and try to come up with some new ideas. Most of all, this groove should feel like a swinging, dirty, funky celebration. Have fun with this one, I know I did!

The Band

Dmitry Ishenko:

"In this particular New Orleans groove, I'm connecting to the bass drum notes and playing a pretty simple bass line of just roots and fifths. I'm leaving a lot of space and also playing a little behind the beat. It's also really important to hear the upbeats that [the drums] play on the snare drum. For me, this is the part of the drum pattern that has the most melodic freedom. I'm also listening to the snare because that influences the way my feel comes across. I'll occasionally do a fill or a walk-up where I switch from playing on beats one and three to maybe four 8th notes leading into the next section. It's really important to do that together with the drums. We have to have the bass and drums together and make things obvious for whoever's playing on top of us. That's why any fills should probably be on the simpler side."

Elias Meister:

"I hear the snare drum as more like the 'free' part. I'm thinking about people walking, dancing, marching in a parade...but it's a loose parade. [On the guitar], I'm thinking about playing fills and also playing a little bit over the bar line. For this 8-bar cycle, it's always nice to hit beat one together with the whole band to mark [the top of the form] and then you can play in-between the beats to fill up more of the spaces."

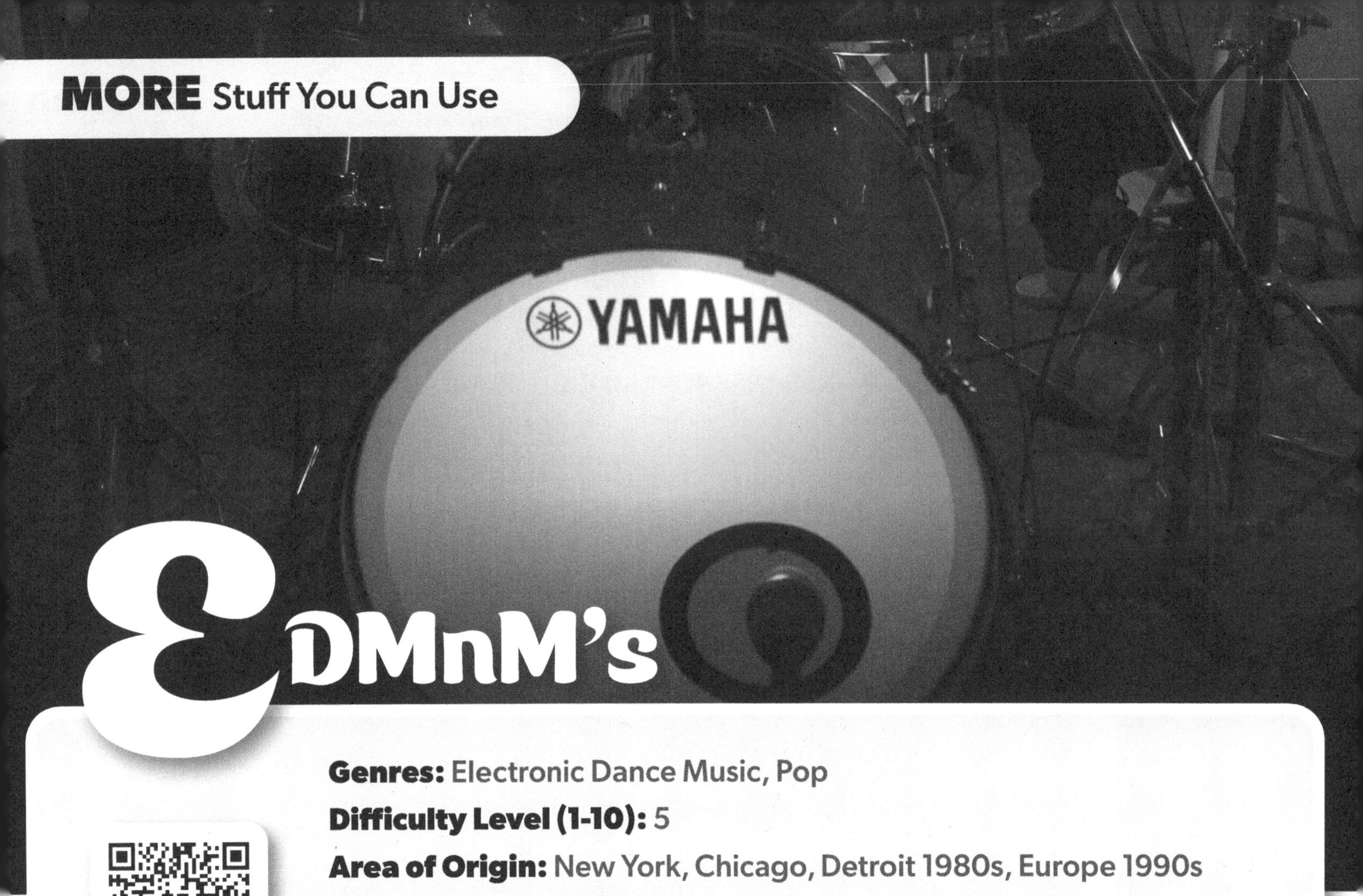

8 EDMnM's

Genres: Electronic Dance Music, Pop

Difficulty Level (1-10): 5

Area of Origin: New York, Chicago, Detroit 1980s, Europe 1990s

Artists to Check Out: STS9, Pretty Lights, Komfortrauschen, Who Made Who

Drummers to Check Out: Zach Velmer, Adam Dietch, Luke Holland, Thomas Lang, Michael Schack, KJ Sawka, Andy Gangadeen

The History

No instrument has endured more changes in the way it's used in modern recorded music than the traditional drum set. Drum machines, programmed loops, sample replacement and quantizing have completely changed our expectations of what drums sound like in pop and electronic music. This has created an interesting reverse effect for acoustic drummers who now need to be able to replicate the sound and feel of these machines on stage. Electronic dance music or "EDM" is a perfect example of this, and drummers who can really play this style authentically have found a valuable niche in the music scene.

EDM is a broad term, encompassing styles such as house, techno, drum'n'bass and dubstep, drawing influences from pop, disco, world music and hip-hop. The beginnings of this music can be traced back to the 1980s in cities such as New York, Detroit and Chicago. EDM typically features inorganic, programmed sounds with the singular goal of getting people out of their seats and onto the dance floor [5a]. The rave scene in Europe in the '90s spawned a new batch of creators like the highly influential French duo Daft Punk, who recorded several tracks and toured with Omar Hakim on drums. However, most of these artists' reliance on technology means that many popular EDM acts do not feature live drums. But some do, and it's important to know how to get the right sounds for this style. Drummers like Zach Velmer (STS9), KJ Sawka (Pendulum), Andy Gangadeen and Michael Schack have become innovators in EDM, seamlessly blending acoustic and electronic drum tones with the intricate programming of these tracks.

The Music

I have four words for you: "four-on-the-floor" (or is that one long word?). In any case, the quarter-note bass drum pattern is the most important element in replicating an electronically programmed groove. The feel should be tight and precise, just like a drum machine. But since we are not actually machines (yet), there are other parts of the pattern that we can use to make it groove even harder.

Make your fills punchy and robotic, almost as if someone has pushed the "fill" button on their drum machine.

Variation #1

Variation #2

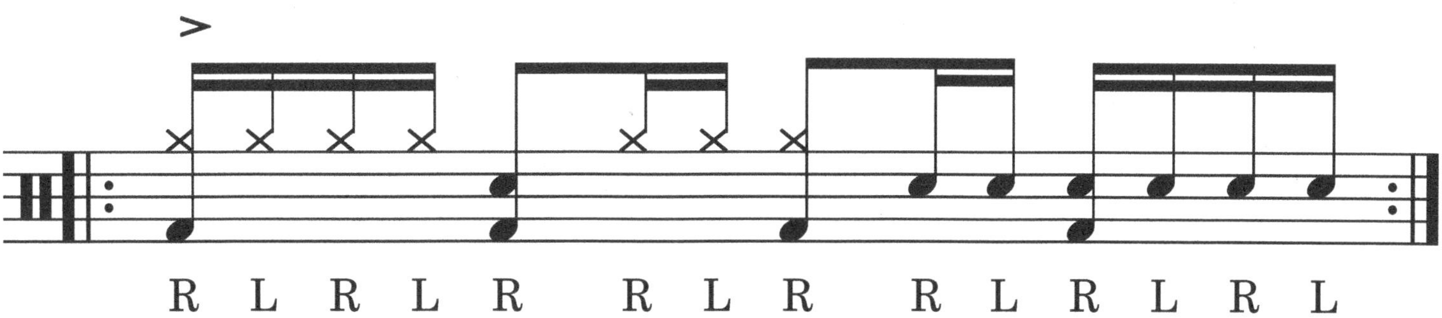

MORE Stuff You Can Use

Regardless of whether you're using 8th-note combinations or fast triplets, it's important to make your phrases fit within the framework of the backbeat.

Fill #1

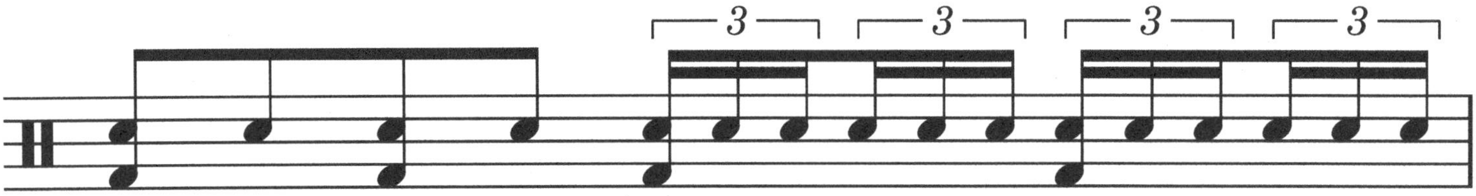

Fill #2

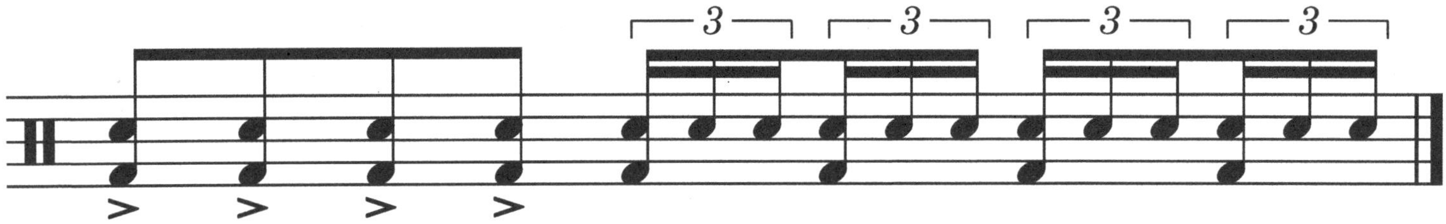

Open and close the hi-hat slightly by lifting your toes inside your shoe. This will help you get the tight sizzle sound to mimic a programmed hi-hat.

Variation #3

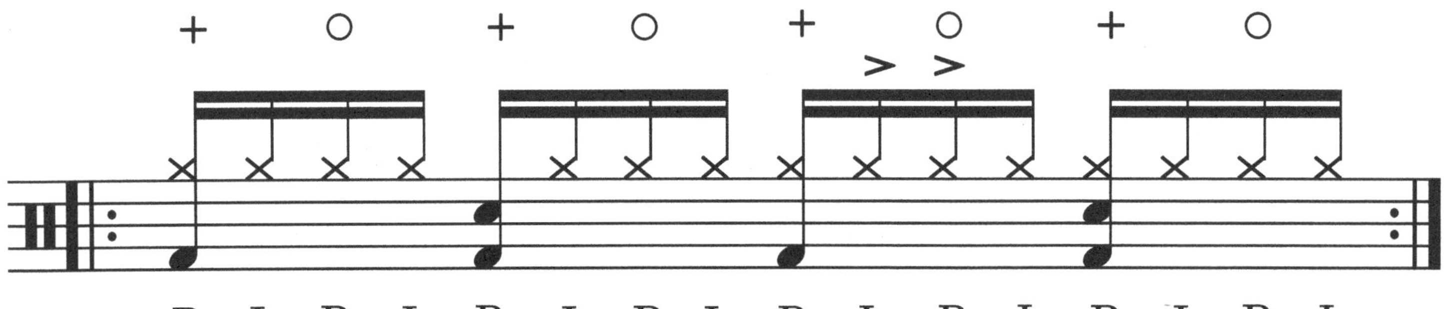

Variation #4

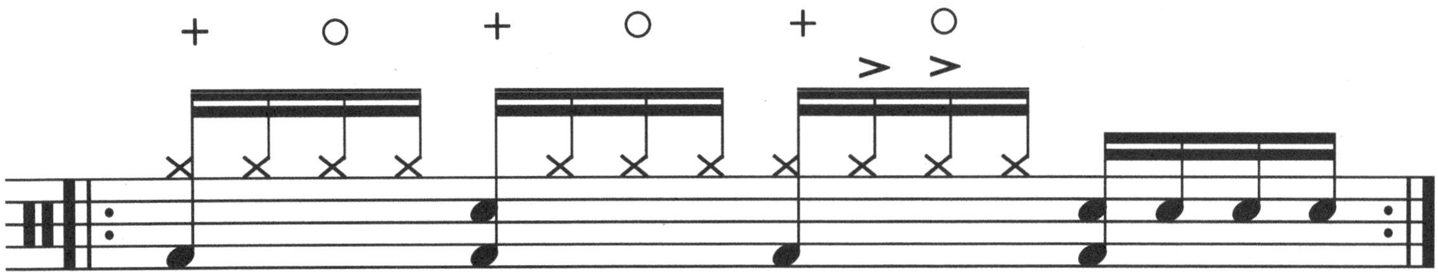

It's also important to choose drum tones that fit this style. Use cymbals with a sharp, trashy attack and minimal decay. The snare should be crisp and deadened so there are no unwanted overtones. It's also a good idea to use the toms less than you might in a rock context since these sounds are not as prominent in programmed beats. EDM is mostly kick and snare mixed with higher-frequency hi-hat effects and loops.

One magnificent innovation in the way drummers record and perform EDM is the creation of hybrid rigs that blend acoustic and electronic sounds. While many drummers use drum machines and pads as side elements, drum triggers have allowed for even more integration since it's possible to mic a drum to get the acoustic sound, then blend in as much of the triggered sound as desired. This is critical in getting live shows to sound like the studio versions of the songs and allows drummers to be onstage in musical situations where they might otherwise be shut out. Hybrid rigs and drum triggers have become an important part of live performances in pop music as well. As times change, it's important for us to evolve creatively too. So, find your inner drum machine and stay on top of the beat to keep them dancing all night long!

The Band

Elias Meister:

"When you play electronic dance music with live instruments, you're thinking about replicating a drum machine or a sequencer. You're thinking about playing very tight, like a quantized kind of thing. Both the timing and the sound should be super-even and more towards that synth vibe, which you can do with a guitar too. It's very simple and repetitive. If you have a fill, it should be simple like something somebody would program by hitting buttons on a machine. [On guitar], you can do a lot with the duration of the notes and the sustain, keeping the voicings and the rhythm exactly the same, but making it tighter or longer to recreate the sound of opening or closing an envelope filter. That will create more of the variation you're looking for."

Dmitry Ishenko:

"I'm trying to replicate a machine, in this case a bass synthesizer. So, the part that I'm playing has to be extremely even and repetitive. If there's any kind of variation, that's more of a timbral or tonal thing...but the part itself remains pretty static. I expect that machine-like quality from a live drummer in EDM as well. I would also say that we're playing more in the center of the beat [to create] propulsive forward motion, but definitely not on the back of the beat. Center or front, as even as possible, as if you're actually programming a grid."

Folky Dokey

Genres: Folk, Country, Americana

Difficulty Level (1-10): 4

Area of Origin: U.S.A., 1940s

Artists to Check Out: Woody Guthrie; Peter, Paul and Mary; Pete Seeger; Bob Dylan; Joni Mitchell; Willie Nelson; Dolly Parton; Johnny Cash; Simon & Garfunkel

Drummers to Check Out: W.S. Holland, Hal Blaine, Paul English, Steve Gadd, Jim Keltner

The History

The modern use of the term "folk music" came about in the 1940s when artists like Pete Seeger and Woody Guthrie began writing protest songs railing against injustices in society. Guthrie's 1940 classic "This Land is Your Land" is one of the nation's most enduring protest anthems and has been covered hundreds of times by artists all over the world [6a]. As the 1960s rolled around and the Vietnam War raged, artists like Peter, Paul and Mary; Bob Dylan and Joni Mitchell took this style even further as the "folk revival" emerged in New York's Greenwich Village. Their acoustic guitar-driven music was filled with raw emotion and outrage, but also melancholy, joy and hope. While this style has deep roots in the traditional spirituals of enslaved African-Americans, it also contains strains of country, blues and bluegrass.

When the Beatles craze hit in the late '60s (termed the "British Invasion,") artists like Simon & Garfunkel; Crosby, Stills, Nash & Young and Dusty Springfield incorporated electric guitar sounds, helping spawn the subgenre of folk-rock. In the south, artists like Hank Williams, Johnny Cash, Dolly Parton and Willie Nelson pioneered country folk, blending elements of folk storytelling with a twangy bluegrass feel.

Another offshoot called Americana appeared in the '90s, combining elements of country, soul, folk and bluegrass. Americana originated with traditional tunes that could be plucked, picked and played on banjo, guitar, fiddle and mandolin [6b]. As it evolved, artists like The Avett Brothers and Mumford & Sons brought this Americana sound further into the pop mainstream with massive radio hits.

The Music

This groove is a combination of a train beat and a light folk backbeat. The feel should be propulsive but gentle and relaxed, since most of the time you'll be playing it behind a singer. Bob Dylan's "Blowin' in the Wind" was the inspiration for the play-along, and it also has a bluesy country vibe. I've frequently used this type of groove with singer-songwriters since it meshes well with the basic strumming pattern of an acoustic guitar.

♩ = 145

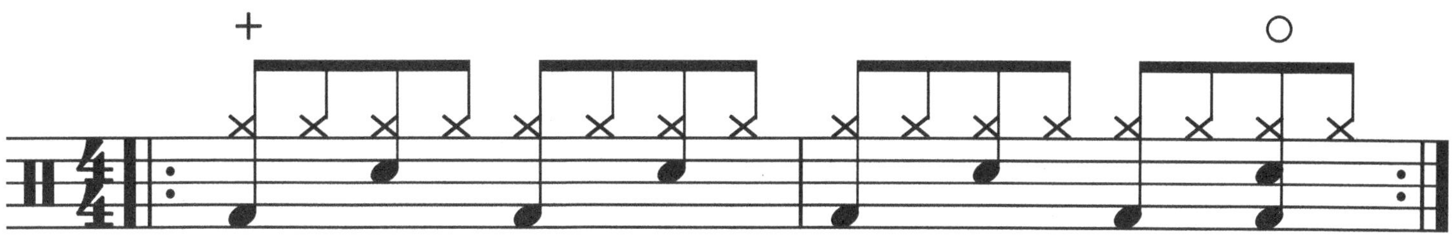

I used a heavy, rigid brush on the hi-hat and a more flexible broom-style one on the snare to create some interesting textures. Hot rods, regular brushes and sticks will all work as long as you focus on keeping a light touch. These musical choices are subtle, but they go a long way towards creating the right feel and energy. You can also integrate a shaker, tambourine or other percussion into your rig for additional textures and sounds. Lock in your bass drum with the bass player on beats 1 and 3, and make sure to feather it (play gently) so the pattern doesn't turn into a heavier 2-beat.

Variation #1

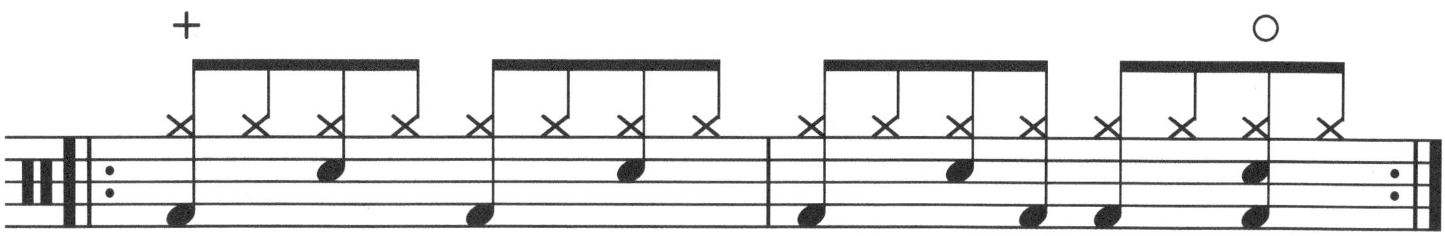

Variation #2

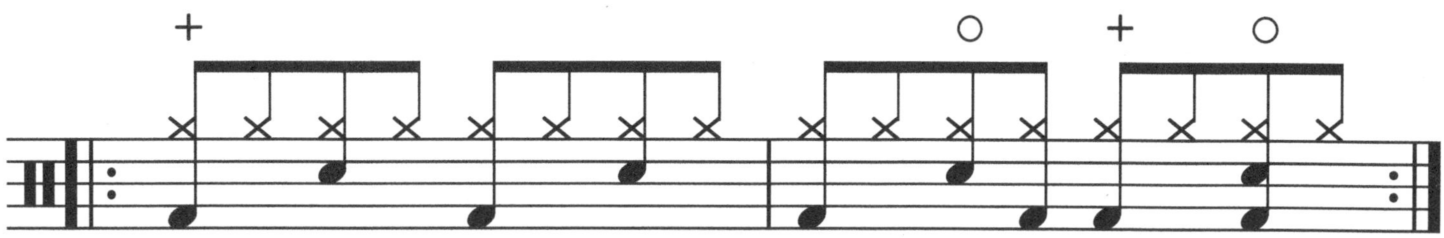

Variation #3

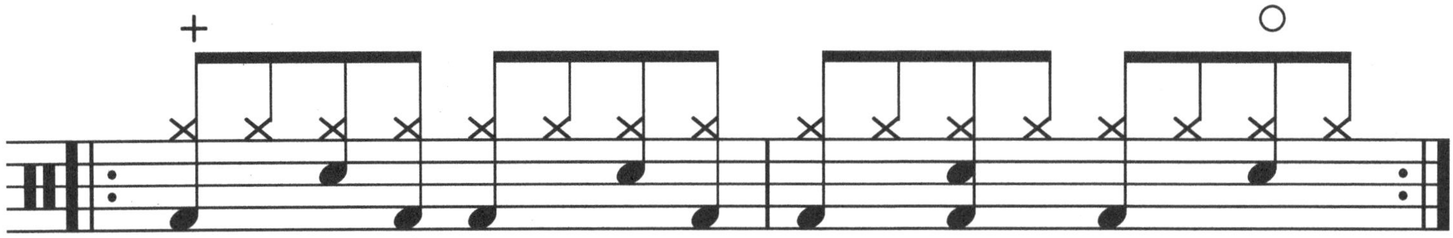

Here's a basic a fill you can use. It's might be super-simple, but the musical language fits this style.

Fill #1

Do a short fill and switch to the ride for a texture change.

Variation #4

Here's the phrase at the end of the play-along track. It's a real classic country folk ending!

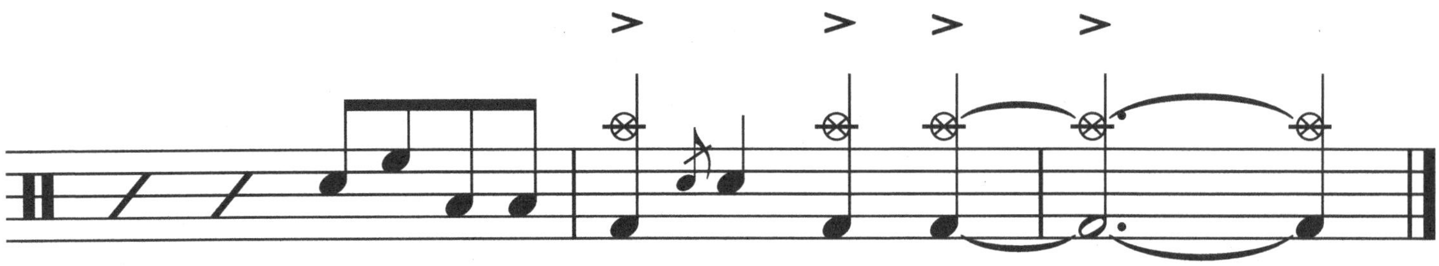

The Band

Dmitry Ishenko:

"In this folk groove, the bass is playing a two-beat. It's basically beats one and three using the root and fifth for occasional fills. The fills are usually just even subdivisions of 8th notes leading into the next chord change. I'm listening to the snare drum a lot because this music swings in a very subtle way. So, the snare placement is very important for me since it determines when I place my next note on beats one and three. That's what I'm listening for in the drums. Mostly kick and snare. [The bass and drums] are just slightly behind the beat and it's important for us to leave enough space for the song so a vocalist can float on top of what we're doing...it's just a very solid foundation with plenty of space."

Elias Meister:

"This is usually pretty light and laid back and you're really trying to tell a story with the song. I have this kind of feeling in my mind when I'm playing. I think simplicity is the key in this kind of music. The less fancy stuff and less frills it has, the better. Whatever is the simplest thing, you can still make it vibey. That's where you should go to. It's kind of a rolling feeling, like a slow walking."

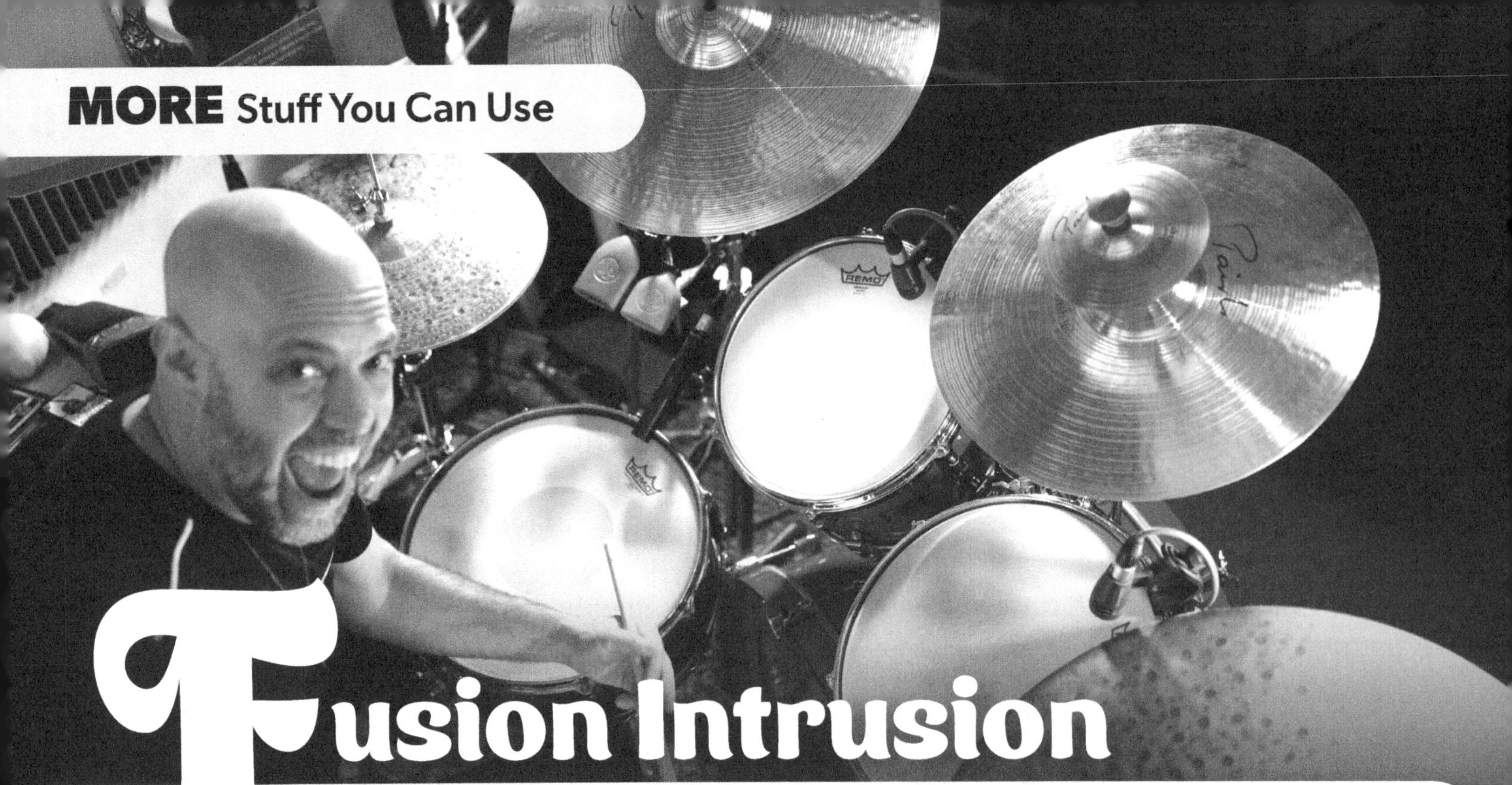

Fusion Intrusion

Genres: Jazz Fusion

Difficulty Level (1-10): 8

Area of Origin: U.S.A., late 1960s

Artists to Check Out: Miles Davis (late career), The Mahavishnu Orchestra, Alan Holdsworth, Larry Coryell, Weather Report, Return to Forever, Pat Matheny, Wayne Krantz

Drummers to Check Out: Dennis Chambers, Billy Cobham, Dave Weckl, Gary Husband, Vinnie Colaiuta, Lenny White, Keith Carlock, Narada Michael Walden, Harvey Mason, Omar Hakim, Mike Clark, Tony Williams (late career)

The History

Fusion emerged in the late 1960s as artists like Miles Davis began combining jazz harmonies with electric instruments more traditionally used in funk, rock and R&B [7a]. While musical experimentation was a primary motivator, fusion, at least in part, came about because jazz musicians wanted to capitalize on the popular appeal of rock music [7b]. The resulting amalgam changed the history of music forever, as groups like Weather Report, Chick Corea's Return to Forever and Herbie Hancock & The Headhunters gained widespread popularity. Electric guitars and synthesizers ruled, while bass players like Jaco Pastorius, Stanley Clarke and Marcus Miller experimented with effects.

This new style also afforded drummers like Tony Williams, Billy Cobham and Lenny White the freedom to delve into a whole new style of improvisation. Casting aside the rules of jazz convention, these pioneers conjured up deep grooves and head-spinning flurries of notes. Their drum sets grew in size to match their massive musical output. This late '60s/early '70s combination of jazz and rock went both ways, as artists like Frank Zappa, King Crimson and Emerson Lake & Palmer used many of the same musical elements to spawn the genre of progressive rock. The linear syncopations of Caribbean and Latin music also had an important influence on early manifestations of jazz fusion.

While many of these innovators had roots in Davis' band as sidemen, the next generation brought a whole new set of ideas to the table. Drummers like Dennis Chambers, Vinnie Colaiuta and Dave Weckl burst on the scene in the 1980s with mind-blowing chops and unmatched precision.

The emergence of jazz fusion is a prime example of how musical genres are rarely self-contained. Everything influences everything else, both consciously and subconsciously as artists hear each other and conjure up new ways to explore their musical creativity. This is precisely why it is so important to become fluent in many different styles!

The Music

This groove was inspired by a track called "Mother Nature" from guitar legend John McLaughlin's 2006 album *Industrial Zen*. Ironically, this tune doesn't even have live drums on it! It's a programmed loop in 5/4 that I started playing over and became totally hooked on. Sometimes just putting on music and jamming can really get the creative juices flowing. As we learned earlier, the best way to tackle odd-meter patterns is to subdivide them into smaller chunks. You can chop up this 5/4 fusion groove into 2 and 3. The first beat of the pattern is a key "check-in point" where the bass and drum play beat 1 and the "a" of 1 together almost every time. Fusion grooves are busy and linear, with lots of stuff happening at once so it's important to have these little spots to tie the music together. Work on getting a really good sound from the hi-hat as you open and hit it on the "a" of 1 and close it on beat 2. This is a small detail in an otherwise dense pattern, but it can make a huge difference in your sound.

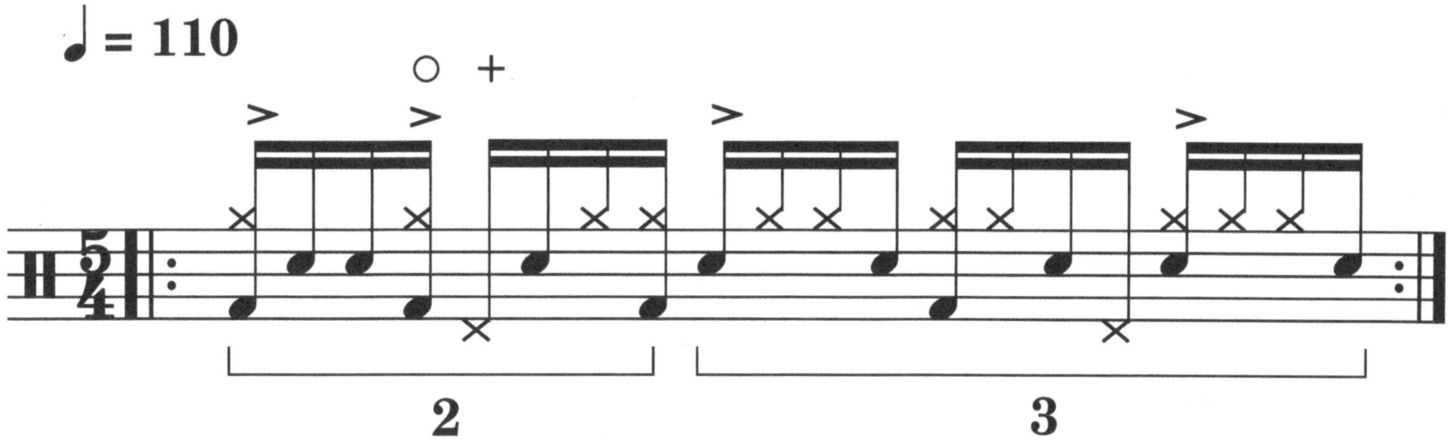

Add some fills around the kit, switch to the ride and try to play a few figures over the bar line for some sweet variations.

Variation #1

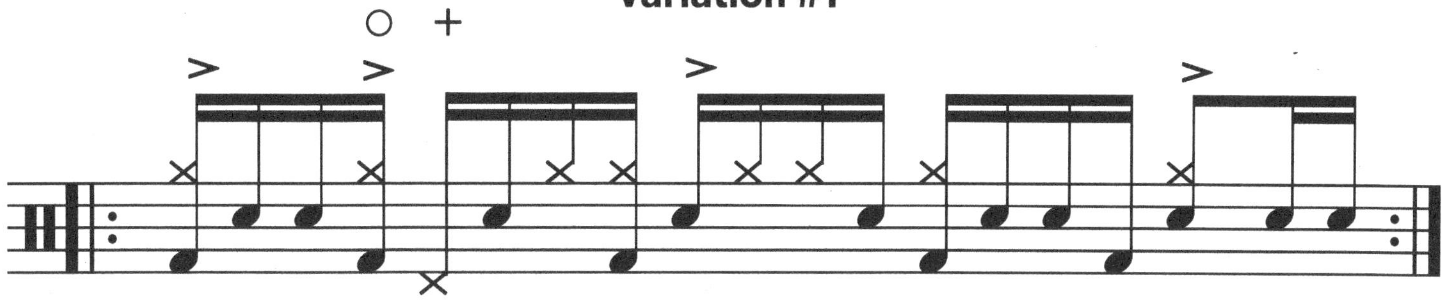

Variation #2

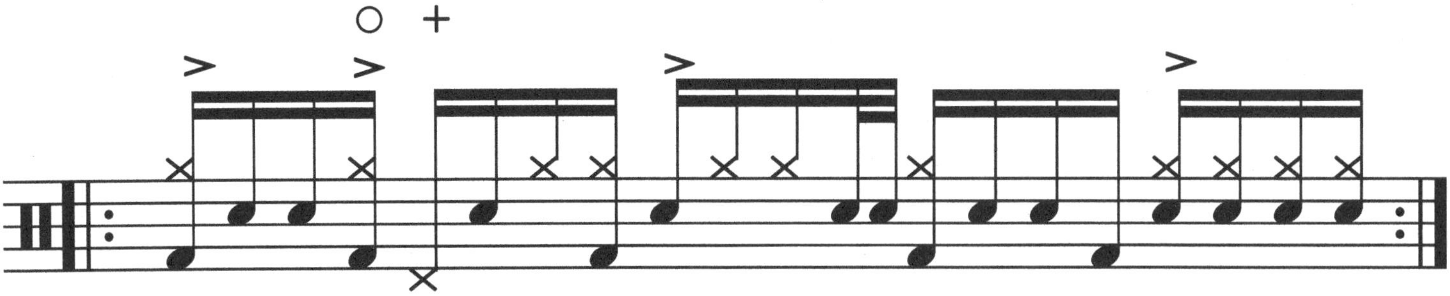

Variation #3

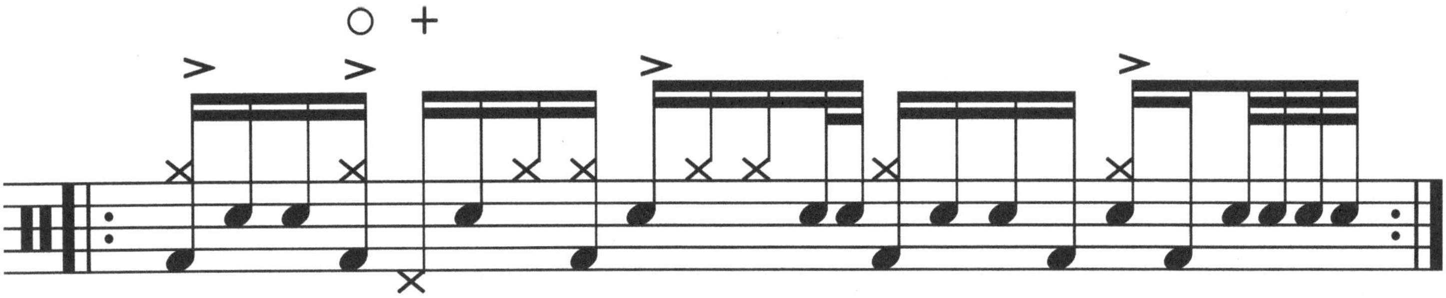

Variation #4

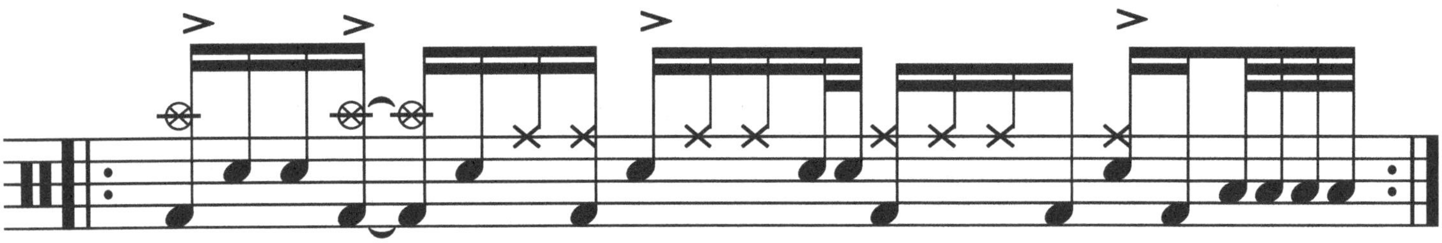

Variation #5

This style is all about listening and communication, so don't be afraid to stretch out and react to what you're hearing. Building and exploring the language of this music with a band can be one of the most liberating and inspiring experiences you'll ever have behind the kit. It's about so much more than fast chops and powerful fills. At its highest level, fusion drumming has an incredible subtlety that combines rich textures, rhythmic exploration and most of all, musical conversation. Happy shredding!

The Band

Dmitry Ishenko:

"I see fusion as something where we're all filling in these different parts of the beat and then landing together...but not necessarily on the downbeat every time where it becomes static and predictable. It's actually good sometimes to omit the downbeat and land on the "and" of one or maybe even beat two. But it's very important that everybody knows where they are [individually], and that there's a certain trust so that no matter how far out we go, we're still feeling the big picture together.

"What I'm looking for from a drummer in this kind of setting is clarity and occasional meeting points. In this song which is in 5/4, the meeting point for the bass and drums is beats 4 and 5. So the bass line can be as busy as you want on the first three beats; then, by strongly stating beats 4 and 5 [or their subdivisions], we're making sure we're in the same place."

Elias Meister:

"In a fusion song where you have a lot of improvisation going on, you want to give each other space to do a fill or musical statement and then respond to that. It can overlap and happen at the same time, but you definitely want to respond to what the other people are doing. In a tune like this where it has an odd meter, you don't want to get too lost in it, but you also don't want to play on beat one all the time because then it gets too obvious. If you can find a way to play over the downbeat for a while, but then when the tension builds up and you're feeling like the music needs a release point (usually on beat one of every fourth bar), then you arrive at that beat together. It's very satisfying to hit that point...and then you can also check in to make sure that you're still in the same spot and keep going."

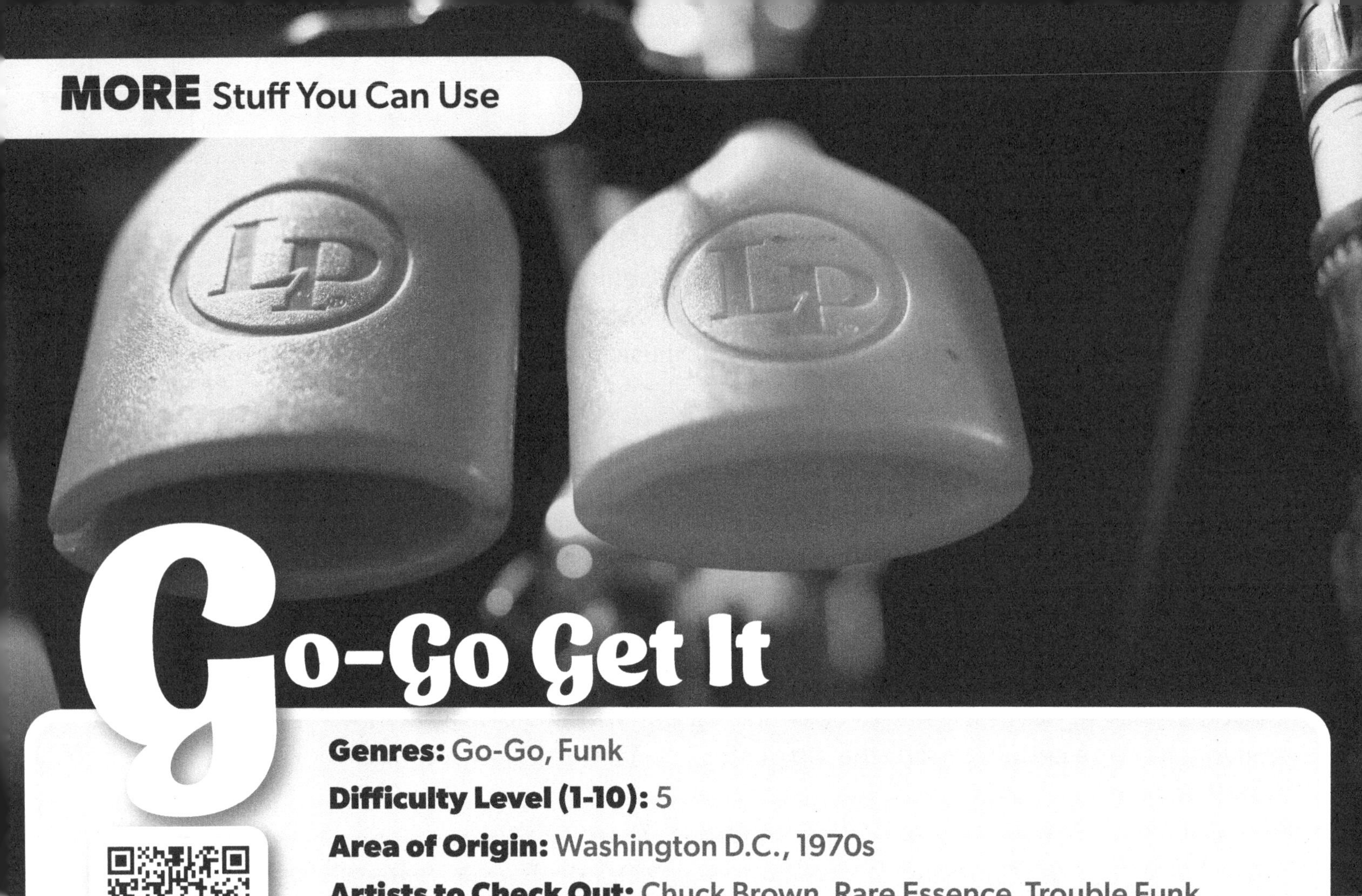

Go-Go Get It

Genres: Go-Go, Funk

Difficulty Level (1-10): 5

Area of Origin: Washington D.C., 1970s

Artists to Check Out: Chuck Brown, Rare Essence, Trouble Funk, Experience Unlimited (E.U.)

Drummers to Check Out: Ricky Wellman, Ju Ju House, Paul "Buggy" Edwards, Kenny "Kwickfoot" Gross, Wes Watkins

The History

It's rare that the beginnings of an entirely new style can be tied to just one artist. In go-go, that artist was the inimitable Chuck Brown. After learning to play guitar while incarcerated for murder, Brown moved to the Washington D.C. area (my hometown) and put his charisma and creativity to good use, releasing several albums in the late 1970s with his band Chuck Brown and the Soul Searchers. While these recordings planted the seedlings of this new style of funk, it wasn't until he met drummer Ricky Wellman that go-go was truly born.

Brown decided that his audience would respond better if he didn't stop between songs, so Wellman (who later went on to play with Miles Davis) devised percussion breaks to connect them. Using cowbells, blocks, shakers, tambourines and hand drums, these breaks evolved into what we now refer to as the go-go beat [8a]. Brown's bands also featured large, tight horn sections, multiple keyboards and synths, plus plenty of call-and-response vocals with the audience. The result was that his shows became raucous, hours-long dance parties where the groove never stopped.

Go-go began as underground music, but after Brown's 1979 mainstream hit "Bustin' Loose," it became inextricably woven into the District's African-American culture. His distinctive scratchy guitar tone and flair for showmanship eventually spawned plenty of successors, as bands like Trouble Funk, Rare Essence, Experience Unlimited and Northeast Groovers have created a vibrant go-go scene that endures to this day [8b].

The Music

This groove is called a socket beat and it's all about laying into a solid pocket and sticking with it throughout the song. Go-go music is usually pretty dense with lots of horns, guitars, keyboards and auxiliary percussion layered on top of each other. The songs also tend to be very long and feature call-and-response vocals with the audience. Sounds like a party! Well amidst all the chaos, the drums provide a foundation that holds the whole thing together. My childhood drum teacher in the DC-area Steve Larrance used to tell me that "the drummer drives the bus." That has never been truer than in go-go music. To put it simply, the more stuff going on around you, the less notes you should play.

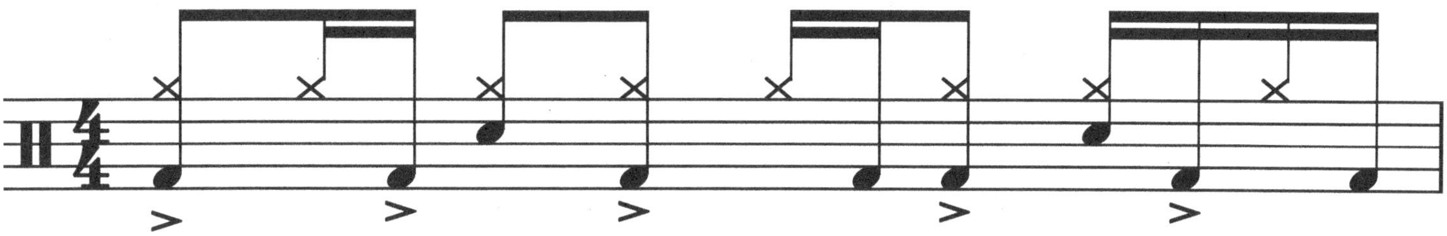

Playing this specific kick drum pattern is what defines it as go-go as opposed to funk or another style. Try to make the feel laid back and slightly swung, but don't let it drag (this is called the "go-go swing").

Variation #1

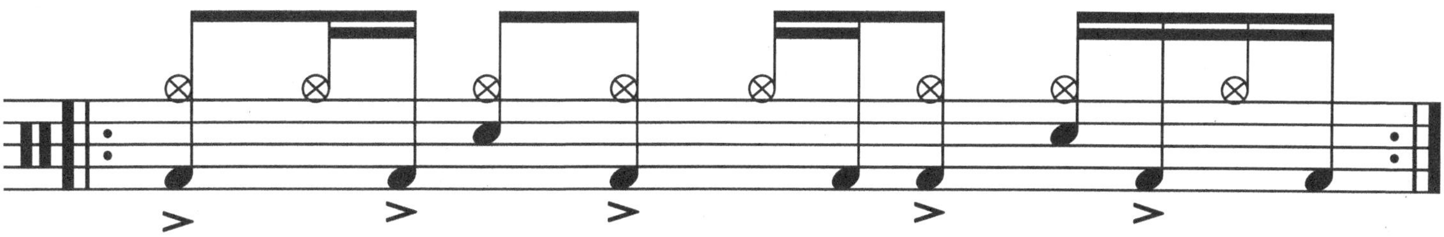

Keep the snare backbeat happening throughout and try varying the hi-hat pattern a bit by playing tight or loose and adding a few funky accents with your left hand (my personal twist on it).

Variation #2

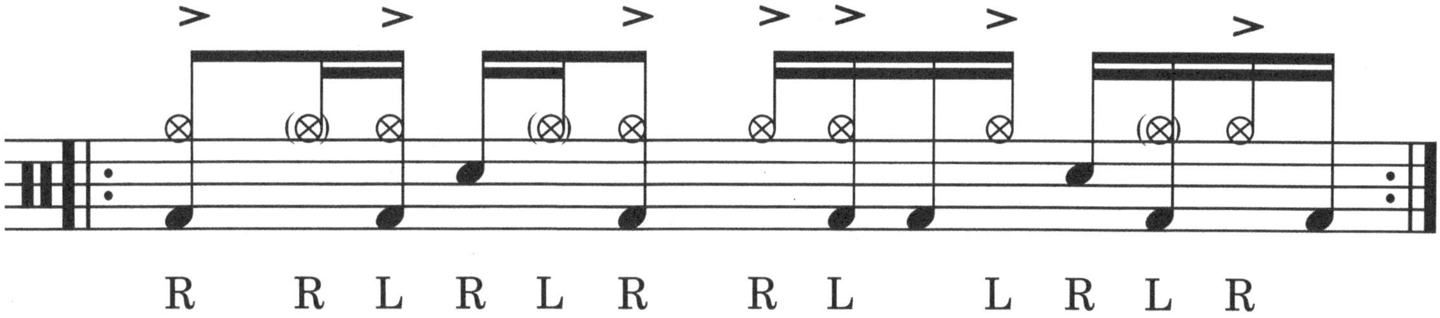

Lock those notes in with the bass player and don't deviate too much if you do a fill.

MORE Stuff You Can Use

Fill #1

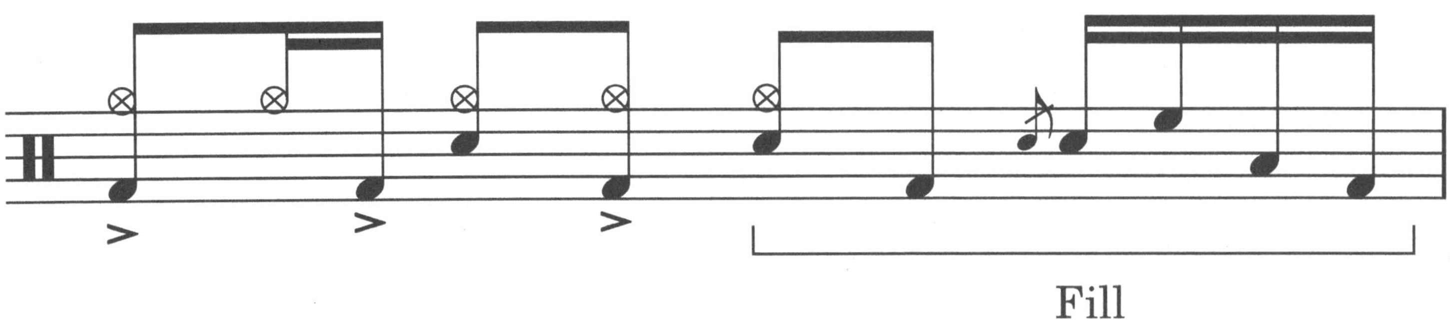

Fill #2

Any variations should be within the context of the main groove, so just sit back and keep the pockets 'n sockets rolling!

The Band

Dmitry Ishenko:

"I'd like to draw a parallel between go-go and Afro-Cuban music, because both have a collection of many parts that all work together to create this beautiful groove. They both traditionally have a drum set and lots of percussionists all playing interlocking parts. [In go-go], the tempo is always on the medium-slow side with a swung 16th note underlying the whole thing. The groove has to be laid back, but the parts are so precise that they're almost on top of the beat. It's kind of a conflicting feel in a way. As a bass player, I'm playing the same thing over and over because there's no need to improvise here. It's more like you're carrying this thing for a long period of time and letting it build through repetition."

Elias Meister:

"It's kind of grooving and moving. It's very swung and bouncy, but also has heavy downbeats on the one. So, I hear these two parts; the bounciness of it and also the weight of the downbeats at the same time. It's not too laid back...you want to get that greasy feel going a little bit, but it's still very driving music."

Wes Maples:

"I feel like the melodies are pretty simple with power chord elements and strong fifths from rock music to create a powerful harmony. The horns get very staccato and aggressive because this is really under the umbrella of funk music, which requires precision. You're almost thinking about it like a sample-based thing where you're coming in with the part and repeating it, building off of it and harmonizing it. You can switch it up every once in a while, but you mostly stay consistent."

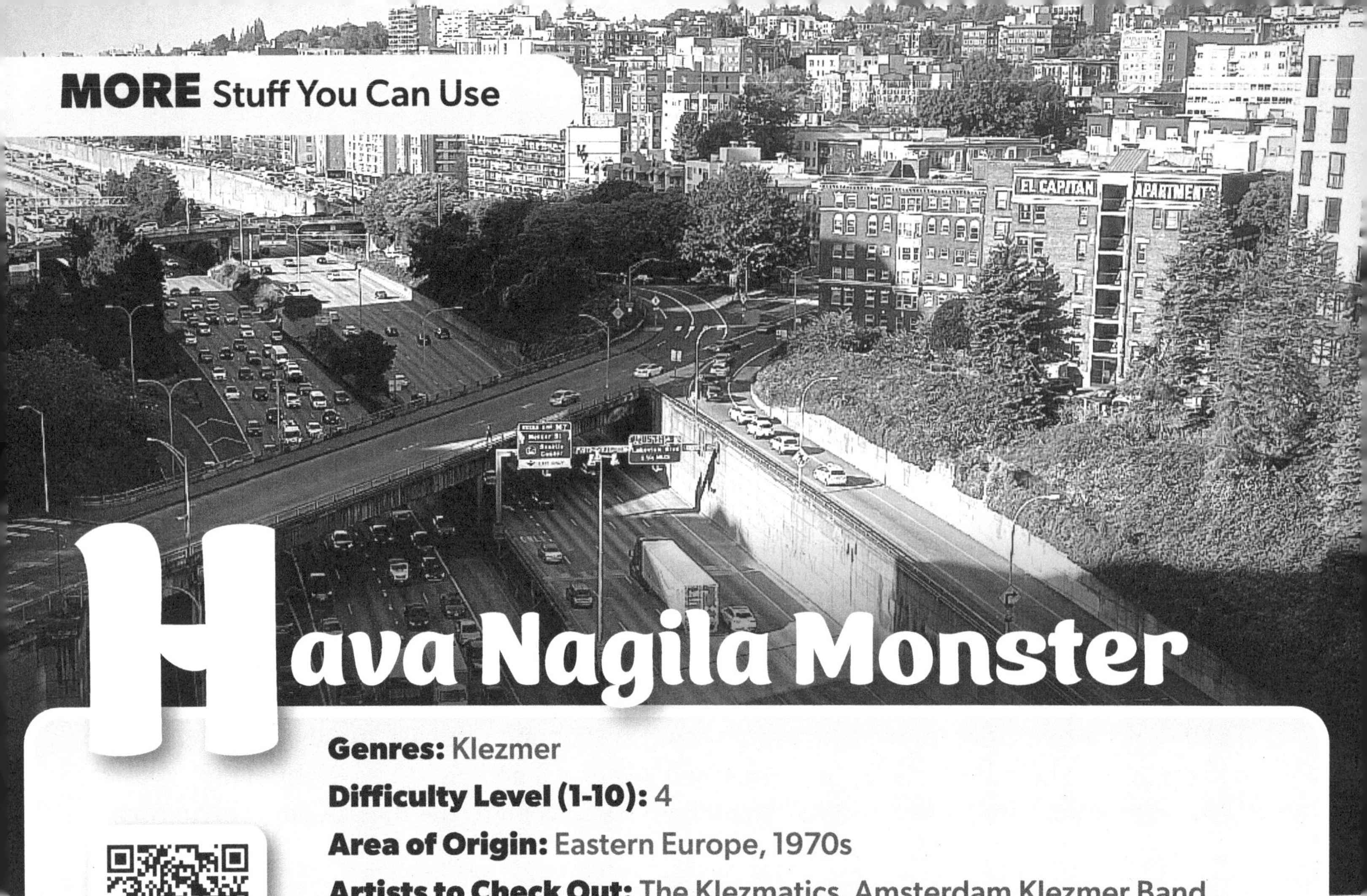

Hava Nagila Monster

Genres: Klezmer

Difficulty Level (1-10): 4

Area of Origin: Eastern Europe, 1970s

Artists to Check Out: The Klezmatics, Amsterdam Klezmer Band, Klezmer Conservatory Band, John Zorn

Drummers to Check Out: David Licht, Aaron Alexander, Larry Eagle, Richie Barshay

The History

While traditional Yiddish klezmer music dates back hundreds of years to the villages of Eastern Europe, the klezmer revival of the 1970s and '80s saw it evolve and grow in popularity. The vast majority of klezmer is made for dancing, with horas, freylekhs and bulgars as a few of the most prevalent types [9a]. These days, every Jewish wedding includes a hora, with guests clasping hands in a circle as the bride and groom are hoisted skyward on chairs amidst the chaotic revelry.

Early klezmer folk bands typically had violin and clarinet, however the modern renaissance featured the addition of instruments like guitar, accordion, brass and percussion. Bands like The Klezmatics stretched the music's creative boundaries by mixing in contemporary sounds while staying true to its traditional roots [9b]. Drummers found interesting new ways to orchestrate these rhythms around the modern drum kit, never losing focus on the primary goal of keeping people dancing.

This melting pot of musical influences cut both ways, as modern klezmer harmony and rhythm began popping up in other genres. Saxophonist and composer John Zorn gained notoriety for using these elements in jazz, while singer Joshua Nelson became the self-proclaimed "prince of kosher gospel." Klezmer's evolution and reinvention within the contemporary music scene has established it as an important style for all drummers to check out.

The Music

This groove is all about keeping a steady pulse, popping the accents and using texture changes to create small variations. The loose hi-hat is a staple of klezmer drumming and both hands play on beat 1, the "and" of 2, the "and" of 3 and beat 4 in unison. That's basically the whole ballgame!

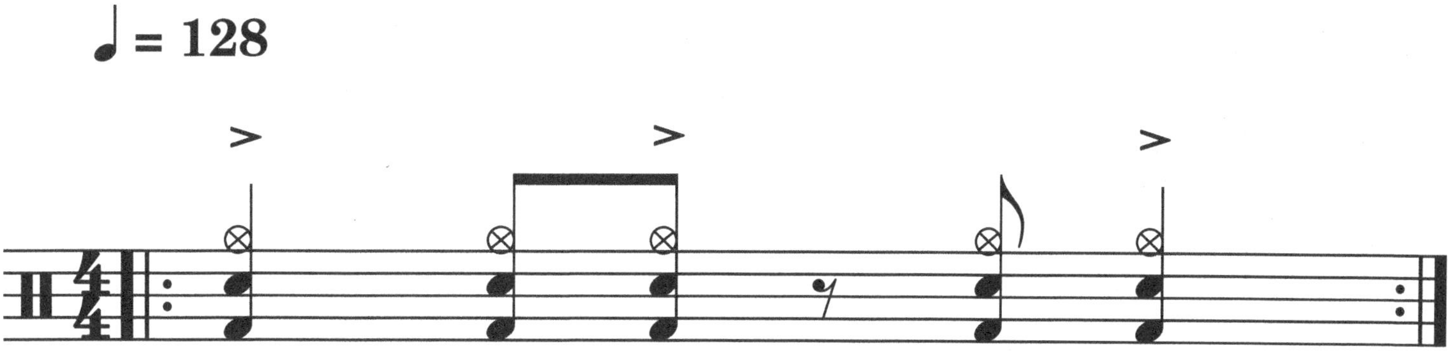

Your kick drum can also mirror this rhythm which really beefs it up, or you can play quarter notes to propel the beat forward. I tend to go and back and forth depending what the other musicians are playing, but I try to make the switch at the beginning of a section and stick with it throughout so it's not too random. This groove is meant for dancing, and it's important not to break the flow (we don't want anyone to fall down!).

Variation #1

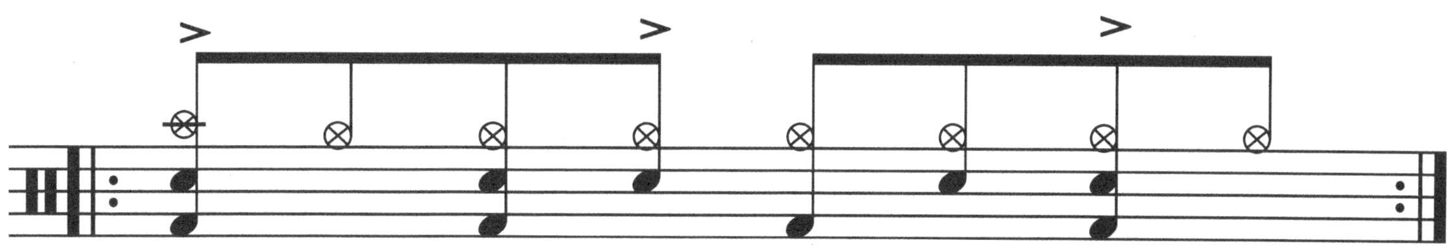

Keep your fills punchy and crisp. Most importantly, always keep the underlying klezmer rhythm in mind so you can smoothly get into and out of musical phrases.

Fill #1

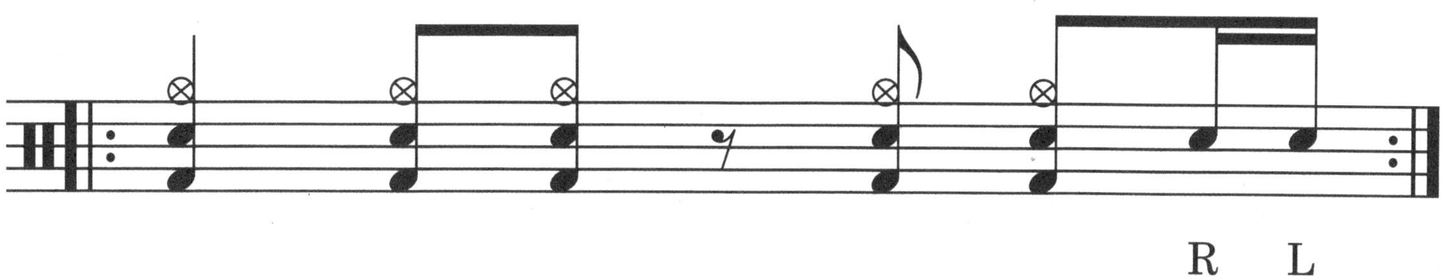

Fill #2

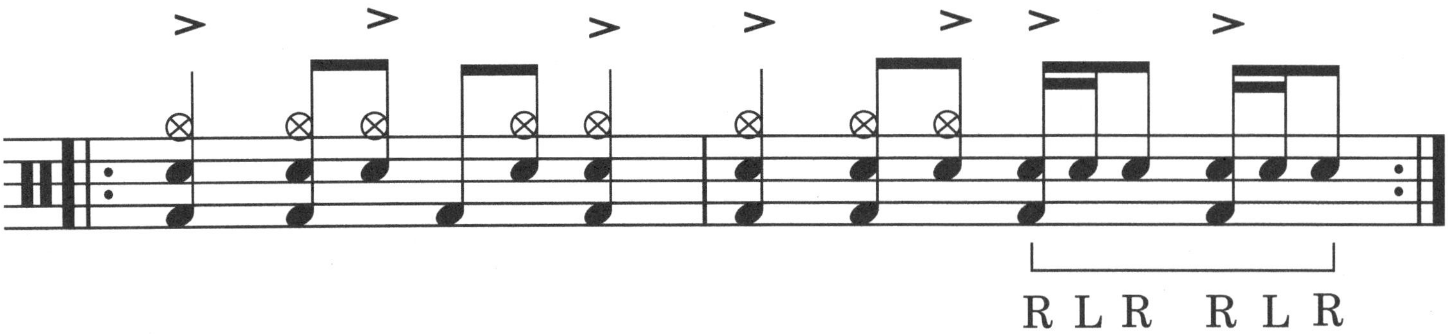

Fill #3

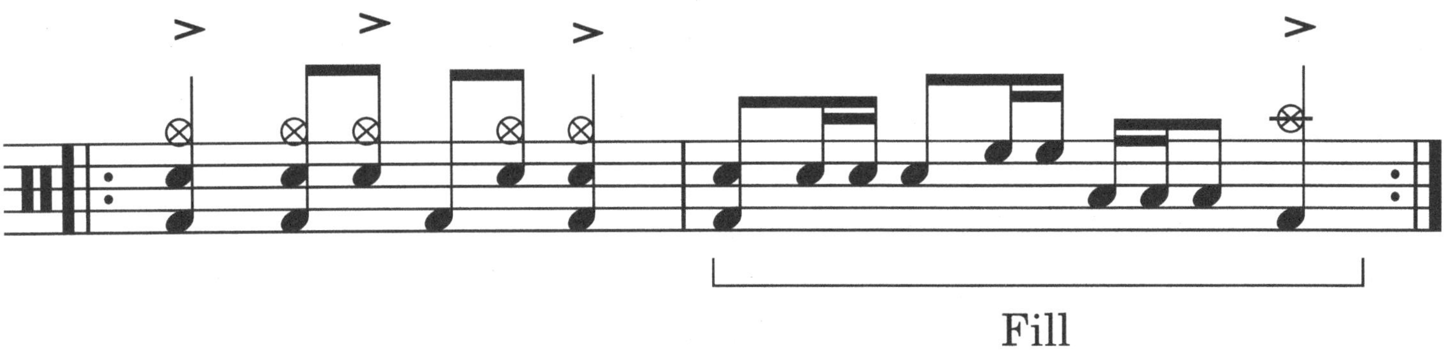

Fill #4

When you're playing live, adrenaline sometimes leads to rushing, but trying to cram too many notes into a short fill can make you late in getting back into the pattern. I always recommend practicing fills with a metronome regardless of what style of music you're playing.

The Band

Dmitry Ishenko:

"Klezmer music really grooves because there are so many interlocking rhythmic patterns. The drums are playing that specific klezmer rhythm and [the bass] is playing just a simple 1 and 3 over it. That creates a certain kind of interlocking groove and then we have the guitar which is playing all upbeats. So, that's three layers of rhythm that create this beautiful big picture and big groove. The only time there is really any kind of improvised input from the rhythm section is at the end of 8-bar phrases where we do a fill into something. Otherwise, we just keep it really solid and groovy."

Elias Meister:

"I'm really feeling the downbeats even though I'm playing upbeats. I'm playing just in the spaces in-between. I feel like the only kind of interaction you would have with a soloist in this style would be marking different sections in terms of intensity. It can be a little bit louder, a little bit softer, a little bit tighter or a little bit more open. Once you pick that intensity or openness, then you stick with it. But the general parts you're playing are very much the same."

Wes Maples:

"I think what Elias said is important. He said he's playing on the upbeats but he's really feeling the 'one' and you can hear that in the melody too. These are really fun, high-energy melodies in unison, but you can feel it always coming back home to land on strong pulses, usually the one. The solo is definitely a device to extend a section and create more energy, and a lot of that is for the purpose of dancers. I feel like a lot of improvisation comes out of that purpose, really."

I Heart the '80s

Genres: '80s Rock, Arena Rock

Difficulty Level (1-10): 4

Area of Origin: Los Angeles, England, 1980s

Artists to Check Out: Def Leppard, Aerosmith, KISS, Bon Jovi, Foreigner, AC/DC, Van Halen, Queen, Journey, Guns N' Roses, Poison

Drummers to Check Out: Joey Kramer, Phil Rudd, Steve Smith, Alex Van Halen, Rick Allen, Tommy Lee

The History

Big hair! Big personalities! Even bigger drums! The 1980s brought about a new era for rock 'n roll as bands like Aerosmith, AC/DC and Van Halen shot to fame with guitar-driven anthems, catchy vocal choruses and a flair for the dramatic. Showmanship took center stage as these bands played to massive crowds in arenas around the world. The shows often featured pyrotechnic displays and costume changes, adding a theatrical element that gave fans a fully immersive experience [10a]. KISS wore outlandish makeup, Def Leppard had one-armed drumming phenom Rick Allen and Aerosmith (my personal favorite) featured powerhouse vocalist Stephen Tyler and guitar hero Joe Perry. Guns N' Roses had Axl Rose and Slash, Van Halen featured brothers Eddie and Alex, while Queen gave the world the inimitable Freddie Mercury.

Drummers hit hard and played BIG. In the early '80s, Phil Rudd brought his massive, thumping drum tone to AC/DC's hit "Back in Black," while long-underrated German drummer Herman Rarebell ripped through Scorpions' mega-hit "Rock You Like a Hurricane." As the decade wore on, Tommy Lee drove the bus on the Mötley Crüe anthem "Dr. Feelgood" and Joey Kramer created the perfect blueprint for power ballad drumming with Aerosmith's "Livin' on the Edge." These were just a few of the many standout performances, and they all had one thing in common: great energy. As the '90s rolled around, this style waned in popularity with the rise of West Coast grunge. But its hallowed place in the history of popular music will always be secure.

The Music

This groove should hit *hard*. I actually grabbed a larger pair of sticks and a heavier bass drum beater when we recorded it. The key is keeping the energy up throughout. I can't tell you how many times I've heard a band play classic rock or '80s tunes in a bar and the drummer got tired and started dragging towards the end of a song. Hitting hard while staying under control and not overplaying is a real art form (Foo Fighters' drummer Taylor Hawkins is a perfect, albeit non-'80s example). The pattern itself is pretty simple, with the ride bell providing that classic '80's sound you'll find throughout this style.

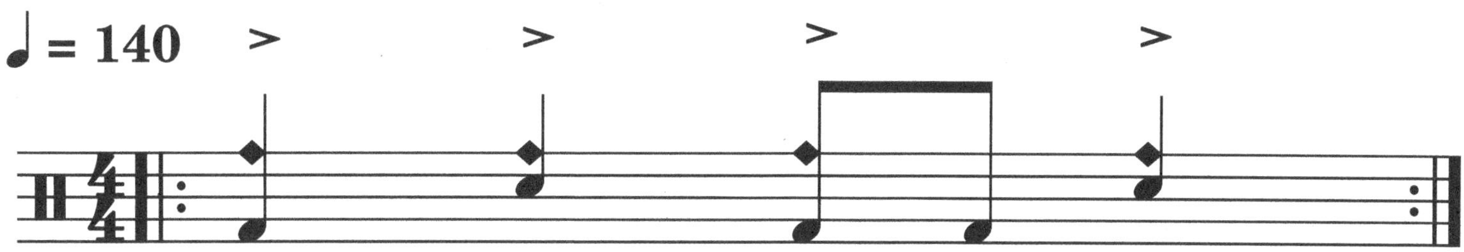

If you check out the play-along track, you'll hear the bassist and guitarist laying into the driving 8th-note rhythms. The bass drum part doesn't perfectly mimic this since it would be way too busy, however it's important to get the pattern locked in with the rest of the band. Try switching to 8th notes on the bell when the B section begins.

Variation #1

Stay on top of the beat to keep things moving forward. You can keep playing the ride bell or switch to loose hi-hat for the C section leading into the hits.

Variation #2

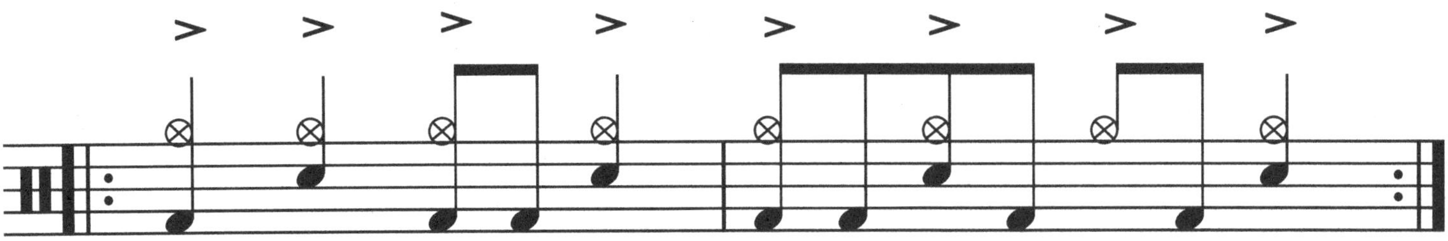

You can add crashes to your heart's content, but remember that your cymbals inhabit a similar frequency as the guitar so you don't want to create a tonal clash by getting too "bashy" and wild.

Variation #3

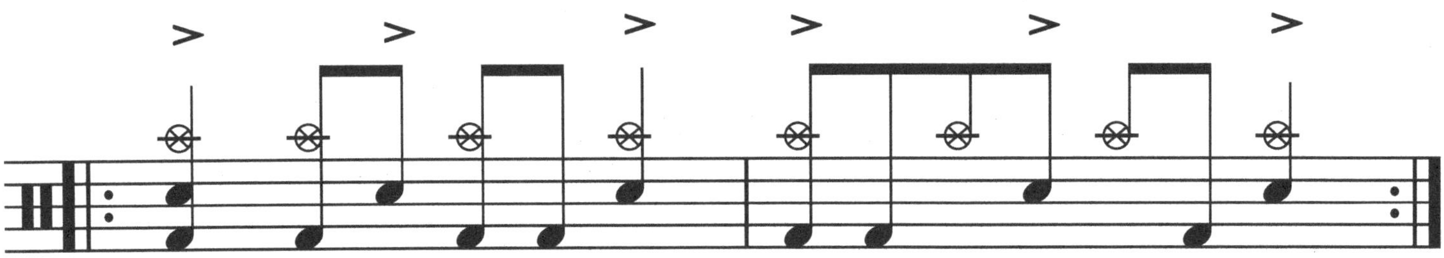

Simple fills that are heavy on the flams can create a beefy texture.

Fill #1

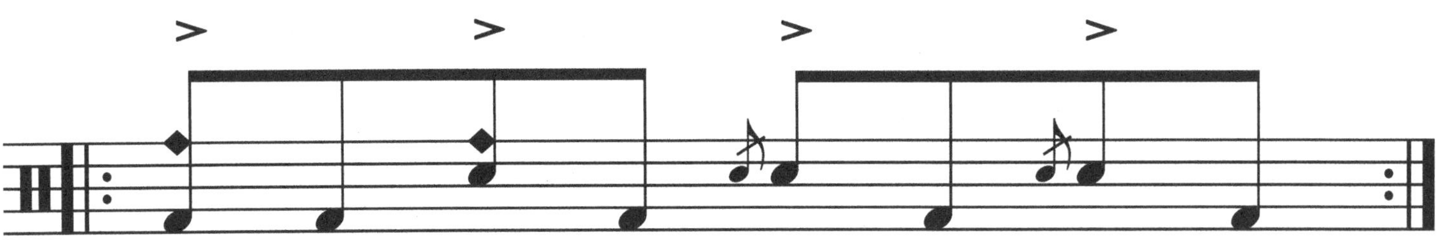

Fill #2

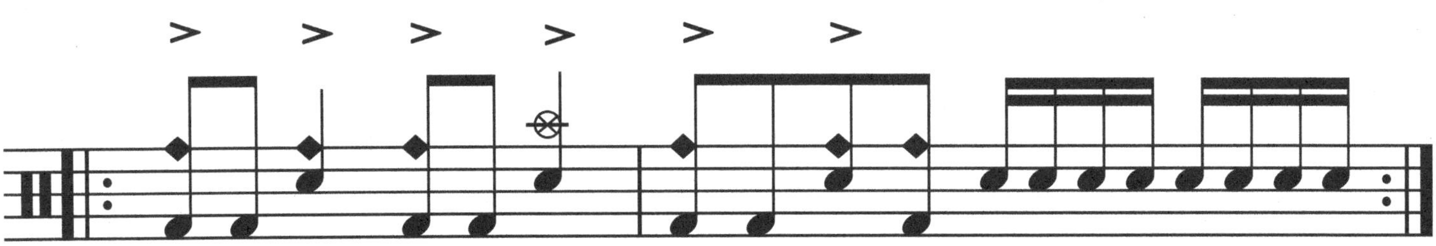

So, grab your flowing blond wig and eyeliner and enjoy a wild ride back in time!

PORCELANOSA

I Heart the '80s Full Chart

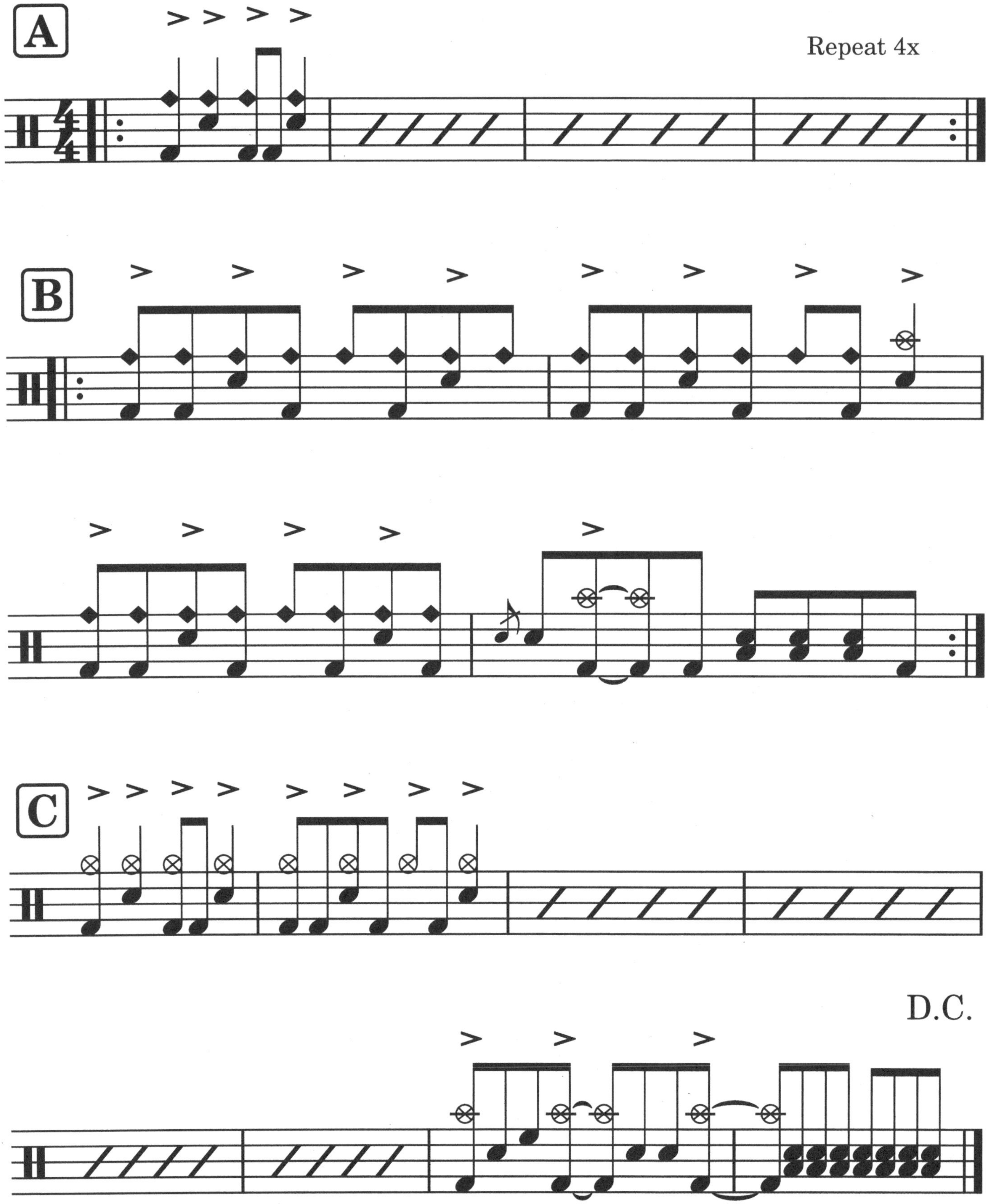

The Band

Elias Meister:

"For the guitar sound on an '80s rock song, you're definitely thinking slightly overdriven but also simple. It's not too crazy and it's very clear. Everything is forward-moving and on top of the beat. It's very downbeat-driven and doesn't have a lot of syncopation. I'm doing a lot of lead parts with arpeggios and stuff. In a setting like this, we're playing pretty hard but we don't want to overdo it.

"When I play this, I'm thinking about a big party happening in a stadium with everybody clapping and stomping and shaking their long hair. One broader point to consider is what a particular kind of music is composed for or where it's meant to be played. If it's a techno club or a stadium or a small rock club or a concert hall or a jazz club, all these styles are adapting to the space and the noise level that's around, plus the amount of people. So, it's good to have that in mind when you're playing a certain style. If I'm thinking about sitting by a campfire or playing in a stadium or a small club, it makes a big difference in how I approach the music."

Dmitry Ishenko:

"In an '80s rock setting, I would play simple and it would be a repeating line. It can be all the same 8th notes, but there could be some melodic variation as long as it repeats bar after bar. It's slightly on top of the beat because you want to keep it driving, but with little variation and no noodling on the bass. The bass and drums stay locked and I'm listening to the snare drum. Give me the two and four. That's really what's determining my note placement. You want to keep things very precise with very little dynamic variation. With the bass part, every note has to be the exact same dynamic with no dips, otherwise the groove is gone."

Jim Black Attack

Genres: Modern Jazz, Rock

Difficulty Level (1-10): 6

Area of Origin: New York, late 1980s

Artists to Check Out: Alas No Axis, Human Feel, Pachora, Tim Berne, Dave Douglas, Endangered Blood

Drummers to Check Out: Jim Black

The History

Jazz is all about improvising, pushing boundaries and conjuring up new avenues for creative expression. One of the major themes of this book is how all styles of music are related and having a basic knowledge of many genres makes you better at each one individually. There is no drummer on the scene today that epitomizes this more than Jim Black. As a renowned jazz drummer and composer, he incorporates rock, Latin, Balkan and avant-garde elements into his distinctive sound. A native of Seattle, Black attended Berklee College of Music in Boston, forming the band Human Feel with saxophonists Chris Speed and Andrew D'Angelo in 1987. After relocating to New York in 1990, the group added guitar innovator Kurt Rosenwinkel. Combining linear rock elements with a loose feel and boundless spirit of improvisation, this band sounded unlike anything the jazz world had ever heard.

After spending time working with jazz heavyweights Tim Berne and Dave Douglas, Black started his own project Alas No Axis with Speed, guitarist Hilmar Jensson and electric bassist Skúli Sverrisson. This group operated and sounded almost like a rock band, featuring group improvisations instead of solos. Jensson's distorted guitar parts and Sverrison's driving 8th-note lines provided the perfect canvas for Black's virtuostic madness.

His drums were tuned so low that you could almost hear the heads rattling. His cymbals had little decay and he played all the parts of the drum set. The rims, stands and anything else he could reach was fair game. He also played with mind-blowing dynamics. The loud parts were *loud*, like he was playing in a stadium. But his quiet moments were equally breathtaking, with flurries of short notes creating a rich tapestry of sound. He played in an almost lyrical way, as a composer.

Later projects like Endangered Blood (with Speed, clarinetist Oscar Noriega and acoustic bassist Trevor Dunn) and the Middle Eastern-influenced Pachora pushed this avant-rock/future-jazz sound even further. The greatest compliment you can give to any creative musician is to say that they sound like no one else. Jim Black is truly one-of-a-kind and an important artist for any aspiring drummer to check out [11a] [11b].

The Music

This pattern is linear and syncopated, but it shouldn't feel too busy if you really emphasize the difference between the accented and non-accented notes. Your first impulse might be to try to crack those accents even harder to create separation, but doing that could make the whole thing too heavy-handed. Try lowering the volume of the non-accented notes instead since dynamics and balance between the limbs is all relative. Think of your limbs almost like faders on a mixing board. The louder everything gets, the less control you have so it's important to find just the right blend.

The right hand has the biggest job in this groove, going between the rim and head of the of the floor tom. The bass drum on the "and" of beat 2 is the "sauce" that makes this groove funky. If you check out the play-along track, you'll hear the bass player emphasizing it too while the guitar melody soars over top.

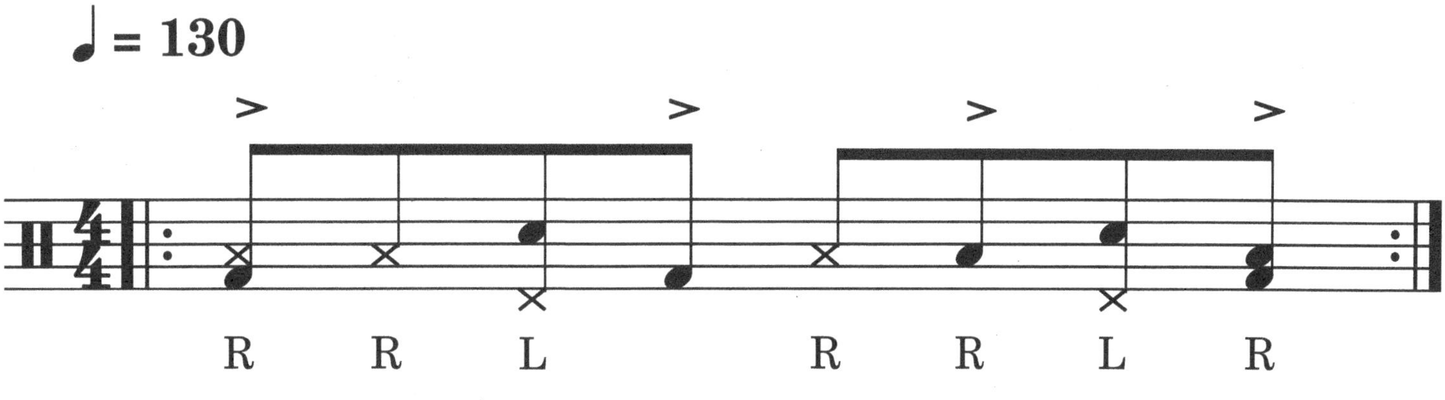

This style of modern jazz/rock has a ton of room for improvisation and musical exploration. The language of the music is super-important (propulsive 8th-note phrases orchestrated melodically around the kit in creative ways).

Variation #1

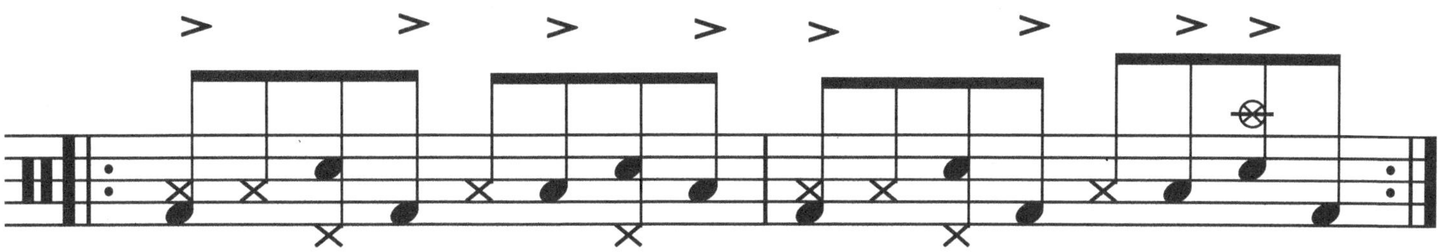

MORE Stuff You Can Use

Once you feel like you've tapped into the vocabulary you can stretch, deviate, interact and be as "present" in the music with your bandmates as possible. Add crashes, do some fills and move freely around the kit.

Variation #2

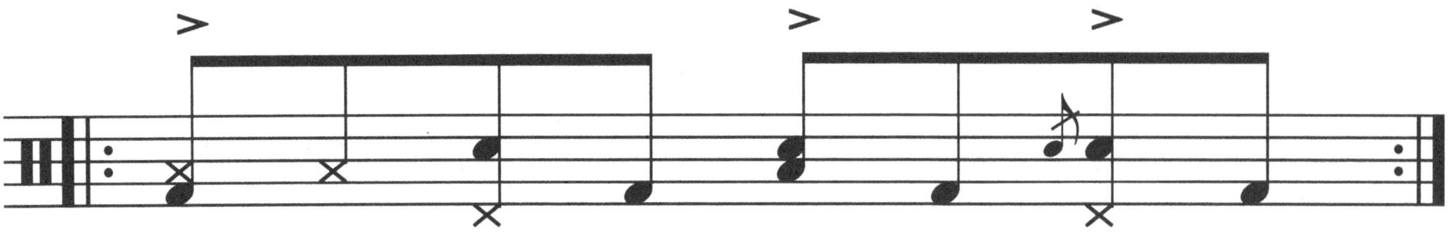

Variation #3

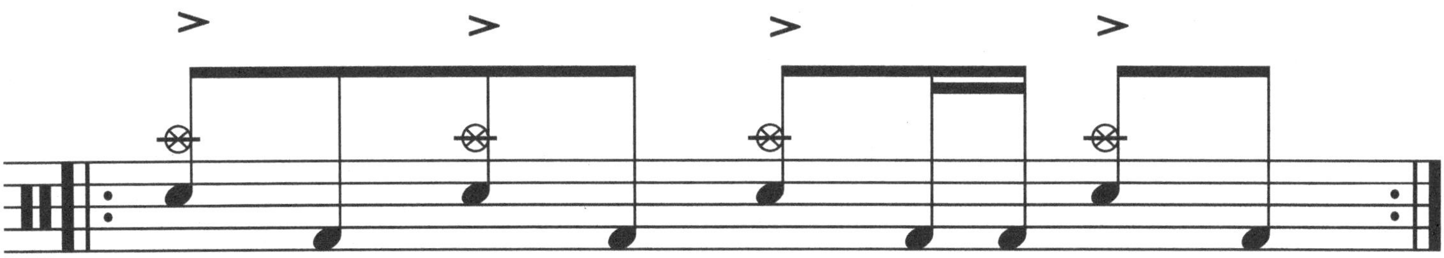

This jazz/rock hybrid is one of my favorite styles to play because it has the solid foundation of a groove at first, but then you can take the music anywhere you want. I hope you enjoy getting into it as much as I did!

The Band

Dmitry Ishenko:

"With this particular Jim Black-inspired piece, we're referencing a lot of what he did with his own solo band Alas No Axis, which is an instrumental project with rock-type compositions. A lot of it is 8th-note based, and so is our example. I'm imitating the great virtuoso bass player Skúli Sverrisson, who in this context is really holding himself back because he has ridiculous technique but he's playing very simply. He plays those 8th notes in a very controlled fashion, kind of short with not much sustain...they kind of bounce. So, that's what I'm channeling...and in the drums, the snare drum and the two and four is important to create forward motion. But at the same time, it's this controlled, delicate feeling as opposed to just a flat-out rock 'n roll '80s sort of groove... and drum-wise, it's pretty colorful. Jim Black is an extremely colorful drummer. He's using every part of the drum set. He can interpret an otherwise standard rhythm, but he uses such colors that it becomes very non-standard."

Elias Meister:

"Playing this intersection between rock and jazz, we're trying to get into this bouncy, cool, sexy thing but you can throw in some weird notes or rhythms that you would not hear in a rock song. When the tension builds, you have the option to go much further than you would in a typical rock song and then resolve it by just going back into that heavy kind of groove...and with the chords and harmonies, I definitely think about trying to find some colors that are not the usual rock colors in how they move."

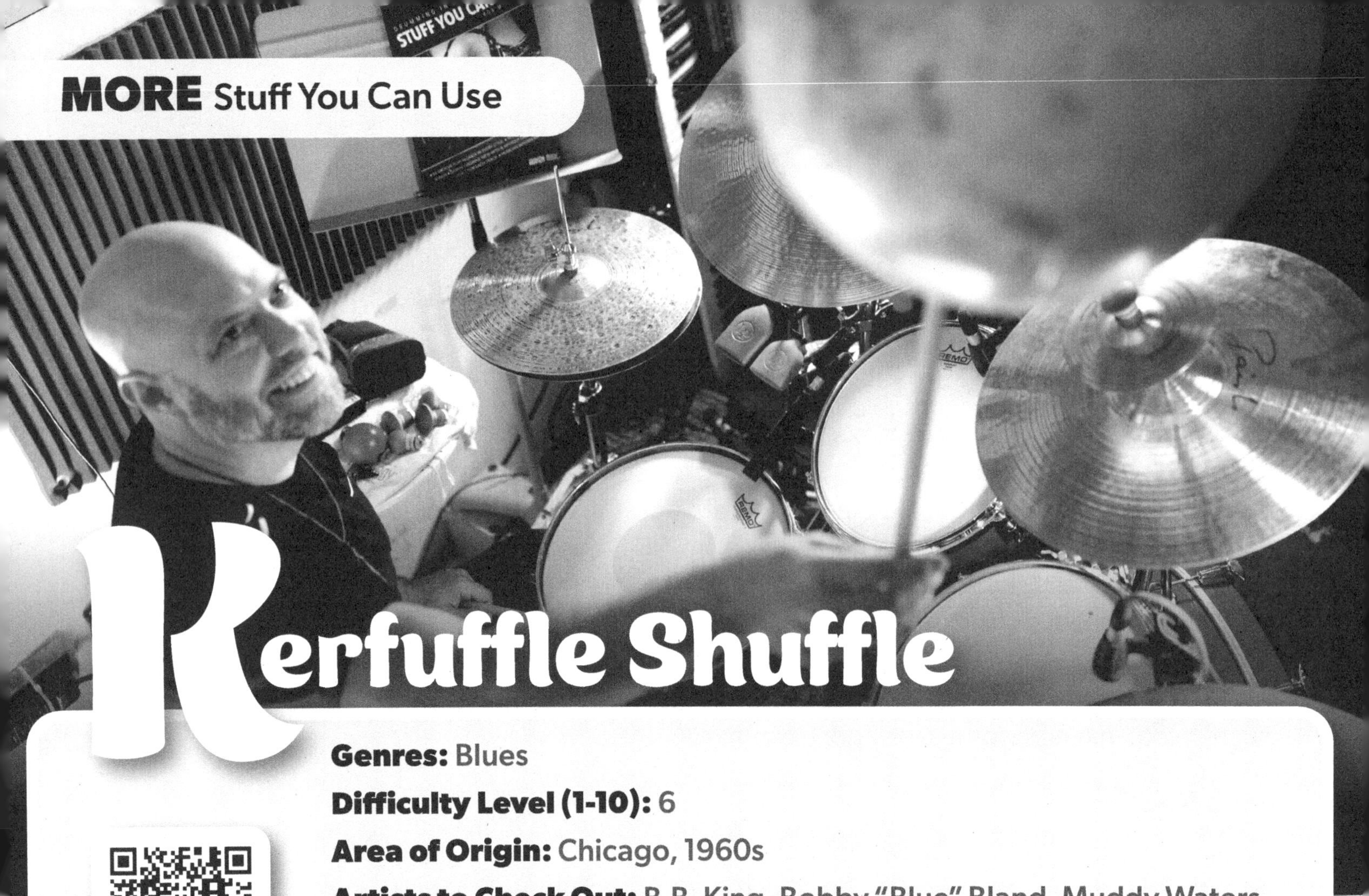

Kerfuffle Shuffle

Genres: Blues

Difficulty Level (1-10): 6

Area of Origin: Chicago, 1960s

Artists to Check Out: B.B. King, Bobby "Blue" Bland, Muddy Waters, Albert King, Freddie King, Buddy Guy

Drummers to Check Out: Tony Coleman, Sam Lay, Odie Payne, John "Jabo" Starks, Fred Below

The History

While there are many different varieties of blues grooves, the Chicago double shuffle became popular in the 1960s, with drummers Sam Lay (Muddy Waters), Odie Payne and Fred Below as early innovators. These grooves combined the swung 8th notes of jazz with the backbeat from early R&B and rock. Legendary blues artists like B.B. King, Muddy Waters and Freddie King all featured this type of shuffle in their music[12a][12b]. Perhaps the most well-known example is Robert Johnson's classic tune "Sweet Home Chicago," which was famously featured in the movie *The Blues Brothers* (1980).

Before we get into the technical stuff, I'd like to explain how this groove came to be in the book. I was in Indianapolis for the Percussive Arts Society International Convention (a joyous annual gathering of drummers from around the world called PASIC) and dropped in on a clinic by the great Tony Coleman, who toured and recorded with B.B. King for over 30 years. Many shuffles I had heard and played up to that point featured a quarter-note "4-on-the-floor" bass drum pattern. T.C. was doing something different! The bass drum was shuffling too, but it was light and bouncy. This is why it's called a double shuffle and it gave the pattern so much forward motion. When I got home and tried it, I realized a few things 1) How delicate a task it was to get the swing on the bass drum just right 2) How tired this made my foot after not very much time 3) How challenging it was to keep it from getting too heavy. All this put me in quite a kerfuffle, thus we have the Kerfuffle Shuffle. For a deeper dive into this style, check out Coleman's own book *AUTHENTIC BLUES DRUMMING* (Hudson Music).

The Music

Besides keeping the bass drum light and accenting beats 2 and 4 on the snare, this pattern is all about being consistent with the time and groove. I'm also doing some variations with my right hand to create texture changes and adjust the intensity to flow with the music: closed hi-hat, loose hi-hat and ride cymbal bell. Try starting with closed hi-hats and then loosen them when the chord change happens. Or play loose hi-hats and switch to the ride to build it up even more. Building and contracting the intensity using textures keeps things interesting without interrupting the pattern.

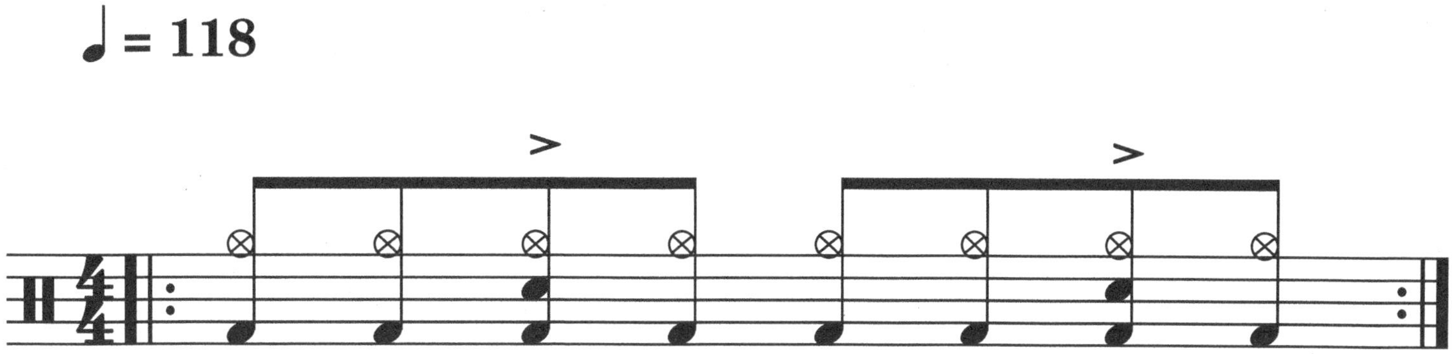

Variation #1

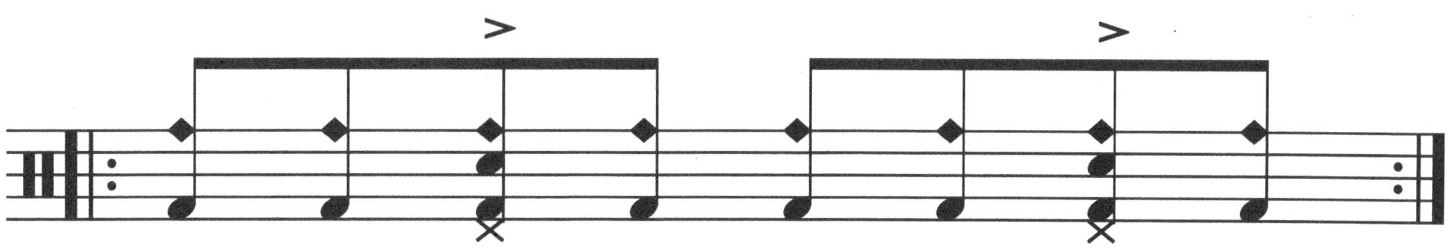

You also can sprinkle some crashes, and they don't always have to be on beat 1. Sometimes it's more flavorful to crash on the "and" of 4 or beat 2. This is a concept I mentioned earlier called creating "station points," and it applies to almost every style of music. Experiment with it using the play-along and try to catch some of the hits with the horn section.

Variation #2

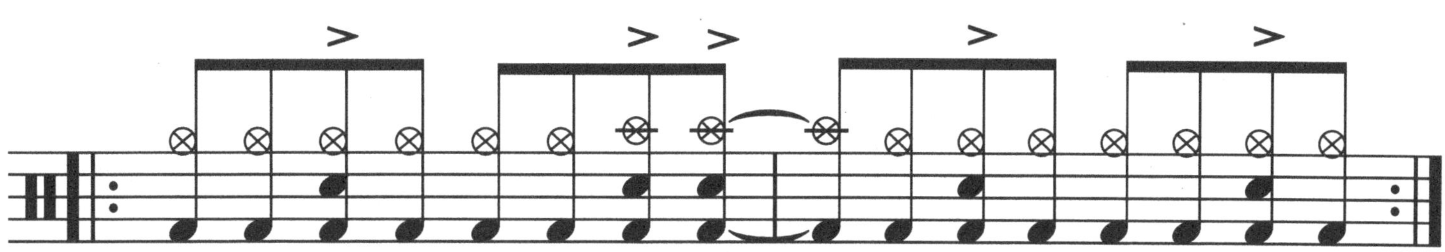

For fills, I like using this simple-but-strong floor tom/snare unison triplet figure in the final measure of a section. However, when you're playing the blues, it's also ok not to do many fills at all and just hold down the beat. The rest of the band will thank you!

Fill #1

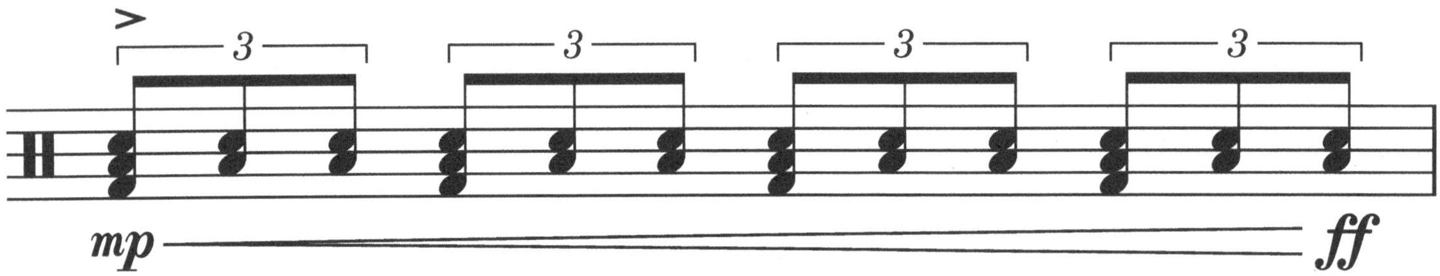

Here's a classic blues ending with my personal twist:

The Band

Dmitry Ishenko:

"From a drummer's perspective, what's tricky about this style is that sometimes the snare can be on top of the beat while the rest of the kit is behind. So, it's almost like a contradiction of itself...but that's how the masters of this music sound. What I'm locking in with as a bass player is the 'behind' part, not the 'ahead' part. From my perspective, it's actually very tight and self-contained. I'm always trying to phrase slightly behind the pattern but be extremely consistent, never varying. That's the key for the bass part. Consistency with exactly the right beat placement, never wavering forward or back. I'm locking in with the first and last triplet of each beat."

Elias Meister:

"On the guitar, you definitely have more liberty in this kind of thing. You don't have to worry so much about marking downbeats. I'm feeling more of a backbeat kind of thing. Other than these big turning points in the form like going to the four-chord, where it's nice to mark the one, that's not something you have to do. It has this loose, laid-back vibe but still has to fit together and move forward and be groovy."

Wes Maples:

"The four-chord is really important in establishing the blues style. As long as you have that, you have the foundation of one and four. So, what I'm listening for [in the drums] is that there will almost always be a fill (especially a triplet), and then you know it's definitely a cue for the rest of the band. That helps keep the band together in making that change to the four and back. There's definitely more room for tonal expression in the saxophone that's very stylistic. The growls and bends and big vibrato are all part of the saxophone tradition in this style. So, that gives a little bit of extra looseness to the texture."

Levon it Be

Genres: Roots/Americana, Blues, Country

Difficulty Level (1-10): 4

Area of Origin: Southern and Midwestern U.S.A., late 1960s

Artists to Check Out: The Band, Ronnie Hawkins and the Hawks, Bob Dylan, Ringo Starr's All-Starr Band, Levon Helm & the RCO All-Stars, Amy Helm

Drummers to Check Out: Levon Helm

The History

Levon Helm, famed drummer for The Band, was born in the Arkansas delta town of Turkey Scratch in 1940. An accomplished singer who belted out many hits from behind the kit, his musicality and melodic approach has made him one of the most important drummers of our time. Though they were a rock band at heart, The Band drew inspiration from many other genres including folk, country and jazz. This melting pot of musical influences practically leaps out at you when you listen to Helm, and you can almost hear his hardscrabble upbringing in his drumming. These are deep grooves, meat-and-potatoes, no-frills, nothing extra. Truly Stuff You Can Use.

Helm adapted his technique to fit the music, often leaving out the hi-hat when he played the backbeat on the snare. This was brand new at the time, but has since been widely copied by drummers like Jim Keltner, Charlie Watts and Steve Jordan. He also didn't use the crash cymbal much, preferring a tighter sound that didn't interfere with the frequencies of his vocals (all drummers should think about frequencies when they play. It's so important!). One thing drummers could not copy was Helm's incredible natural feel which powered hits like "The Weight," "The Night They Drove Old Dixie Down" and "Up on Cripple Creek" (which was the inspiration for our play-along track).

Keltner explains, "he didn't play the drums exactly like a normal drummer would...he didn't hit really hard but he got plenty of volume out of the drum set. He played traditional grip and he played loose but he had a tightness. It's so paradoxical…that's the mystery, that's the beauty of it. It helped that he was such an incredible singer with the most amazing phrasing and so because of that, the playing of the drums was enhanced even more. So, it was the whole package that he had there [13a]."

The Music

The more laid-back and greasy this groove is, the better. The tempo is slow and the backbeat steady, but all the extra "e's" and "a's" are the secret sauce that gives it forward motion. The snare part in particular has lots of room for doubles, drags and ghost notes.

Try to create a large difference between the volume of your accented and non-accented notes. Dynamics is all relative, so rather than just playing the accents louder, try also lowering the volume of the non-accented notes. It can sometimes be hard to play lots of little notes precisely at such a low volume, but practicing quietly and then really popping the accents is the ticket to getting this one right in the pocket. The metronome on the play-along track is clicking 8th notes since a quarter-note pulse at this tempo would be too slow and difficult to lock in with.

Variation #1

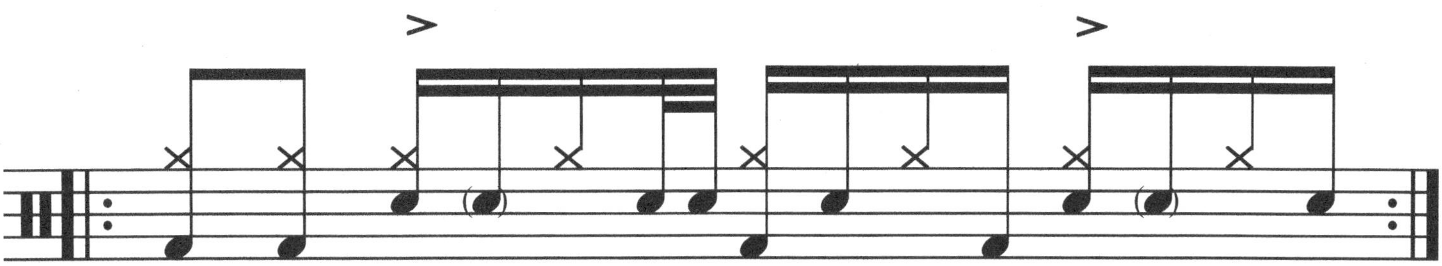

Variation #2

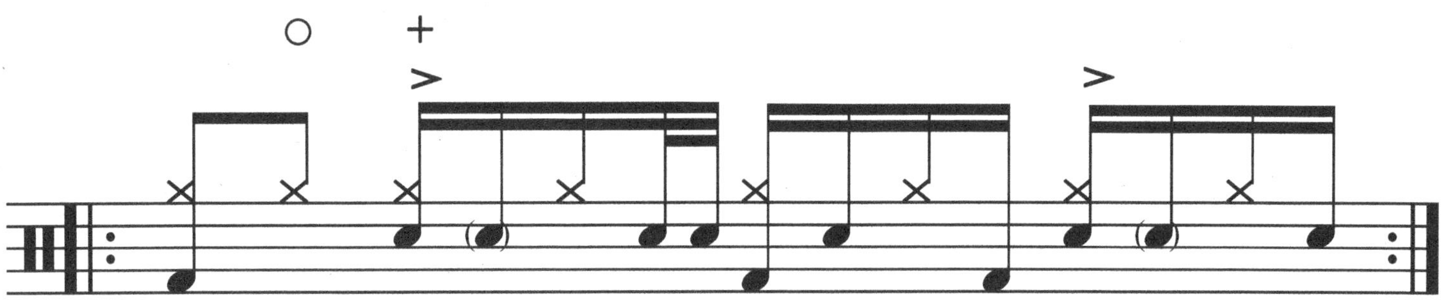

Variation #3

This groove is also very melodic, so it's important that your fills use the musical language of this style. Anything too busy, jarring or flashy simply won't sound right. Try drawing from the vocabulary of the pattern itself and then orchestrate it around the kit.

Fill #1

Fill #2

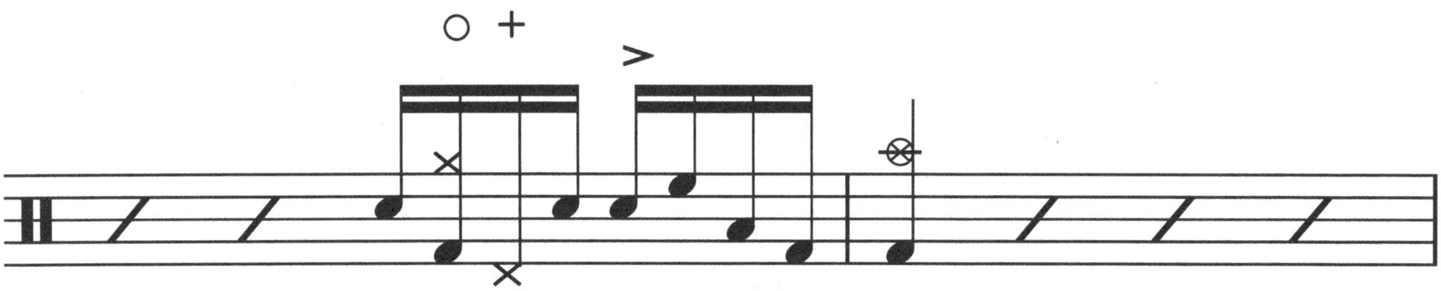

Fill #3

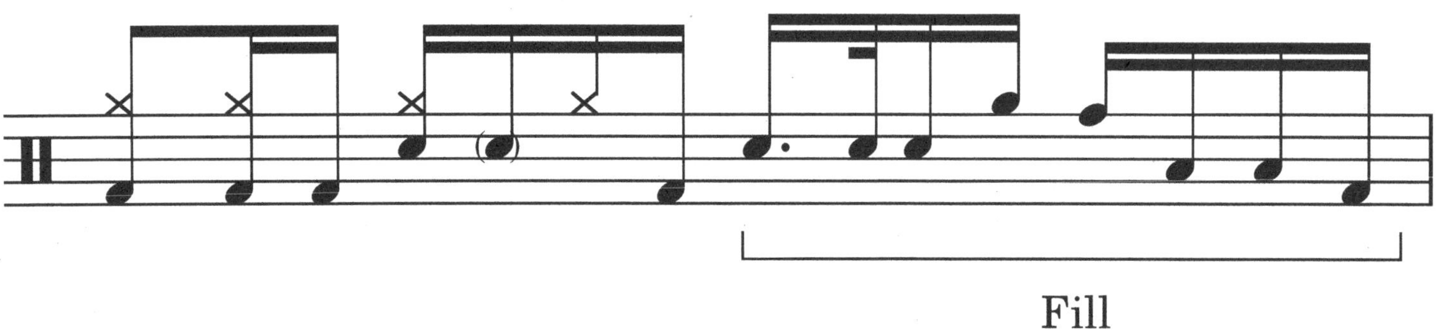

A lot of these fills are "tried and tested" but if you deliver them smoothly and avoid interrupting the flow of the groove, they'll work out great. Slow and steady wins the race on this one!

The Band

Dmitry Ishenko:

"I think this groove is deceptively hard. It sounds kind of effortless and simple, but to make it really work you have to put in some effort. I'm kind of channeling the great bassist from The Band, Rick Danko (a fellow Ukrainian). His style was very locked in with Levon Helm's thing. They were amazing, one of the greatest rhythm sections ever. [Danko's] signature style is that the notes are really short and behind the beat, and he's really locking in with Levon's snare, especially the second hit of every measure. So, that's what I'm listening to in the drums, especially the hi-hat and the snare. Sometimes we need to be in unison and we also need to be laid back enough where it feels like we're pulling, but not entering the 'beat before' territory. Space is really important. You cannot be afraid of space in this groove and you have to really play with the space. Let it breathe."

Elias Meister:

"It's very behind the beat. The two things that I try to keep in mind are first, you don't want to slow down and second, you don't want to be 'too together' with everybody else. It's not like I'm saying it should get messy. You're laying it back but you still want to land together and keep the whole thing moving forward, which is not easy to do. It definitely has a bounce, and the landing point [of the phrase] is often on beat 2, almost like a real Brazilian samba that lands on the two. It makes it much bouncier.

"This is a style where the simplicity is totally the key. You can't clutter this thing up with too many fills or notes. The simplicity makes it really beautiful but also makes it very bare. Feeling the groove being laid back, but still moving it forward is really what you want to focus on."

Mambo Jambo

Genres: Latin Jazz

Difficulty Level (1-10): 7

Area of Origin: U.S.A., 1940s

Artists to Check Out: Dilly Gillespie, Paquito D'Rivera, Tito Puente, Kenny Dorham, Gonzalo Rubalcaba

Drummers to Check Out: Ignacio Berroa, Chano Pozo, Toto Puente, Teddy Stewart, Elvin Jones, Walfredo Reyes Sr., Bobby Sanabria

The History

The genre of Latin jazz emerged in the 1940s when Cuban and African-American musicians in New York began combining jazz harmonies with clavé rhythms. Dizzy Gillespie's hit "Manteca" was one of the landmark songs in bringing this new genre to the forefront [14a]. Its mambo cymbal bell pattern and 3/2 clavé proved irresistible to dancers and alluring to bebop connoisseurs (the drummer was Teddy Stewart, who played on many of Gillespie's hits from this era). Jazz critic Gary Giddins opined that "Manteca" was the first tune rhythmically based on the clavé to become a jazz standard and called Gillespie's album "one of the most important records ever made in the United States [14b]."

Gillespie's classic "A Night in Tunisia" became another pillar of the Afro-Cuban jazz canon, deftly switching back and forth between a mambo and swing groove. "Afro Blue" by percussionist Mongo Santamaria was another landmark of this style, especially after John Coltrane recorded it in 1963 with Elvin Jones on drums. Drummer and bandleader Tito Puente's tune "Oye Cómo Va" also became a huge crossover hit when rock guitarist Carlos Santana released a cover version in 1971.

As the 1980s rolled around, Cuban drummer Ignacio Berroa joined Gillespie's band, becoming one of the most accomplished and important figures in Afro-Cuban jazz drumming. Like much of the music in this book, the brilliance of Afro-Cuban jazz lies in how it combines different musical and cultural elements from around the world to create a groundbreaking new idiom.

The Music

This jazz mambo requires a nice, light touch but still drives forward. The right hand stays on the ride bell while the left creates the melody by moving between the toms and cross-stick. Practice the limbs separately at first, starting with the feet. Then add the left hand and finally, put it all together. When you work with the play-along track, you'll hear the importance of that accent on the "a" of beat 2. The bass player and guitarist are often playing it too and then diverging into other ideas. Latin jazz tends to be rhythmically dense and a little busy, so this accent is like a band "check-in" point within the pattern that ties the music together.

This is another style where using the concept of "station points" can make you sound way hipper. When I'm playing a mambo, I sometimes like to end my fills on the "and" of beat 4 instead of the downbeat. You don't necessarily want to do this every single time or it'll become a cliché. But sprinkling in this type of language can really give the music a jolt and make it interesting. You'll hear the bass player joining in sometimes too.

Variation #1

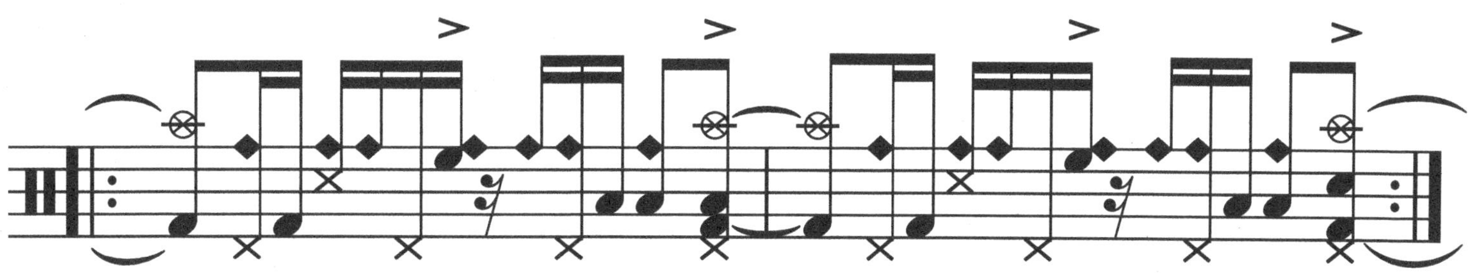

MORE Stuff You Can Use

The toms are a good textural choice for fills in this genre. They can be simple or more complicated as long as you don't break the flow too much and ensure a smooth landing back into the groove. This one is a lot of fun to play once you get comfortable with it.

Fill #1

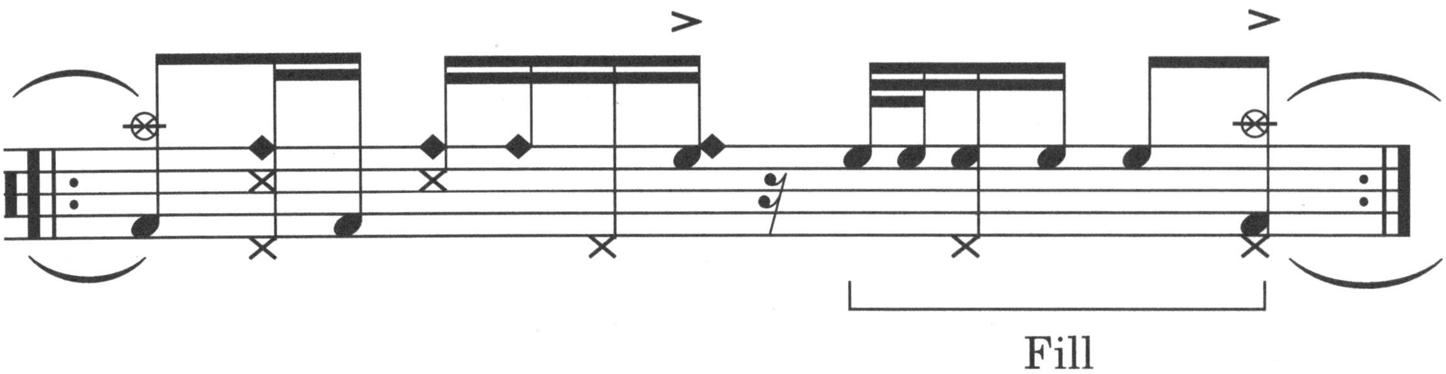

Fill #2

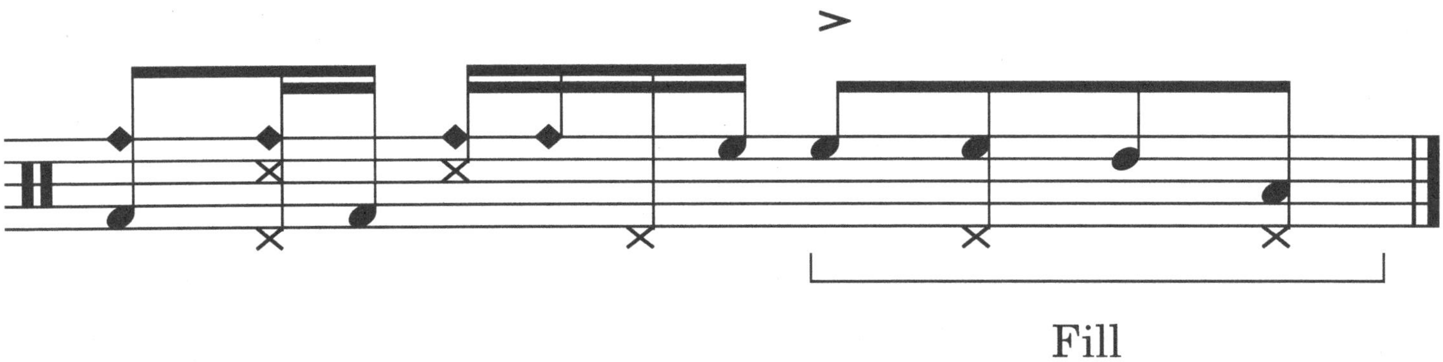

The Band

Dmitry Ishenko:

"I'm playing a tumbao-style bass line which ideally, is never on the downbeat. It's a repeating rhythmic pattern and I'm playing it lightly, but also really pushing it ahead of the beat. An Afro-Cuban bass line has to really push the beat and move forward. As soon as you start dragging, you might lose your place because it's a lot of interlocking parts and they're all in very different places in relation to the measure...so every part has to be very precise. My line is basically a three-note pattern where the third note is always on beat four. So, if I'm coming into a chord change I'm always playing it on beat four of the previous bar. The bass is always anticipating and pushing the rhythm forward. What I'm really listening for in the drums is the ride cymbal, probably a lot of it on the bell."

Elias Meister:

"I feel like the guitar is very on top of the beat and moving ahead. It's almost being pulled back by the percussion which is not laid back, but in the center. It's like the bass and guitar are both pushing it ahead. We're very much playing parts and there's not a ton of improvisation or variation going on. The rhythm and the chords are very specific things, so that keeps it simple and clear in the form. There's definitely a lot of interplay between syncopated rhythms and playing the downbeats, which is a stylistic thing that's appropriate for this music."

Mike Clark Spark

Genres: Jazz, Fusion, Funk

Difficulty Level (1-10): 7

Area of Origin: Oakland, CA, 1970s

Artists to Check Out: Herbie Hancock, Tower of Power, Sly & the Family Stone, Graham Central Station

Drummers to Check Out: Mike Clark, David Garibaldi, Lenny White, Greg Errico, Gaylord Birch

The History

As a bevy of Miles Davis' former sidemen ushered in the jazz/fusion era of the 1970s, a whole different strain of funky jazz was emerging in the San Francisco Bay area. Called "Oakland Funk" or "East Bay Funk," this groundbreaking style combined the linear vocabulary of post-bop jazz with the funky grooves of soul artists like James Brown. The result was music that sounded and felt completely new, as drummers like Mike Clark (Herbie Hancock & The Headhunters), David Garibaldi (Tower of Power) and Gaylord Birch (Graham Central Station) led the way.

As Clark explains in a 2017 interview with pianist George Colligan, "I would say it was the next logical place for forward-thinking drummers of that time to go. For me, I listened to Clyde Stubblefield, Jabo Starks and Bernard Purdie and found my own way of kind of negotiating what I thought they were doing and added bits of that to my own sensibilities...and that became my signature grooves. As far as the blowing, improv or even fills, I used bebop or post-bop language instead of the type of stuff you would hear most funk drummers playing...people all identified with it as the 'Oakland Thing' and we all felt united in this understanding. Musicians and non-musicians alike talked about it all the time, like we all shared this thing and the whole town got it. This was really exciting! When you went to hear the music, everyone was trying to push the envelope and taking chances. There was no playing safe, it was all exploratory [15a]."

Clark and bassist Paul Jackson brought this signature sound to the wildly popular Herbie Hancock albums *Thrust* (1974) and *Flood* (1975). At the same time, Garibaldi's innovative and funky drumming fueled

Tower of Power's landmark record *Back to Oakland* (1974), while the chronically underrated Greg Errico laid down some nasty East Bay funk with Sly & the Family Stone. After spending time in the Bay area, New Yorker Lenny White brought the Oakland sound back east in his work with Chick Corea's Return to Forever. Oakland funk was here to stay, leaving an indelible imprint on the history of jazz, funk, soul and everything in-between [15b].

The Music

This style of drumming is all about creating musical interplay and conversation within the groove. While the pattern itself is busy and linear, each note you play should really mean something beyond just shredding licks. My hope is that working with the play-along track inspires you to get out there and try this with other musicians. It's not easy, but it can be incredibly rewarding! Since you're playing almost every 16th note with one of your limbs, it's important to create a big difference between the accented and non-accented notes. This will make the pattern sound less robotic and groove harder.

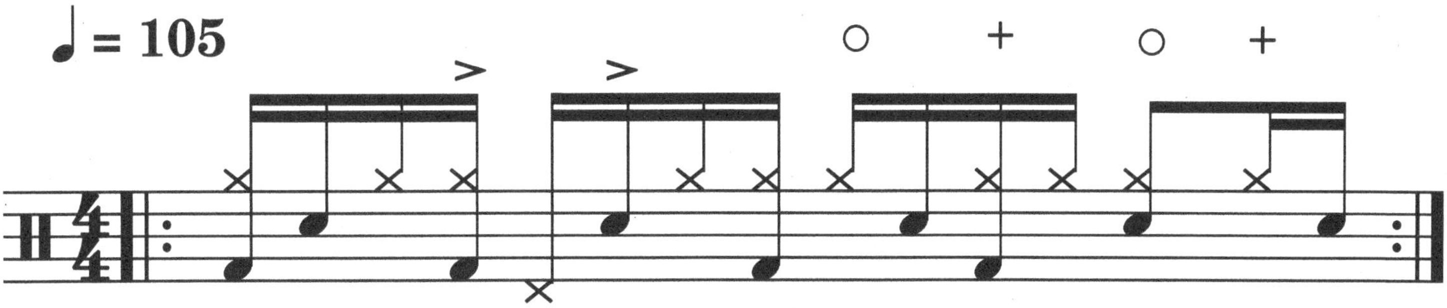

The feel should be loose and relaxed, but also tight and focused...(head explodes). But stick with me here! The way we do this is by blending textures and using appropriate musical language.

For example, when you open/close the hi-hat on beats 3 and 4, make it quick and tight but still relaxed. Really pop the snare accent on the "e" of beat 2. If this were a jazz pattern, you might use a looser, broader articulation; if it were soul/R&B you'd want to tighten it even more. Since this style is a blend of all these things, try to find the perfect sweet spot that really fits the flow of the groove.

Also note that that bass and drums aren't playing exactly the same rhythms or locking together like they might in other styles. They're playing more across and around each other while staying in touch and trading musical ideas. Try to go beyond mimicking what others play and think about developing musical phrases even further (the classical concept of motivic development is something all improvisers should check out).

Variation #1

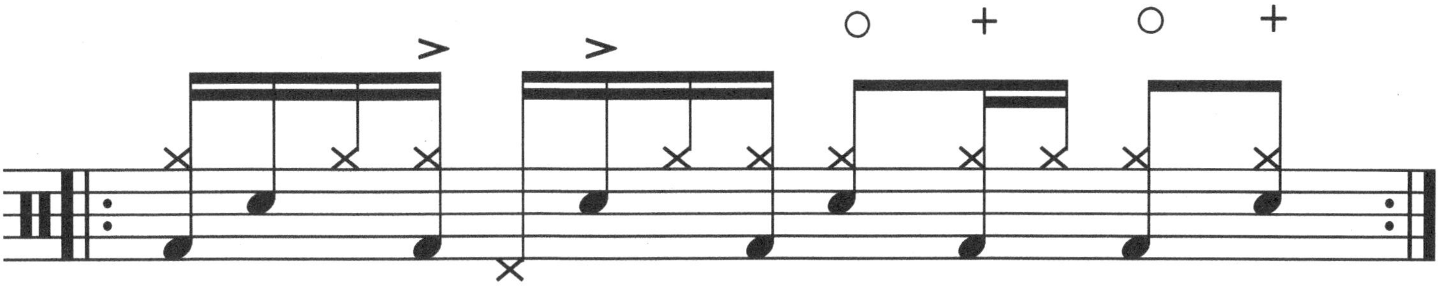

MORE Stuff You Can Use

Switch to the ride, add some crashes and tom fills or try phrasing across the bar line. It's important to build energy as the track goes along, so don't play all your good stuff at the very beginning and try to leave yourself some room to grow.

Variation #2

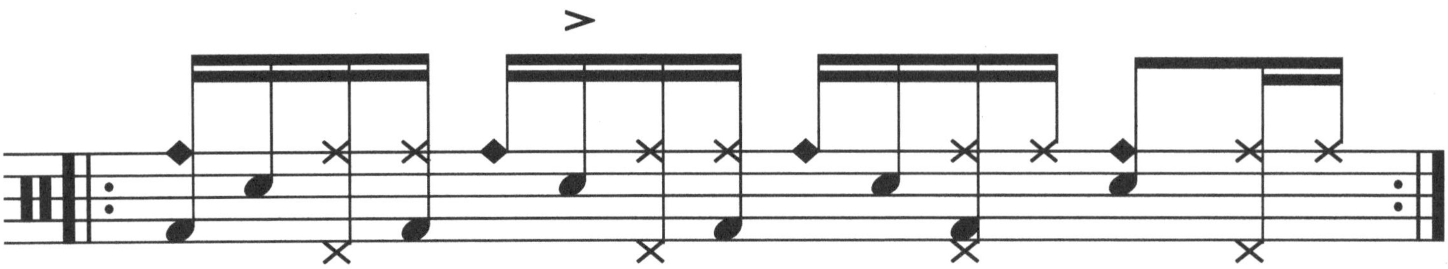

Fill #1

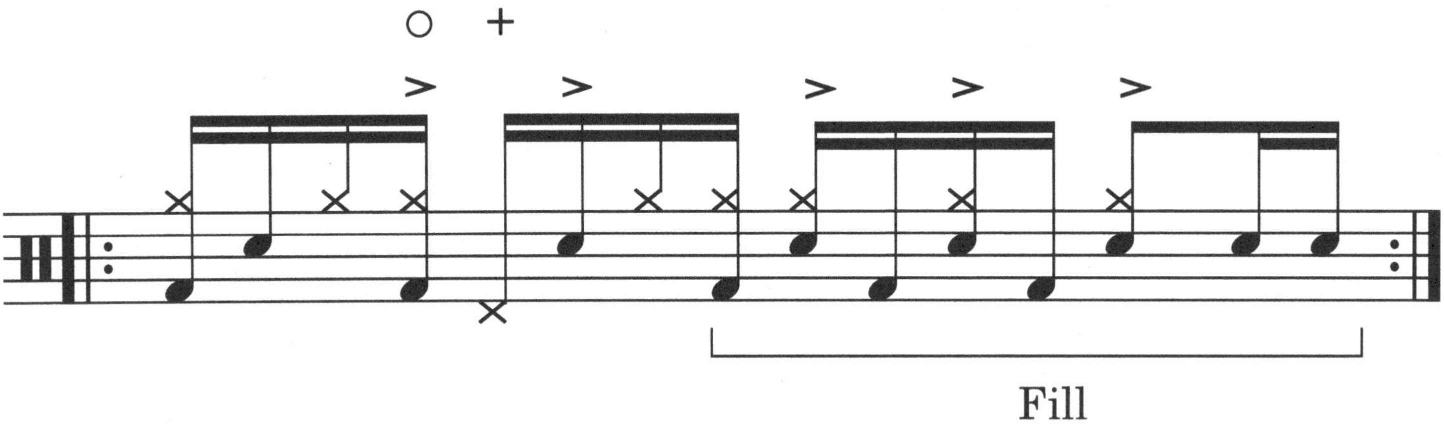

Fill #2

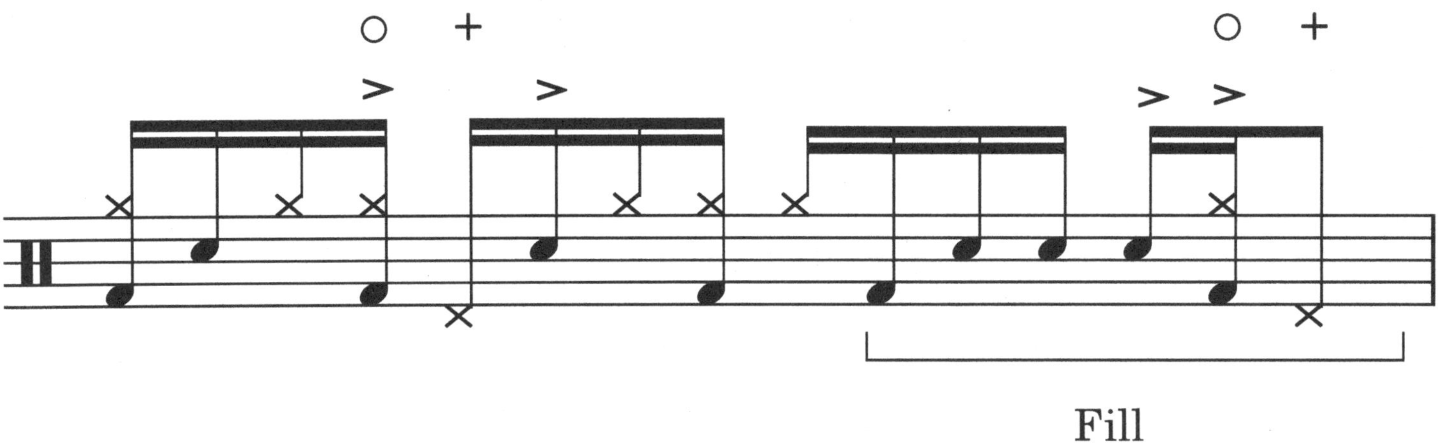

Here's the ending phrase for the play-along track.

You should play this music with joy and freedom, but you don't want to get tired or run out of ideas before the song is over. Above all else, keep the groove steady and always keep listening. In jazz/funk (and every other style in this book) your hands and feet are delivering the message, but your ears are the key in deciding what that message actually is.

The Band

Dmitry Ishenko:

"It's a very straight (not swung) feel and very 16th-note based...and within those 16th notes, there's a lot of syncopation going on which is usually done in two-bar patterns. It can start and stop anywhere on the beat and doesn't have to begin on beat one. It could be starting on beat two. It's really interlocking 16th notes that we're talking about here between the hi-hat, snare and the bass guitar. Paul Jackson from the Headhunters is actually my favorite electric bass player of all time and I've studied him tremendously. He was always kind of mixing it up as far as where the bass line starts. What also really makes a difference is the register change. He tended to play a lot in the higher range of the bass and very percussively, so when those sections would happen he would drop everything down an octave and all of a sudden, the thing had a lot of weight behind it. We're also (of course), missing the fifth ingredient here in our track which is Herbie Hancock, who would start building up on the synthesizer and adding sustained voicings."

Elias Meister:

"I'm trying to hear where people are leaving space in the 16th-note groupings to add in the guitar...moments where the bass and drums are not playing. Everything is very tight and centered on the beat and it's very downbeat-driven too...so the guitar can complement what the drums and the bass are doing with the opposite kind of accented 16th-note rhythms. That usually works really well. I also try to think of things to slowly add intensity to the groove over time without changing the parts too much. Obviously, you could just play a little bit louder. That's the easiest thing, but what's more interesting is to play the notes a little bit longer, less staccato, play fuller voicings or higher/lower pitches to add volume and intensity."

Wes Maples:

"I'm trying to find the space in-between and create a counterpoint, especially with the guitar, and trying to imply some interesting harmonies. It's kind of like boxing...throwing little jabs here and there. It's very much influenced by the great Benny Maupin [Herbie Hancock's sax player] who would play short, melodic phrases and little ideas that really are more textural and imply a little bit of form. But it's not a full-fledged solo. It's semi-improvised and trying to impose a little bit of form on the music too. You can hear how the energy builds nicely over the length of this track and you can hear some of the counterpoint get more complicated between the sax and the guitar. It also builds more rhythmic and harmonic tension which adds to the energy overall. But we keep it simple in the beginning."

Nineties Nails

Genres: Industrial Rock, Metal

Difficulty Level (1-10): 8

Area of Origin: England, U.S.A., Germany, 1970s

Artists to Check Out: Nine Inch Nails, Ministry, Rammstein, Marilyn Manson, Skinny Puppy

Drummers to Check Out: Ray Mayorga, Ilan Rubin, Gene Hoglan, Joey Jordison, Chris Vrenna, Josh Freese, Brian Viglione

The History

Though it originated in England in the mid-1970s, industrial music truly gained widespread popularity in the '90s with the commercial success of artists like Nine Inch Nails and Marilyn Manson. A cross between techno and heavy metal, these songs featured abrasive tones, repetitive machine-like grooves and dark, explicit lyrics. This genre was all about pushing the envelope and breaking free of the traditional confines of electronic, metal and pop music. It was almost as if you had entered a dystopian factory.

While some studio recordings had programmed drum loops, live performances were a different story. Trent Reznor's Nine Inch Nails assembled a band to recreate his music for touring while bands like Ministry, Rammstein and Fear Factory had a more metal-based guitar/bass/drums configuration but incorporated industrial sounds. Manson embraced the theatrical elements of the genre with outlandish outfits, jaw-dropping pyrotechnics and absurd stage antics. Canadian band Skinny Puppy blended harsh, industrial sounds with synthesizers, evoking electro-pop.

While there are many subgenres within the umbrella of industrial music, all share a penchant for the avant-garde and a severe distaste for the establishment. This was protest music against the machinations of society, but still drew strong influences from popular music. It was both discordant and groovy at the same time, becoming one of the most consequential new styles of its era [16a] [16b].

The Music

Integrating electronic sounds into acoustic patterns is not only fun and challenging, it's an important way for us to stay musically relevant in an age where programming has become such a big part of modern music. Blending in triggers is one way to get this happening, while another is to divide your limbs between acoustic and electronic pads. In this pattern, the left hand plays a drum machine, while the right handles the hi-hat and snare. It's a real workout, but if you can get everything organized it'll sound great. It's almost like two drummers playing at once! If you don't have a drum machine, you can put a second snare to the left of your hi-hat and use the rim/head as your two surfaces. It'll still be awesome.

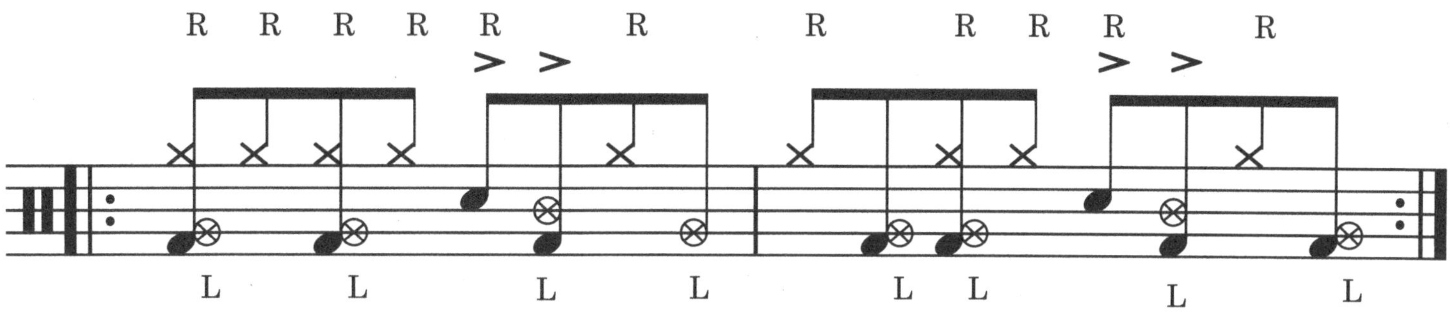

If you do have a drum machine, find a patch with industrial-sounding kick drum and snare pads. The way these sounds interact with their acoustic counterparts is what makes this pattern really cook. Practice the hands separately at first and you'll discover it's not as challenging as it seems.

Right Hand

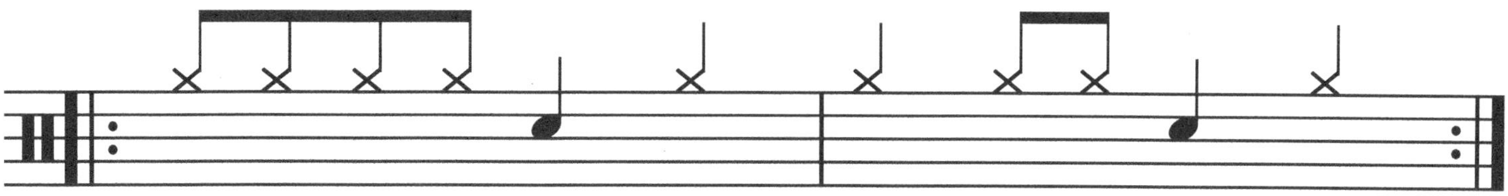

Left Hand

You can also try practicing just the left hand and right foot. The more independence you can build, the more fluent you'll be with this musical language.

Left Hand/Right Foot

When you use the play-along, try to lock in your bass drum part with the bass player. One of the most challenging aspects of this pattern is not necessarily adding the fills themselves, but getting out of them and back into the groove without breaking the flow. Keep your fills rhythmically simple and focus on textures since there's already so much going on. You can play a left-hand fill on the snare pad, a right-hand one on the snare/toms or combine both options.

Fill #1

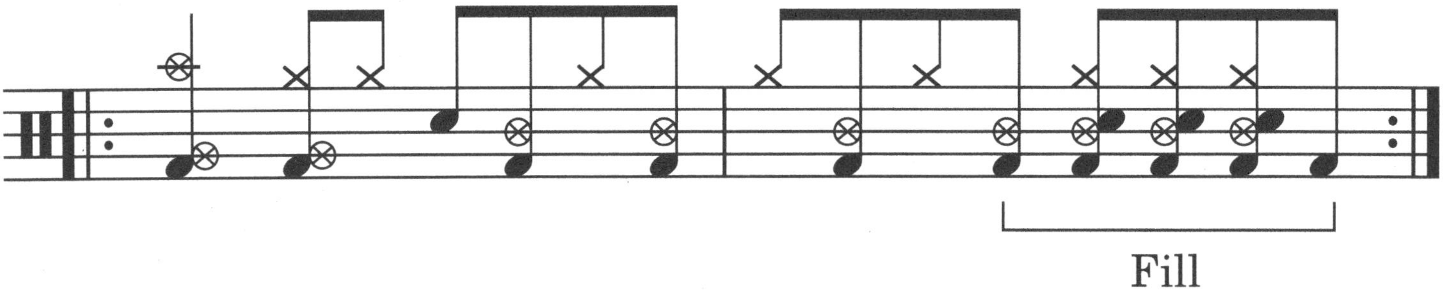

I also tried to make the acoustic kit sound more industrial by using cymbals with short decay and creating a trashy cymbal stack. Move your right-hand hi-hat part over to the stack for even more ultra-weird '90s fun.

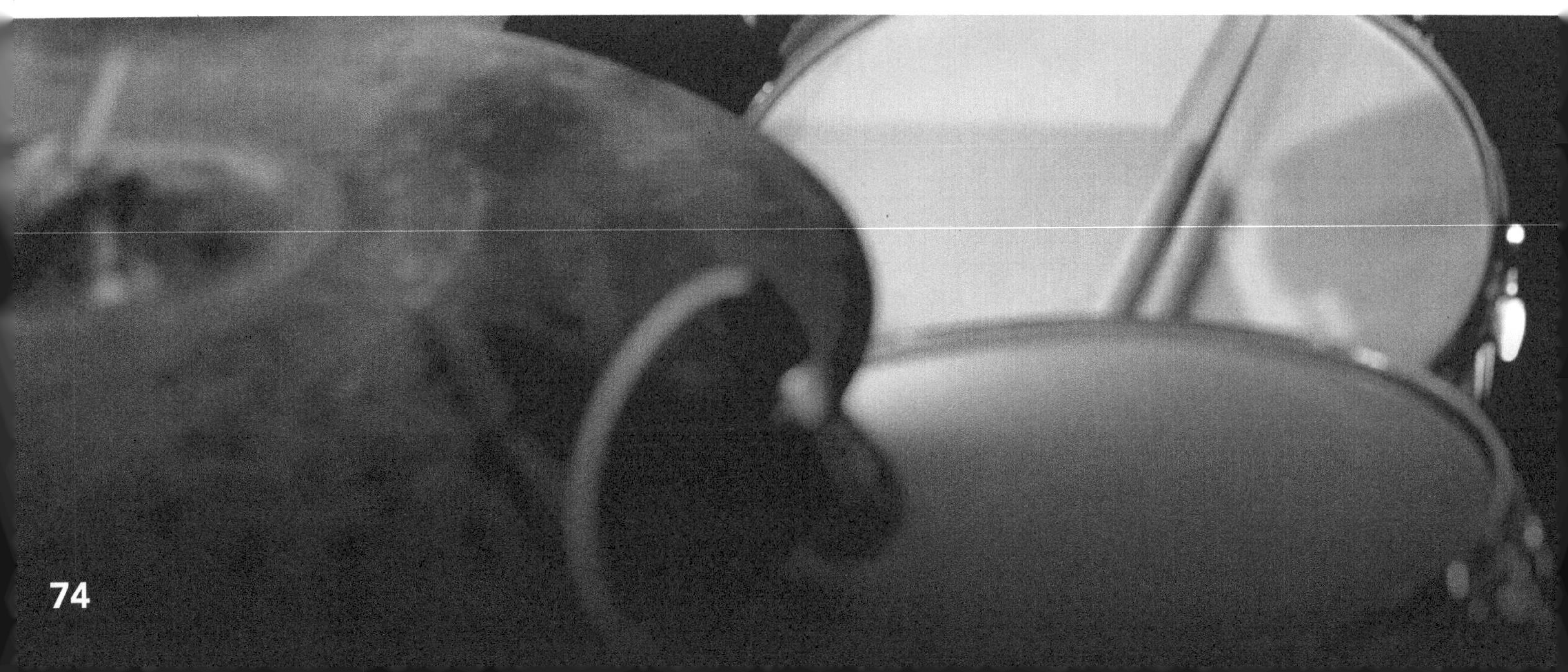

The Band

Dmitry Ishenko:

"We're talking about industrial music, which is a cross between heavy metal and techno. It has a lot of elements of techno, specifically the repetition. From a bass perspective, it's a repeating pattern and the track I recorded here is emulating a synth because most bass parts in industrial music are synthesizers. I used an octave pedal and I'm playing pretty much the same thing over and over. It's a two-bar phrase with occasional fills leading into certain dynamic resolutions, but it's pretty much the same part. I'm really just listening to the bass drum, hi-hat and snare to give me the right time because my part is pretty static. I also completely distorted my bass sound with an octave pedal so you're not even hearing the real bass tone."

Elias Meister:

"When you're talking about this industrial sound with the busy drums, it's nice to play something very active and then leave a lot of space for the drums to propel the groove. Everything is very tight. Sound-wise I'm using a bit less distortion with a slap-back or bathroom reverb sound which makes a big difference in getting that kind of effect. In the bridge we open it up a little bit by playing longer notes, but that's the only variation... it's very repetitive and tight. The sound I'm thinking about is like somebody in a big room in a warehouse hitting a piece of metal. What would that sound like? It's kind of a strong attack and then a weird, long decay, but it's tight, dry and away from the attack. But then it has this decay in the guitar and drums that adds this feeling to it."

Orleans Machines

Genres: Jazz

Difficulty Level (1-10): 6

Area of Origin: New Orleans, 1940s

Artists to Check Out: The Meters, Allen Toussaint, Professor Longhair, Jelly Roll Morton, Preservation Hall Jazz Band, The Neville Brothers

Drummers to Check Out: Herlin Riley, Zigaboo Modeliste, Stanton Moore, Idris Muhammed, Johnny Vidacovich, Jamison Ross, Shannon Powell

The History

Years before artists like The Meters and Fats Domino brought New Orleans music into the mainstream, there was trail-blazing pianist Professor Longhair. Known to his friends as "Fess," he was one of the first to combine Afro-Caribbean clavé rhythms like rhumba and bossa nova with American rhythm and blues in the 1940s. The result was funky grooves and jaunty, playful songs. As journalist Amanda Petrusich cheekily puts it in her profile of Longhair, "when Fess sang, he did so in the punchy, precise style of the postwar blues shouters, but on occasion he warbled like a deranged songbird [17a]."

While he never achieved widespread commercial success during his lifetime, Longhair's influence on the next generation of New Orleans musicians was undeniable. Dr. John, Allen Toussaint, James Booker and Huey "Piano" Smith all drew deeply from this musical combination of clavé and blues. This music was a melting pot of influences, incorporating elements of Dixieland, boogaloo and jazz. Famed New Orleans drummer Johnny Vidacovich who played with Longhair described the feel as "a camel walking through the desert [17b]." As time went on, New Orleans drummers like Idris Muhammad, Herlin Riley and Stanton Moore have continued Longhair's musical legacy in the world of jazz, blues, funk and beyond.

The Music

I think of this groove as a N'awlins bossa nova since it combines a 2-3 clavé with a funky swing feel that makes you feel like grooving your way down Frenchmen Street (Bourbon Street is just for tourists these days!). That feel is what makes this pattern really cook, so practice the limbs separately at first and try to get it locked in the pocket. While it's important to stay relaxed and play a little behind the beat, try not to slow down or get too sloppy. While your ride cymbal provides the greasy swing, your feet and left hand should be precise. Keep the groove light and buoyant.

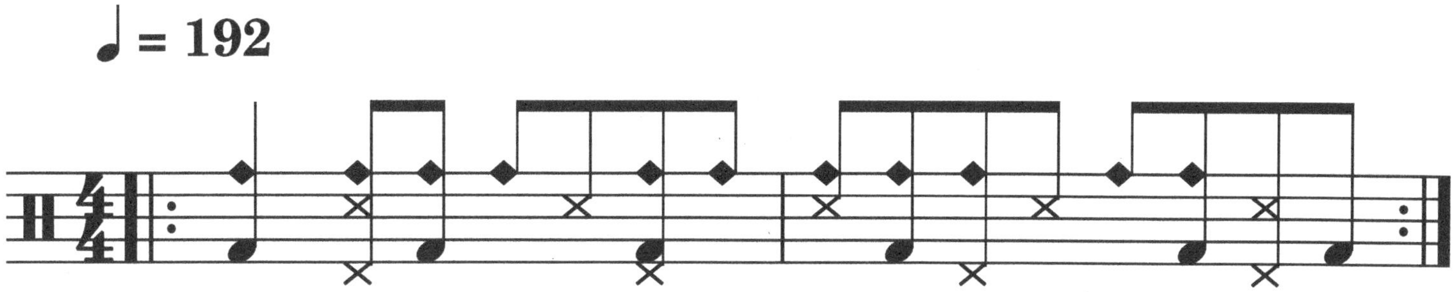

It's also important to use the correct musical vocabulary when you improvise and develop musical ideas. Drags and snare buzzes are great tools in this style since this groove is like a jazzy cousin of the traditional New Orleans street beat. You can mix up the cross-stick and snare, sprinkle in some toms and keep your ears open for opportunities to interact with the bass and guitar.

Variation #1

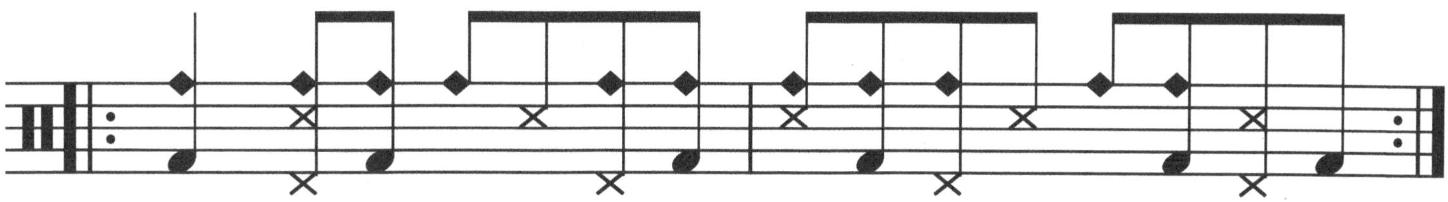

It's also nice to use the concept of "station points" to end musical phrases on beats other than 1. Playing this short fill with a crash on beat 4 is a perfect way to create forward momentum.

Variation #2

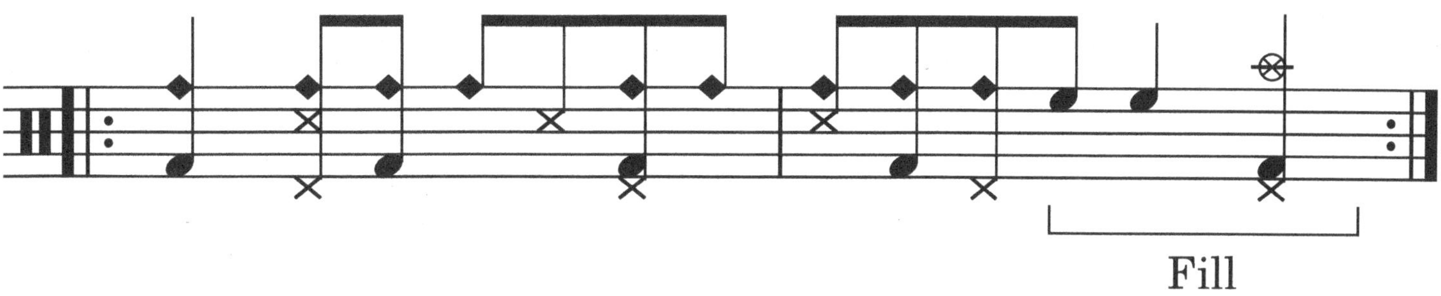

MORE Stuff You Can Use

There's a lot of musical "crosstalk" going on here since the bass line and drum part come together in certain spots and then diverge. The drum part is busier, while the bass is very simple.

Variation #3

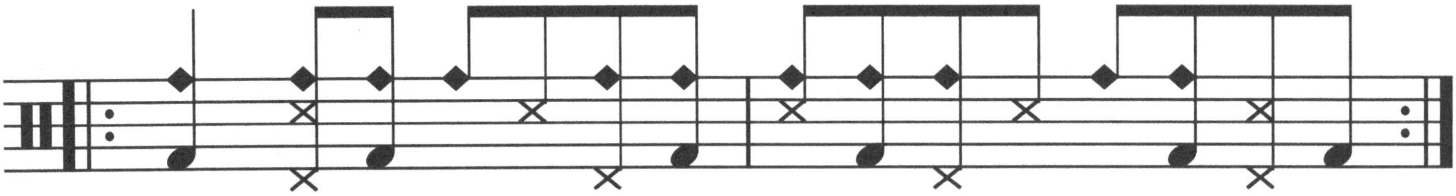

Variation #4

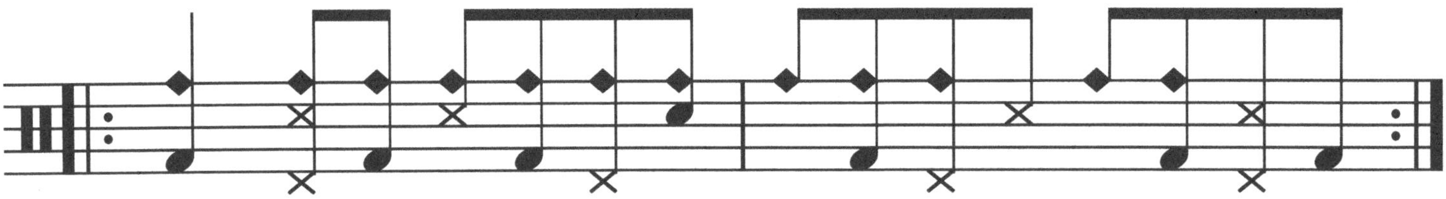

Once you get it locked in, this groove should feel like party time! I can almost smell the gumbo.

The Band

Dmitry Ishenko:

"So, the classic New Orleans-type of bass line would adhere to a 3-2 clave in Afro-Cuban music. It all goes back to Africa, all those rhythmic styles. I'm just playing off of what [the drums] are doing. It's a lot of different layers and I'm just bouncing off the off-beats [the drums] are playing. That's the best way to describe it. I'm a bit stricter about it from a bass perspective, since I'm trying to play beat one every two bars and also trying to make it busier in the second part. But we still have that clavé as an underlying rhythmic figure, so I'm playing off of that but making it slightly busier."

Elias Meister:

"I'm thinking about a similar underlying rhythm. The guitar is very simple and steady. It's kind of loose, but dancing and driving at the same time. It's definitely a 'holding-it-down' situation where you just want to dig into the groove...and if you feel a change or an inspiration from the drums, you can respond with a very slight variation. If you keep the part very steady, then the slight variation will stick out and add some excitement or new information. It's just experimenting with the timbre of longer or shorter notes and playing slightly more busy or syncopated rhythms. That will do the trick to create a contrast with the first part and mark it as a really different thing.

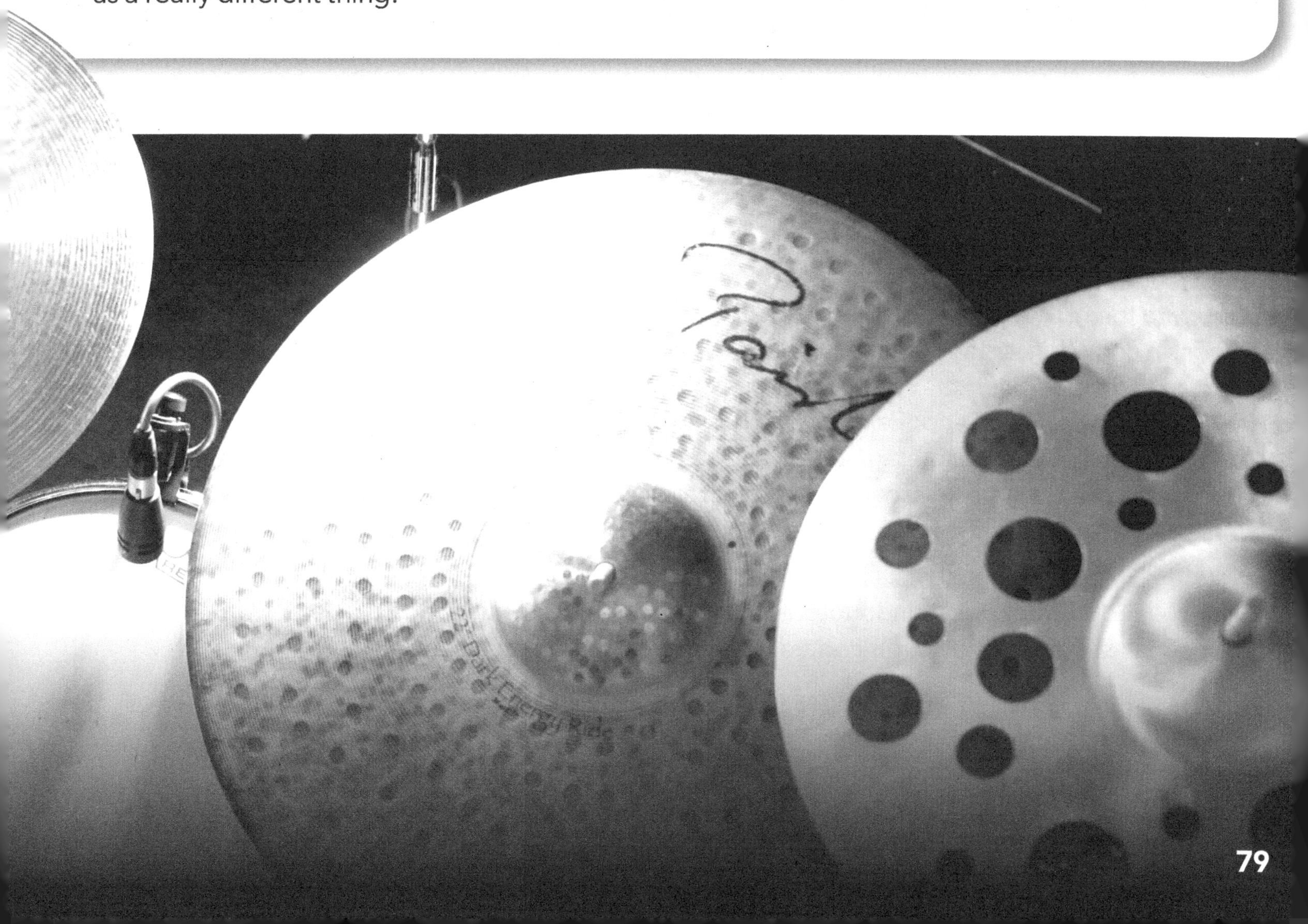

Polka Party

Genres: Polka

Difficulty Level (1-10): 4

Area of Origin: Czech Republic, Europe, Midwestern U.S.A., 1950s

Artists to Check Out: Jimmy Sturr, Polkacide, Walter "Li'l Wally" Jagiello, The Six Fat Dutchman, Frankie Yankovic, Joe Oberaitis, Polkaholix

Drummers to Check Out: Dennis Coyman, Ken Yash, Roger Lichwala, Rich Berends, John "Bermuda" Schwartz

The History

Polka music originated in a region of Europe called Bohemia (now the Czech Republic) in the mid-19th century. As European immigrants made the journey to America they brought this festive, upbeat dance music with them. Modern-day polka is especially popular in the Midwest, with northeastern Ohio, Wisconsin and Minnesota as major hotbeds [18a]. As the 1950s and '60s rolled around, artists like Frankie Yankovic, dubbed "America's Polka King," rose to popularity with iconic hits like "In Heaven There is No Beer," "Beer Barrel Polka" and "Pennsylvania Polka," which was later featured in the film *Groundhog Day* (1993). Walter "Li'l Wally" Jagiello and Six Fat Dutchmen were other important artists of the era, as polka bands performed at state fairs, dances and festivals throughout the country. Polka also remained popular overseas with artists like The German Polka Band and "Berlin Speed Polka" group Polkaholix carrying on this rich tradition.

Today, "Weird Al" Yankovic is undoubtedly the most well-known musician associated with this style, gaining mainstream appeal for his comedic polka mashups of popular tunes.

The Music

This pattern may seem simple at first, but it's actually harder than you might think to stay consistent throughout an entire song. In this style, the other musicians will be relying on the drums to keep a steady pulse so they can layer their parts on top. So, the main thing to remember is that the bass drum should never stop playing quarter notes. If you miss one, someone might fall down (hopefully not!).

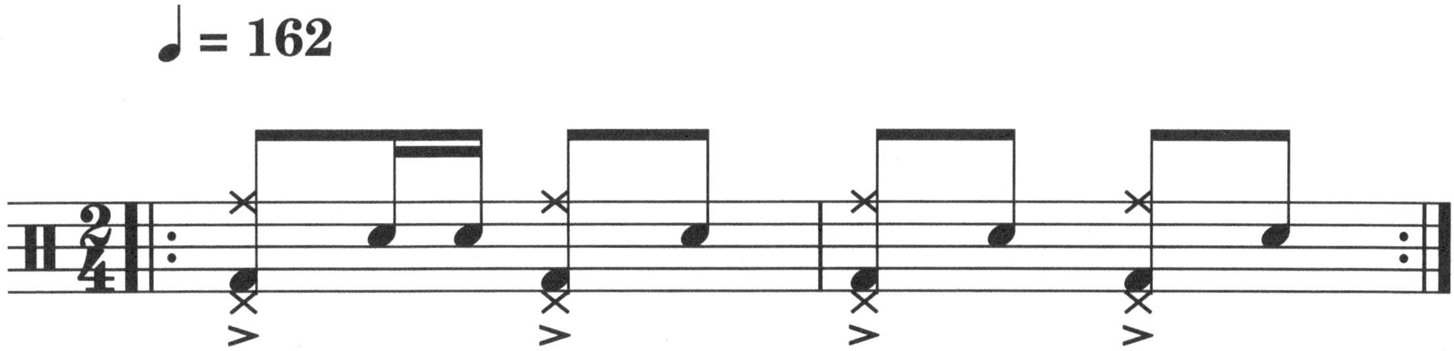

Add in some subtle texture changes with your right hand to change the flavor in different sections. You can play the ride, the bell, loose or closed hi-hat or even the rim/side of the drum. You can also step on the hi-hat and release it quickly for a "crashy" variation.

Variation #1

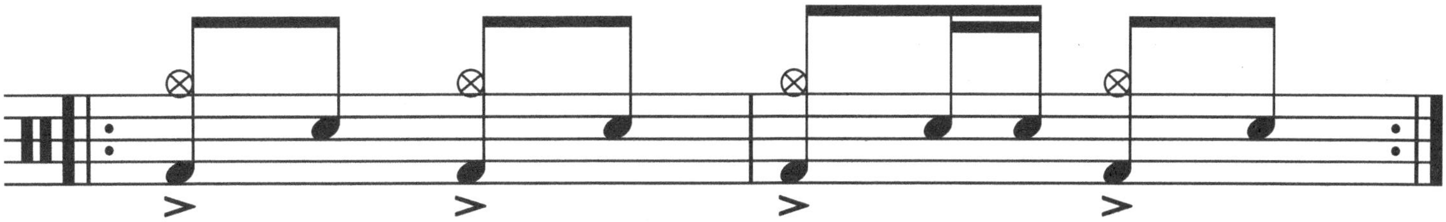

Variation #2

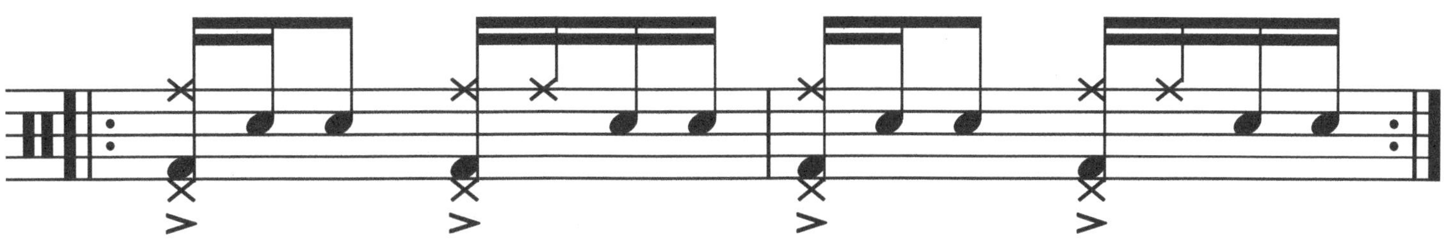

Variation #3

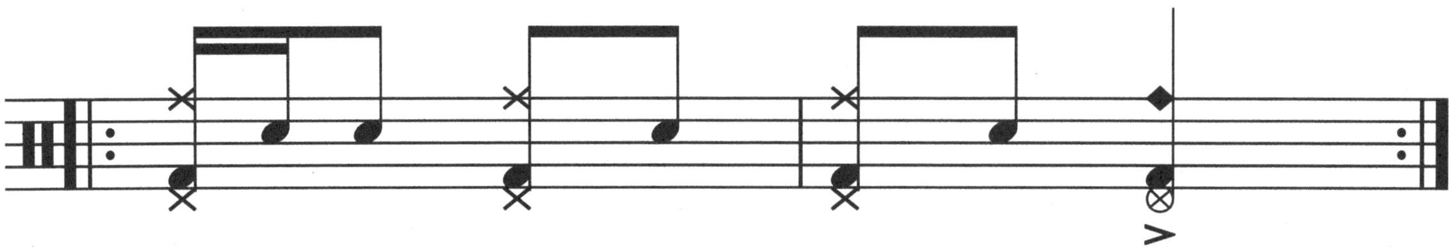

Variation #4

Keep it pumping even when you play a fill. Your fills should be crisp and clean so they fit within the pattern. I like to use open double-strokes instead of buzzes or drags since the musical language of polka drumming is almost like an exaggerated marching style. Keep things rhythmically simple and clear. This music should be fun and a bit playful.

Fill #1

Fill #2

Here's a lead sheet for the play-along track. Try to focus on the information that is relevant to the drum part like the form, hits and melody.

Polka Party

While polkas can have a wide range of tempos, you'll notice that the play-along track is quite fast. This can make it feel like a mad scramble, so it's important to play with a light touch to keep it from turning into a metal blast beat. The real challenge is remaining steady and focused on every single note you play. This requires both mental concentration and physical endurance since it's easy to lose steam as the tune goes on. So, dig in and keep the Polka Party rolling and you'll see clogs on the ground and steins in the air! As the Germans like to toast, "Ein Prosit!"

The Band

Dmitry Ishenko:

"In a polka, it's all about endurance. I'm playing a very simple part. It's just beats one and three, and the root and fifth usually. I do occasionally throw in a fill on spontaneous parts of the beat, but not the obvious spot like the last two beats before a chord change. What I'm really doing is almost imitating a tuba player in a Mexican 'Banda' [brass] band, which is heavily influenced by German polka. The German immigrants are the ones that brought those brass instruments to Mexico, so I'm kind of channeling that music along with polka itself...but I'm really trying to imitate a tuba and just stay on top of the beat, grooving hard with the drums. The one thing you always have to remember is that this is dance music. You have to be super-consistent if you want people to dance."

Elias Meister:

"The one thing I'm looking for in this kind of music is playing very simply with no frills or anything that makes it too complicated and takes away from the driving rhythm. If we're talking about getting that tuba feel, it's nice when the bass plays short notes. I'm really feeling both the downbeats and the upbeats. In some other grooves, you might feel the downbeats more or the upbeats or the backbeats. In this one, I'm feeling both. It's also good to mark the different sections of the tune by playing with the dynamics a little, but not too much. You can go higher or a little lower to mark a new section. You can open up a little or go a bit more closed...just enough to make it different. Once you find a new way of performing that section, you stay there for 8 or 16 bars before you move to the next one."

Wes Maples:

"It's like a dance, but it's also like a sing-along. I'm approaching the sax part by thinking about it almost as a vocal where you would emulate the context where people are singing and dancing. You're really keeping things simple so it's accessible. I think that's a big part of this style."

PAiSTe
PST X
18" SWISS MEDIUM CRASH

Power Ballad Salad

Genres: Classic Rock, R&B

Difficulty Level (1-10): 3

Area of Origin: Great Britain, U.S.A., 1970s

Artists to Check Out: Aerosmith, Guns N' Roses, Styx, Pearl Jam, Journey, Mötley Crüe

Drummers to Check Out: Joey Kramer, John Panozzo, Steve Smith, Steven Adler, Matt Cameron, Tommy Lee

The History

As rock bands of the 1970s sought a wider audience and greater radio airplay, they began experimenting with slower, more emotional music. This led to the emergence of the power ballad with its heavy, distorted guitars, massively reverbed-out drums and romantic, heart-rending vocals. Bands like REO Speedwagon, Journey and Styx led the way, with the latter producing one of the first hits of this style with Dennis DeYoung's song "Lady" (1973). Aerosmith's classic "Dream On" was released that same year and as the '70s came to a close, it seemed like even the heaviest rock bands had a power ballad or three in their sets.

Scorpions, Foreigner and Whitesnake became power ballad pioneers in the 1980s, while Poison scored a massive hit with "Every Rose Has Its Thorn." In the early '90s, there was the Guns N' Roses classic "November Rain," and even metal bands began getting in on the act with Metallica's "Nothing Else Matters" and Ozzy Ozzborne's "Mama, I'm Coming Home" topping the charts. Pop singers like Celine Dion ("My Heart Will Go On") and Meatloaf ("I'd Do Anything for Love") joined in, while R&B acts like Boyz II Men, Whitney Houston and Mariah Carey proved that this formula could transcend many genres. Besides the slow tempos, the one thing they all had in common was the emotional intensity of the music. Power ballads typically had lots of dynamic changes, soaring solos and a certain overwrought, grandiose quality. As bands discovered that embracing their softer side was a pathway to commercial success, the power ballad cemented an enduring legacy in the history of popular music[19a] [19b].

The Music

This is another one that might appear simple on the surface but actually requires a high level of musical skill and attention to detail. If you can believe it, of all the play-along tracks in this book, this one took us the longest to get just right! Your bass drum pattern should lock right in with what the bassist plays so the guitar and organ can soar freely overtop to create layers and rich musical textures.

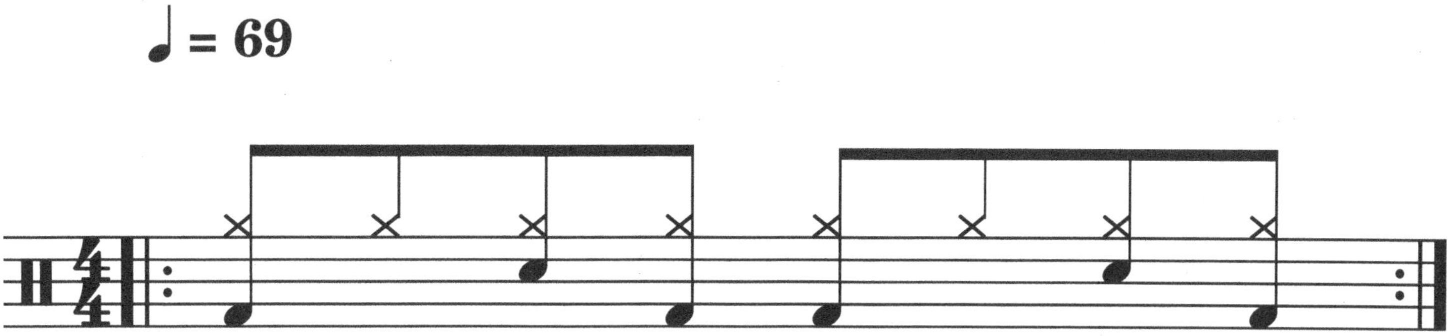

The opening fill I did on the play-along track was heavily inspired by Ringo (even though he pre-dated most rock power balladeers, he definitely influenced them a lot). This fill is highly syncopated and should be played far behind the beat, but always comes back on beat 1. It's also very melodic, which is an important element of good ballad drumming.

On the B section, we switched up the rhythm of the kick drum/bass pattern. Lock it in tight!

Variation #1

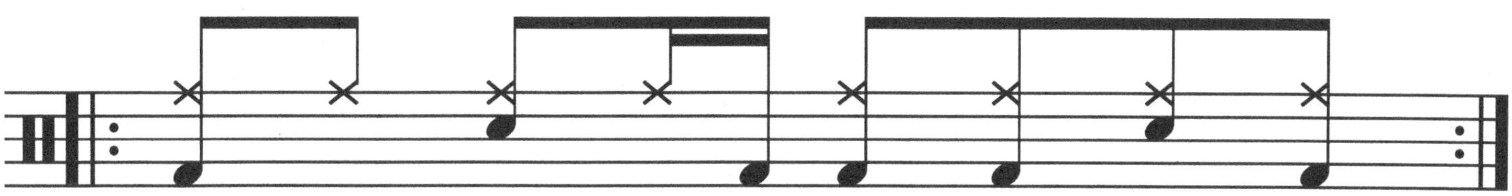

Variation #2

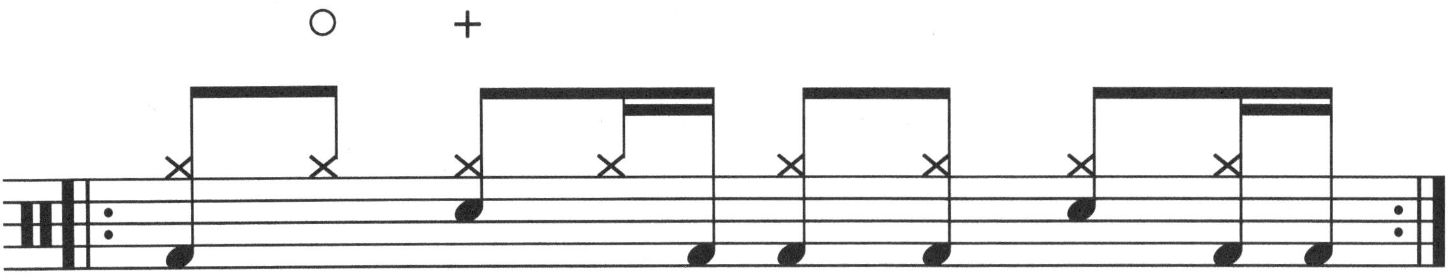

You don't want to get too deep into mimicking musical clichés, but I've found that when you're playing a fill in a ballad, if you can sing it, then you can play it. If you can't sing it, then it has too many notes and won't be a good fit. This pattern is like a dish with only three or four ingredients, but they're the best ones in your kitchen.

Add some descending tom fills, open the hi-hat or put in some carefully placed crashes for variation. Use flams to thicken up the texture of your phrases and get a nice, fat tone out of the kit. When drummers hear the term ballad, their first impulse is usually to play quieter. This is good place to start, but it's important to avoid being tentative and tip-toeing around it. The "power" in power ballads doesn't come from the volume, it's more about intensity. Learning how to really crush a ballad can help you in so many musical situations.

Fill #1

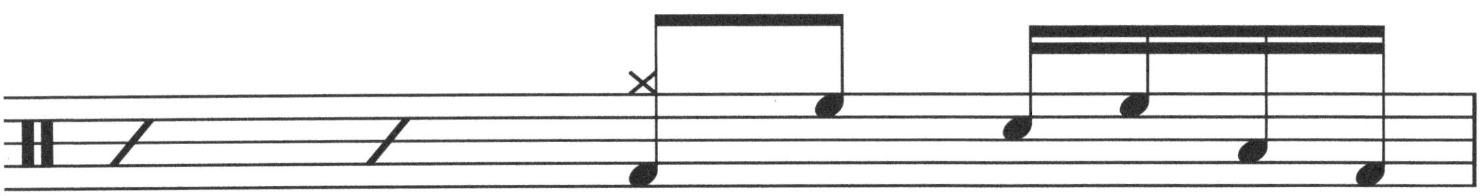

Fill #2

Power Ballad Salad

Here's a chart for the play-along track. Notice that a variation of the opening fill comes back at the end of the form each time.

The Band

Dmitry Ishenko:

"From the bass perspective, it has to be very simple and lock in with the bass drum. We really have to establish a kick drum/bass guitar pattern and choose a particular rhythm to stick to. In this case, we played two sections and both have a slightly different pattern to contrast them. The part where [the drums] can make it interesting is every 4th or 8th measure where you can deviate from the pattern. Maybe I can do a bass fill too, but we need to make sure not to step on each other's toes. It helps to know the other person's style and be able to predict what they're going to do...so that'll decide whether you're going to be on the busier side or play really laid back and let the other person take over with the fill. I think that's what makes it interesting. Otherwise, you just adhere to the really strict groove, a strict rhythmic pattern. But we still have to play with precision and forward momentum. We're laying back slightly but we're not playing in a neo-soul/R&B ballad behind-the-beat fashion. We're still being very forward and direct."

Elias Meister:

"I'm thinking about hitting a lot of downbeats with the chords and keeping the rhythm really steady and heavy on the beats. But then in-between, you've got a little space to do smaller harmonic fills to make the chords sound a little bit more interesting than just strumming. In the arc of this tune, you can definitely have some dramatic development as it goes along. [You can] start a little bit lower in register and intensity and develop this upwards. We also have this bridge part which is naturally a higher point... so you can raise the intensity a little bit, both with the density of the playing, the register and the material that you're playing...and then come back towards the end of the song to a more solid, 'home' feeling. It's not just a ballad that's quiet in the background. The tempo is slow, but it has a feeling of rock epic-ness and drama and intensity... it's not in-your-face or over the top, but it's definitely loud and full."

Questlove's Best Love

Genres: Funk, R&B, Hip-Hop, Neo-Soul

Difficulty Level (1-10): 4

Area of Origin: Philadelphia, 1990s

Artists to Check Out: D'Angelo, John Legend, The Roots, The Sugarhill Gang, Stetsasonic, Kurtis Blow

Drummers to Check Out: Questlove

The History

In the years before drum machines became widely used in hip-hop production, artists like The Sugarhill Gang, Kurtis Blow and Stetsasonic used live musicians to create their beats. In the early '90s, bands like The Roots brought this practice back into vogue, with drummer and bandleader Ahmir "Questlove" Thompson at the forefront.

As the child of Philly blues musicians, Questlove spent his youth listening to classic records by Prince, Stevie Wonder and The Ohio Players, later discovering hip-hip pioneers like J Dilla and A Tribe Called Quest. This melting pot of musical influences shaped his unique approach to the drums. His early work with The Roots features tight and vibrant grooves that provide the perfect backdrop for rapper Tarik "Black Thought" Trotter's musical explorations. As the group gained popularity with the albums *Things Fall Apart* (1999) and *Phrenology* (2002), Questlove's sound continued to evolve, becoming rawer and more open while retaining its unmistakable groove.

This was also the same time period when he recorded the landmark album *The Philadelphia Experiment* (2001) with bassist Christian McBride and pianist Uri Caine. This was one of the most important records of its era, blurring the lines of hip-hop, jazz and R&B in a funky tour-de-force of musical brilliance. His drumming on neo-soul singer D'Angelo's hit album *Voodoo* (2000) was another example, drawing inspiration from early hip-hop, jazz and R&B. These recordings are living proof of how all musical genres are related and learning about many styles can make you better at each one individually.

Questlove's Best Love

Keeping an open mind musically and continuing to evolve has been one of Questlove's most enduring and appealing qualities as an artist. It's allowed him to achieve mainstream success as a musician, producer and cultural visionary while still staying true to his drumming "Roots" [20a] [20b] [20c].

The Music

This groove is all about the pocket and feel. There's a steady 16th-note pulse that simmers beneath the surface, pushing it forward even when you're not playing every single note. While most of the 16ths are divided between your limbs, the syncopation between the kick and snare gives this pattern its shape, so make sure to really pop those accents.

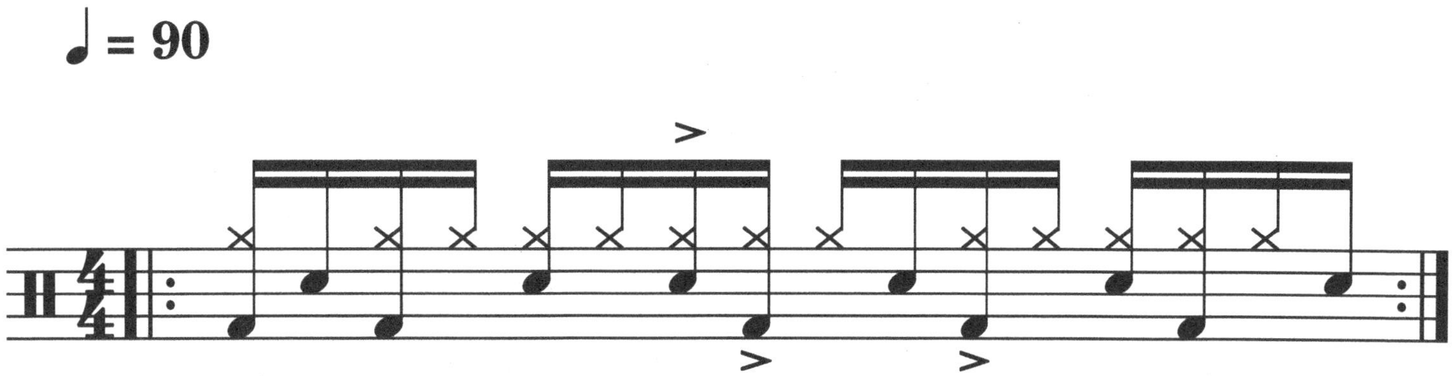

One of my favorite things about Questlove's drumming is how he uses quick moments of open hi-hat to expand and contract the texture. It never gets too loose or messy and creates a nice variation. Throughout it all, the feel stays relaxed but precise. Most importantly, we never lose the backbeat. Everything else is built around that foundation, so it's a good idea to simplify at first and add the syncopations later when you're working with the play-along track. All those little notes are just ways of enhancing the groove without destabilizing it.

Variation #1

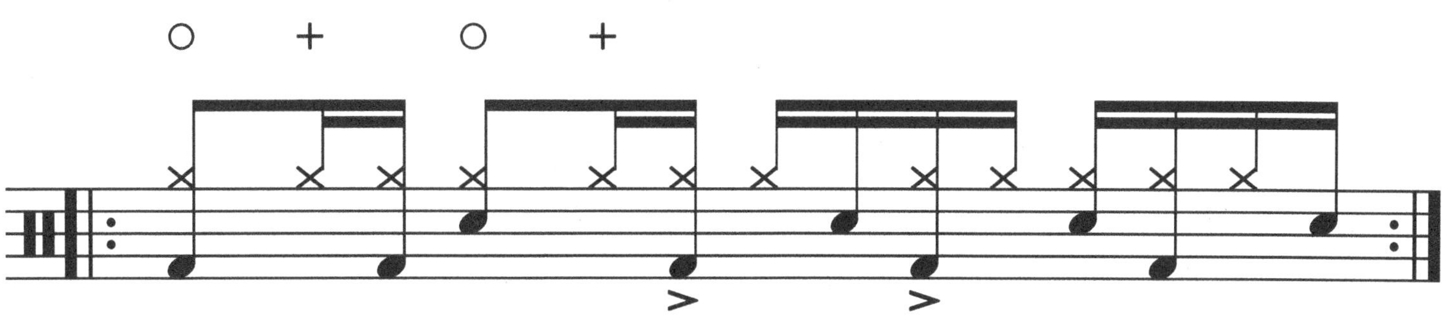

Variation #2

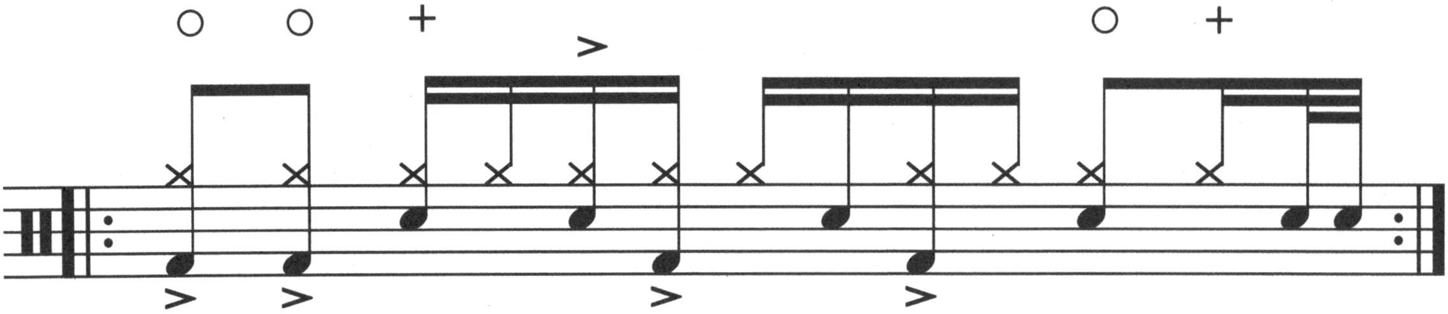

Switch to the ride for a texture change.

Variation #3

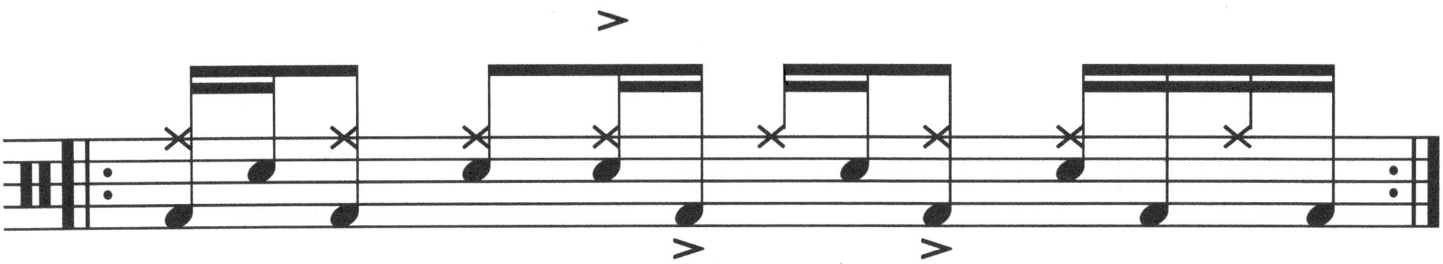

Variation #4

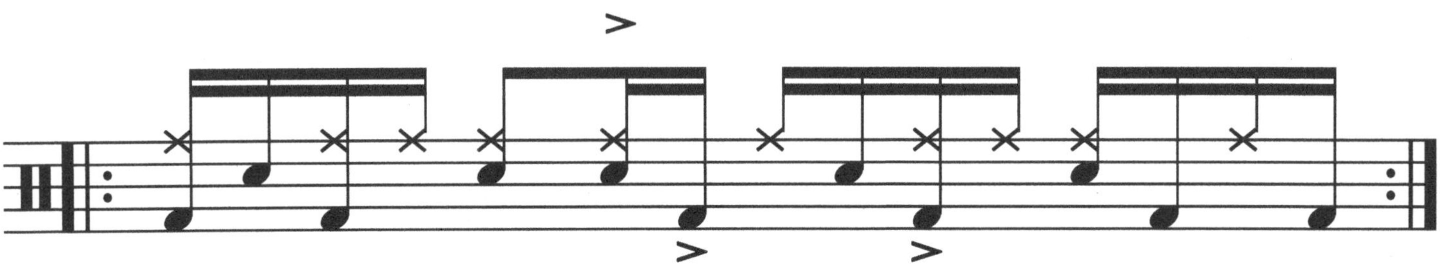

Questlove's Best Love

When I'm playing a fill in this style, I try to do it within the groove as opposed to leaving and returning to it. It's even more important to create a clear pocket in situations where you're working with a larger band. This will help everyone stay on the same page, and I know horn players always appreciate a drummer who marks the sections and shows leadership and confidence. It makes their job so much easier.

Fill #1

Fill #2

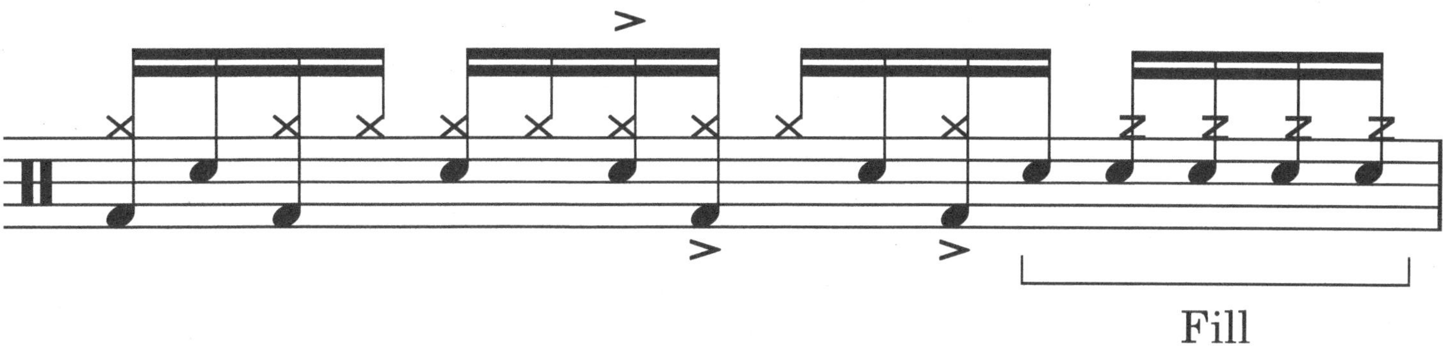

MORE Stuff You Can Use

Here's the whole form for the play-along track. Try to focus on making subtle texture changes when a new section begins.

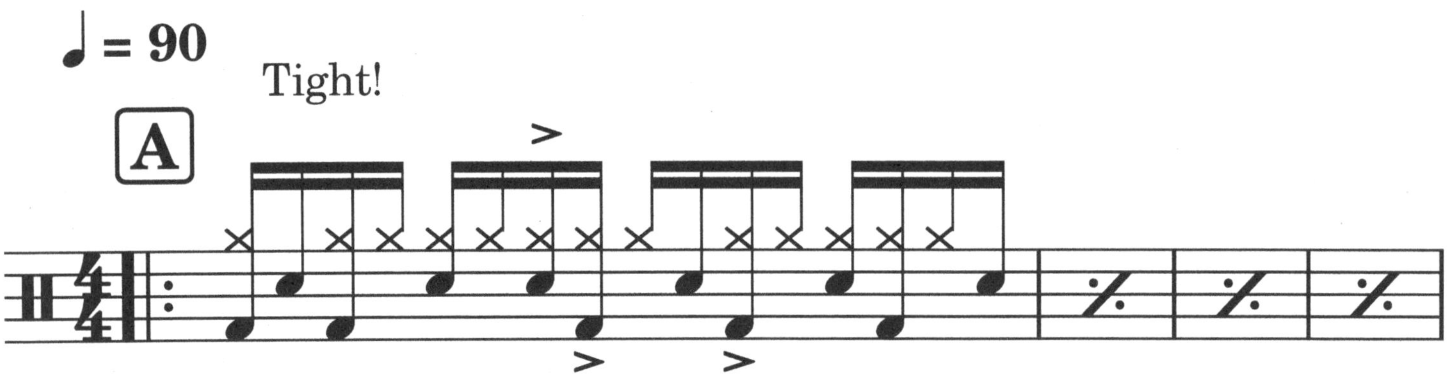

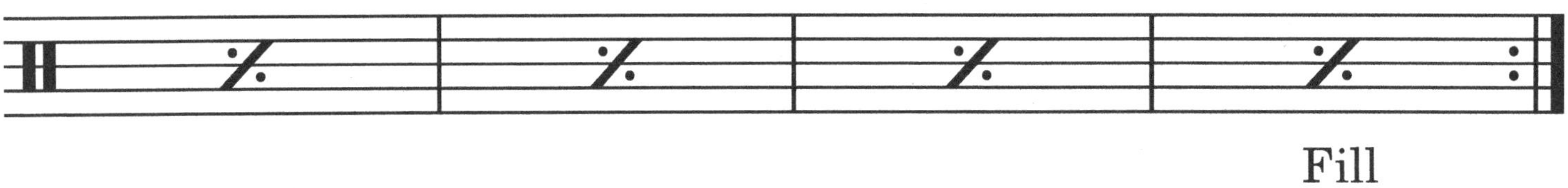

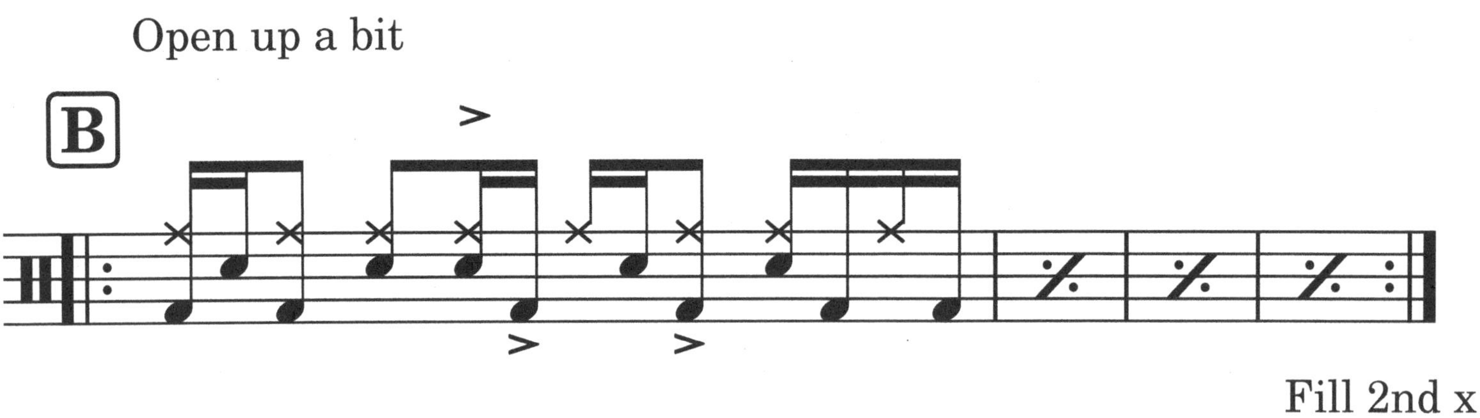

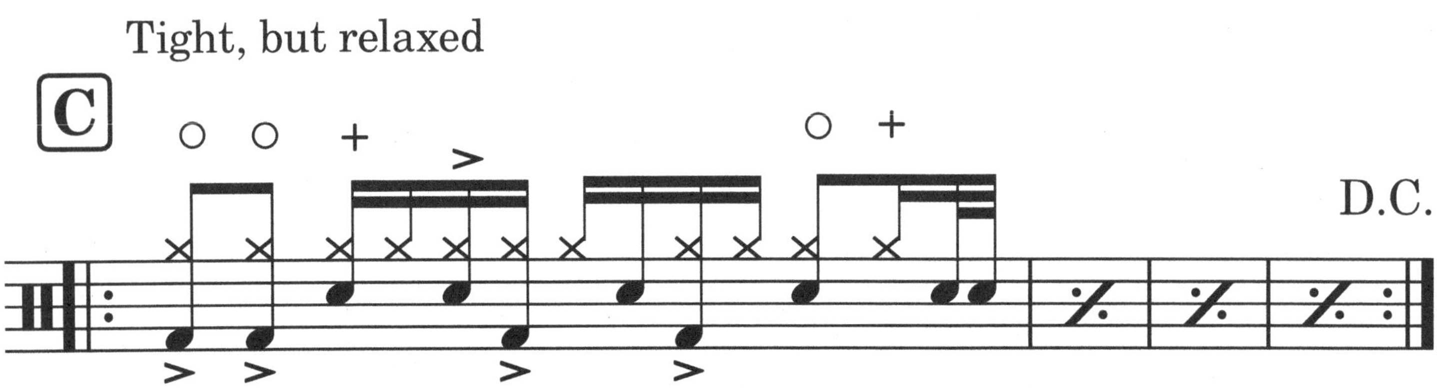

Playing funk, soul, R&B or hip-hop on the drums is just like decorating a house. You start with a solid foundation (your feet), put up some walls (the backbeat), then haul in your furniture, add some pictures and make it your own (the hi-hat and snare syncopations). So, show your bandmates your best love by building them a nice groove house and inviting everyone over for dinner!

The Band

Dmitry Ishenko:

"I'm playing a two-bar pattern with a repeating bass line with occasional variations, but it's pretty much the same thing. The 16th note definitely swings a bit and I'm pretty laid back on the groove even if the drums might be pushing ahead in certain parts. As it goes on, you can add elements, little things here and there...and then it morphs into something slightly different with a few more elaborate notes. But overall, it's still the same thing we started with."

Elias Meister:

"I'm feeling like this kind of groove can be very laid back on the guitar. I'm really counting on the rhythm section to keep the time and move it forward while I add this element of looseness to it. I think it's important to mark different sections with small variations in what you're doing but keep the same part. The key for me is those subtle variations that build it up. You keep the same pattern but get slightly busier, open the sound up a little bit or go higher up in the register. The development in the drums is a similar thing. It doesn't change much, but those little variations will raise the intensity over time through different sections."

Wes Maples:

"Questlove is very much a disciple of James Brown, so that approach to horn arranging is very important here. It's really coming from a lot of jazz influence because that's where a lot of those horn players got their lines. If you listen to Pee Wee Ellis or Maceo Parker with James Brown, it's a lot of simple jazz elements. It's almost like a 'So What' Miles Davis kind of vibe."

Ride the No Wave

Genres: No Wave, Punk, Disco, Jazz

Difficulty Level (1-10): 6

Area of Origin: New York, 1970s

Artists to Check Out: James Chance and The Contortions (James White and The Blacks), Bush Tetras, DNA, Teenage Jesus and the Jerks (Lydia Lunch), Suicide, *No New York* Compilation (1978), Theoretical Girls, Mars, Arto Lindsay, The Gynecologists, UT, The Lounge Lizards, 8 Eyed Spy, John Zorn, Sonic Youth, Ornette Coleman's Prime Time

Drummers to Check Out: James Christensen (James Chance), Dee Pop (Bush Tetras), Jim Sclavunos, Wharton Tiers (Theoretical Girls)

The History

New York City was a gritty place in the late 1970s. Critics charged that moral decay had swept the population into a psychologically twisted vortex of violence and vice. From this supposed blight emerged some of the most groundbreaking and edgy music ever created. Fashioned as an adverse reaction to the synth-driven New Wave genre, the no wave scene was the epitome of rebellion and counter-culture. Combining punk energy with avant-garde jazz and disco funk, this music was unlike anything that preceded it. It was raw and totally unbound by musical convention. It was punky and it was funky. It was noisy and weird and it didn't care what you thought!

Artists like illustrious saxophonist and impresario James Chance took all the chances, critics be damned. Drummer Don Christensen's tight and wildly innovative beats were the backbone of Chance's band The Contortions (he also performed under the moniker James White and The Blacks). Bush Tetras, DNA, Mars and Teenage Jesus & the Jerks were also at the forefront of this burgeoning downtown scene. The latter band featured singer and poet Lydia Lunch, who became one of the most important figures in the no wave movement, later collaborating with Sonic Youth (which was not technically a no wave band but borrowed many of its musical elements).

The genre gained even wider popularity when renowned musician and producer Brian Eno put out the landmark no wave compilation album *No New York* in 1978 featuring many of these artists. Though this style was eventually absorbed into post-punk, noise rock and other subgenres in the '80s, its massive influence on the history of the New York music scene and city itself can never be denied [21a, 21b].

The Music

This style of drumming can be best described as controlled chaos. It's like you've entered an insane disco! No wave drumming is a combination of disco-dance and rock, with a dash of punk and hints of avant-garde jazz. The main word here is energy. It's important to keep building the intensity of this groove as it goes along and not run out of gas. The four-on-the floor bass drum and snare backbeat remain consistent throughout, but everything around them can change.

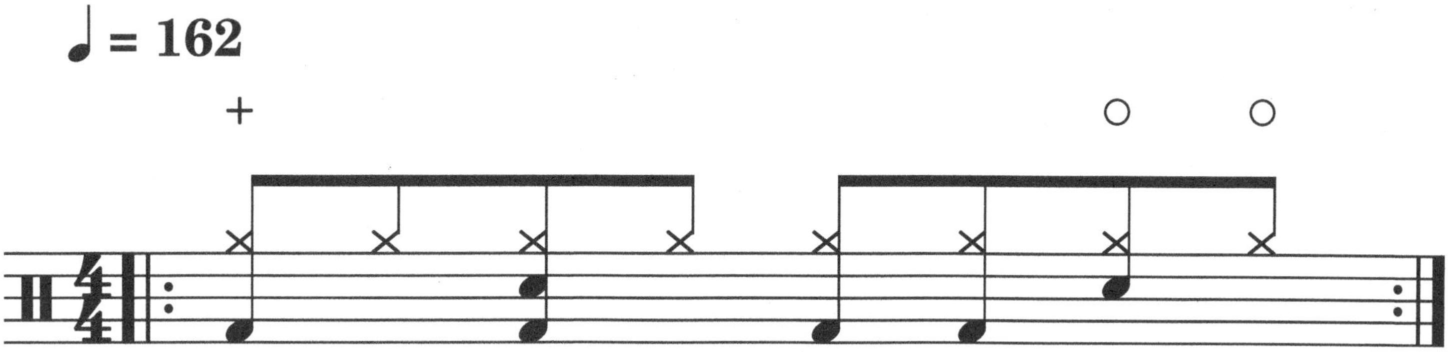

Open the hi-hat on the upbeats for disco vibes or use both hands to switch to 16th notes. You can loosen it entirely to introduce some punk energy or add some punchy snare fills for an EDM or pop aesthetic. As long as you stay on top of the beat and keep the kick and snare pumping, anything goes!

Variation #1

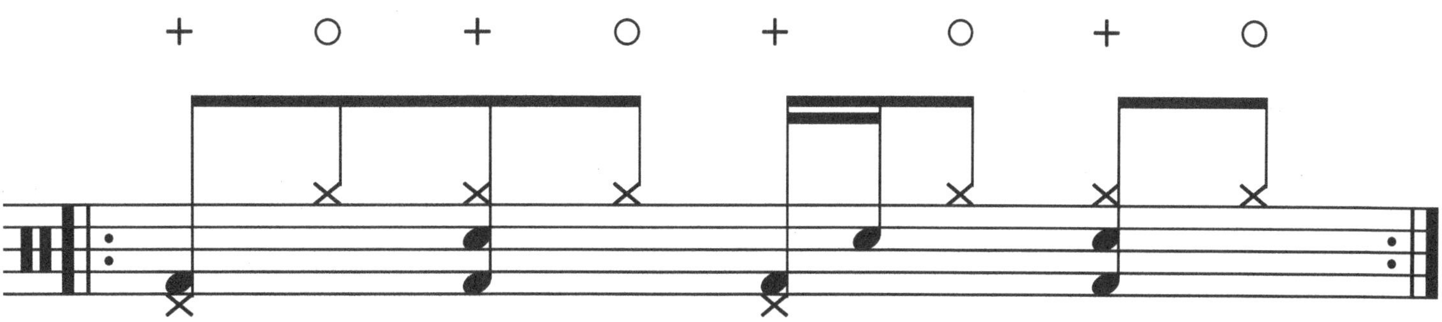

Variation #2

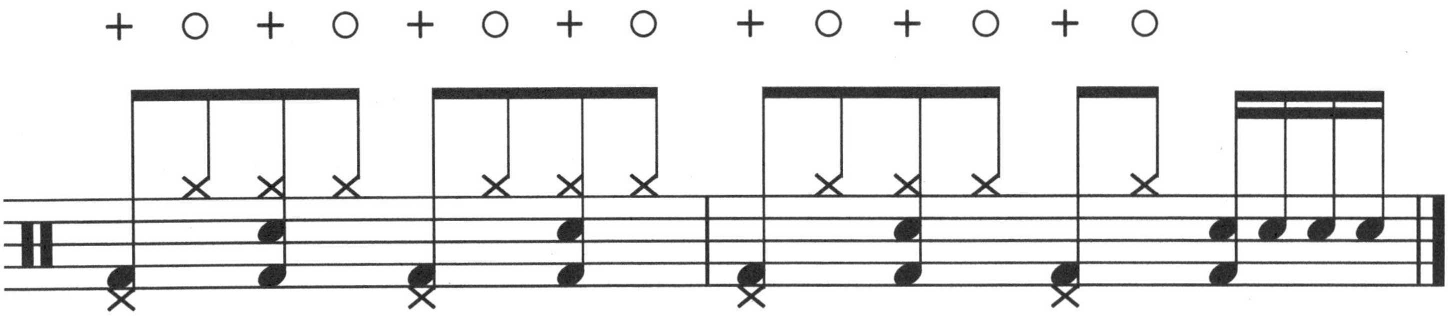

Variation #3

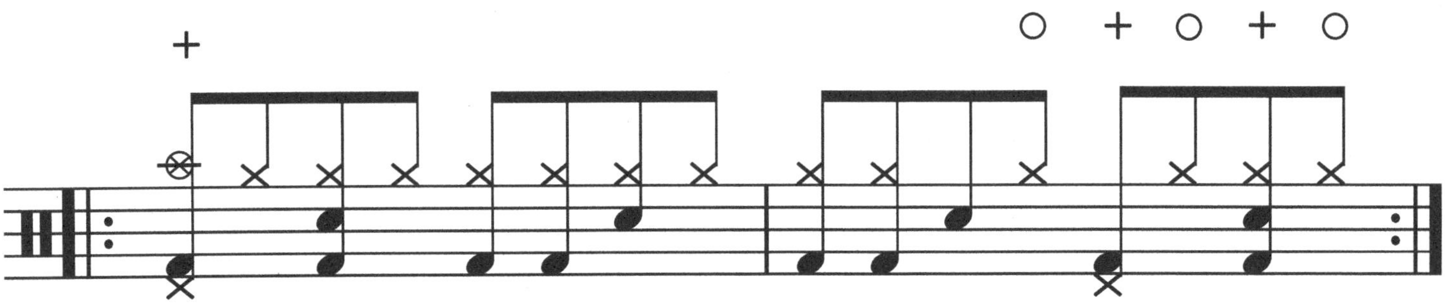

Variation #4

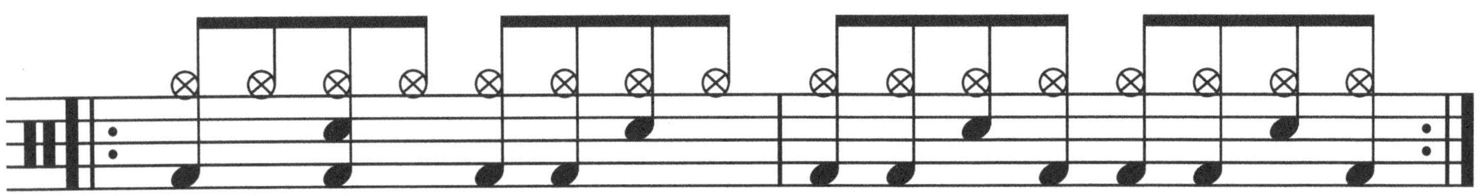

Variation #5

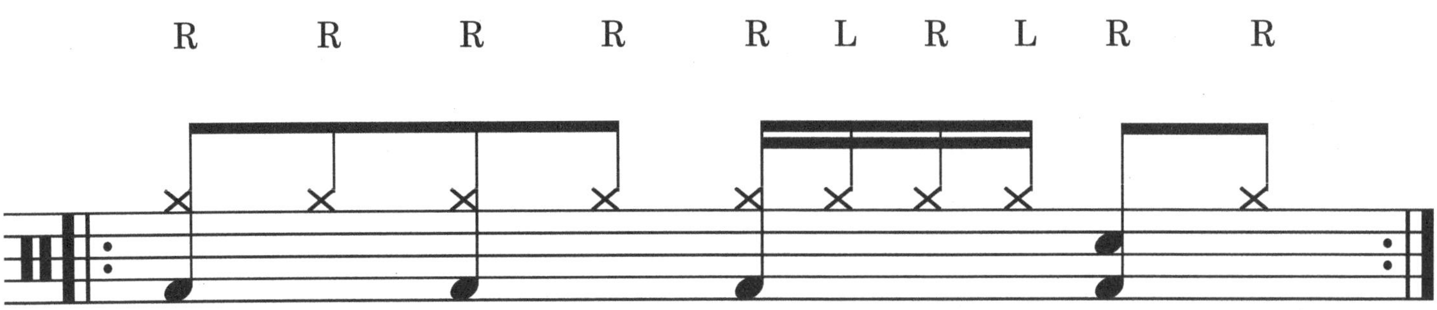

Variation #6

Variation #7

Once you've got a few variations dialed in, work on using them to interact with the other instruments. Since this music is like a conversation, your part won't lock together with the bass and guitar in a traditional sense. This track is atonal and has an open form, so it's the drummer's job to bring a sense of order to the mayhem while also joining in and contributing to it.

Fill #1

Fill #2

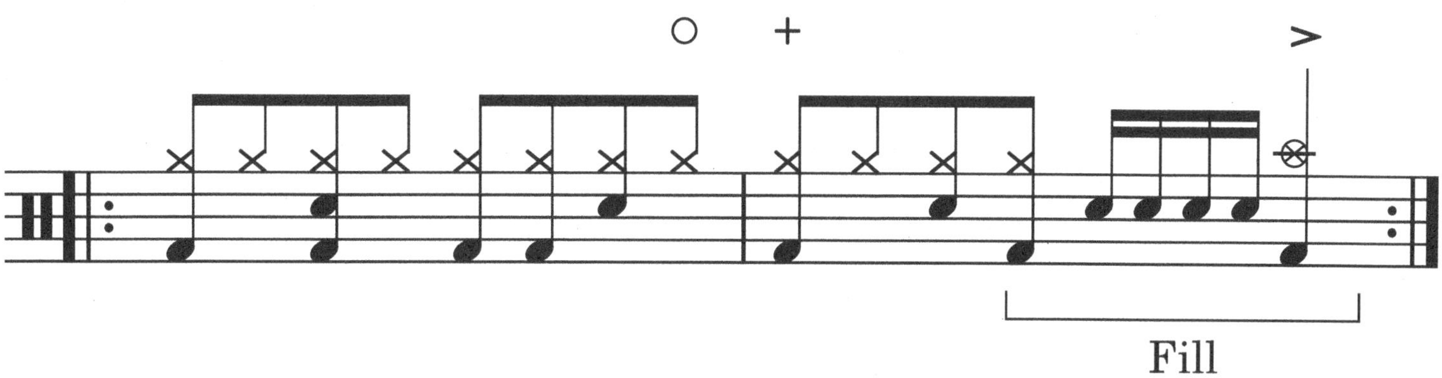

Fill #3

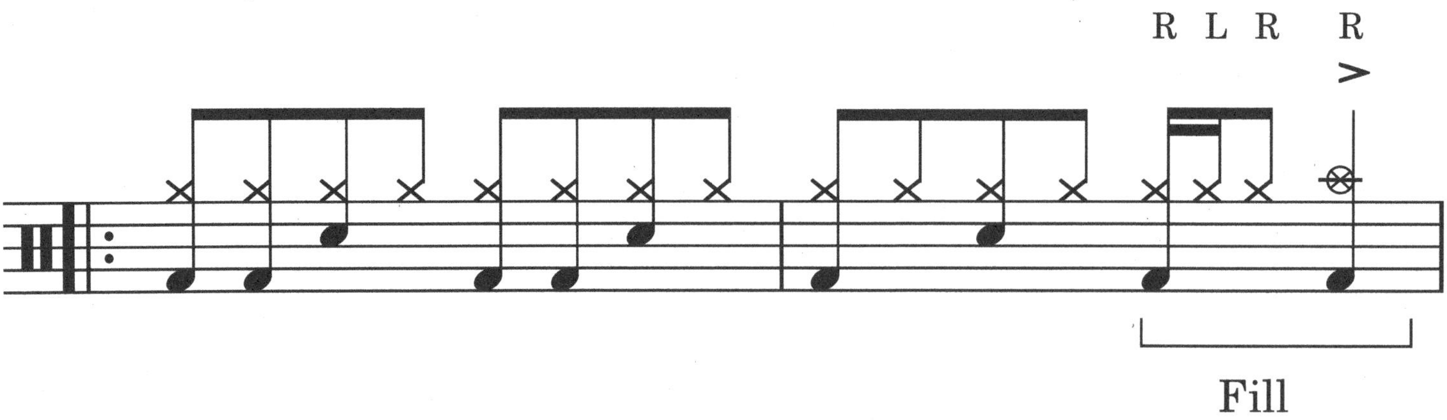

Fill #4

Playing this way can be incredibly inspiring because it frees you from many of the musical rules and responsibilities in other styles. Creativity is the name of the game, so keep the beat cranking and ride the no wave in to shore!

The Band

Dmitry Ishenko:

"The no wave style that emerged in New York City in the late '70s was basically a bunch of punk musicians who decided to get dance-y. So, the underlying groove is almost like funk/disco but very, dare I say, 'spastic,' with a lot of elements of noise on the top. It's also often very fast. Musically, we are moving in blocks, meaning that we are playing sections of two to four bars for a certain period of time and then moving on to the next section.

"From the drums, it's the kick drum with four-on-the-floor. That's the glue and if you take it away, it becomes like these spastic, spontaneous patterns that are interlocking but without being grounded. As a bass player, I'm playing a lot of syncopated lines, but still being aware of the four-on-the-floor, disco/funk, late '70s-early '80s style. I'm also throwing in some really wacky notes once in a while. Part of it is embracing the absurd, because it's supposed to be that way. It's supposed to be jarring, in-your-face and really unexpected stuff that takes you by surprise. So, the more absurd the better, especially from the guitar."

Elias Meister:

"It's a very on-top-of-the-beat, angsty, strong thing and I'm going to some weird, atonal places. When the section flips and the four bars are over, you go into something new that can be very weird and different...and then you just start again with that, and go with it. It also has this short and loud reverb with a slapback delay sound on the guitar to give it more of an industrial vibe.

"There's a lot of improvisation happening in terms of the parts. We're going away from the harmony (especially the guitar), and going all over the place, but it's still like a part. You're choosing a color that you're putting into the next section and then just going there. The repetition is what makes it into a part, even if it's something very weird. Sometimes, I'm really taking a chance. I might make a noise with the guitar where I don't even know what's going to come out or just run my fingers up the fretboard... and you hear that sound and the next section comes and you're committed to it. It'll work because of the weirdness and the fact that we're keeping the groove going. It's almost like going into a different room when you change it up, but it has a lot of power to it."

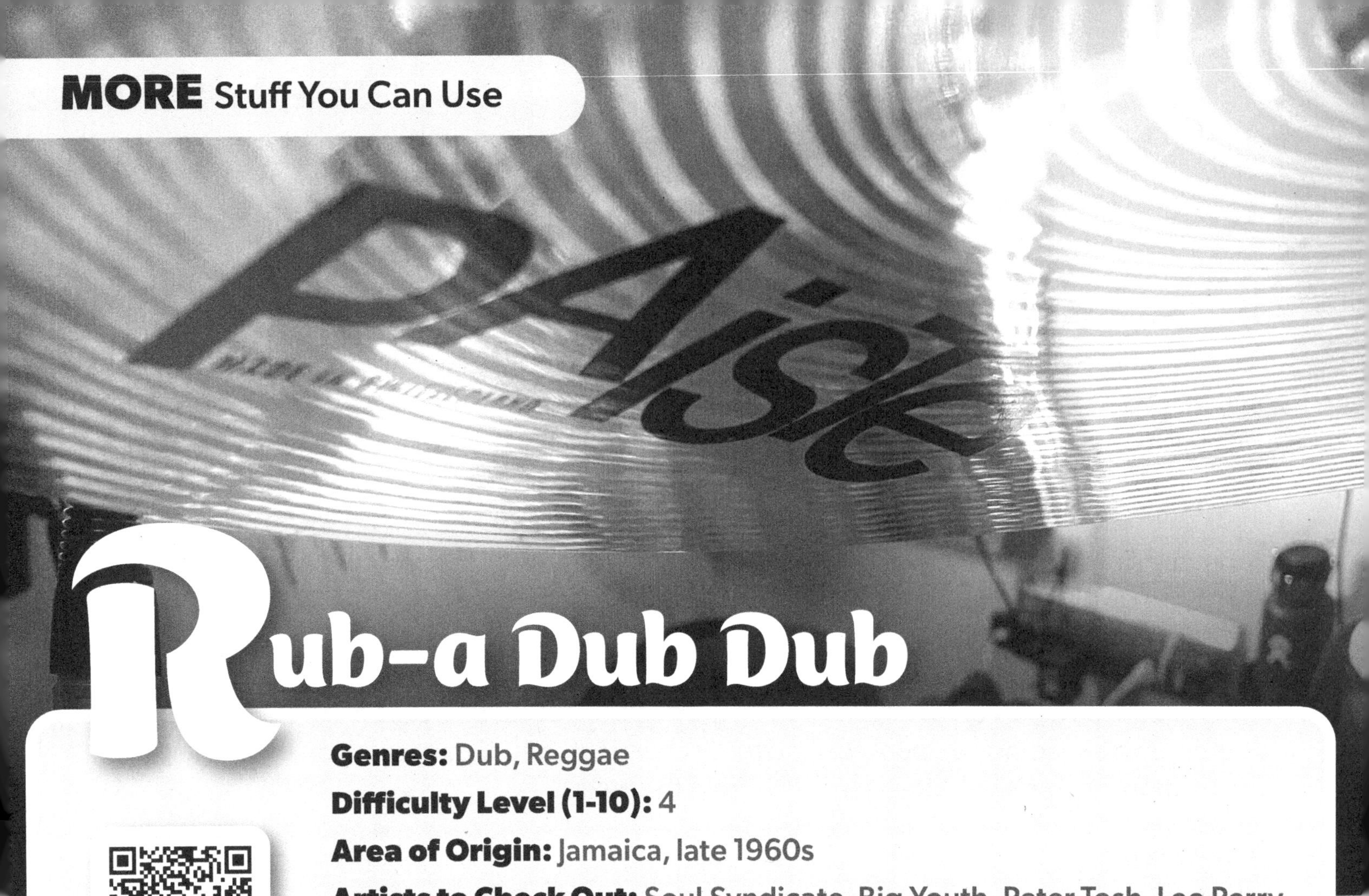

Rub-a Dub Dub

Genres: Dub, Reggae

Difficulty Level (1-10): 4

Area of Origin: Jamaica, late 1960s

Artists to Check Out: Soul Syndicate, Big Youth, Peter Tosh, Lee Perry, Augustus Pablo, King Tubby, Sly & Robbie, Easy Star All-Stars, African Head Charge, Mad Professor, Keith Hudson, Burning Spear, Bill Laswell

Drummers to Check Out: Sly Dunbar, Style Scott, Angus "Drummie Zeb" Gaye

The History

As the reggae craze swept the world in the late 1960s, producers and artists looked for new ways to take advantage of this burgeoning musical phenomenon. Multi-track recording was becoming more widely used at the time, and many Jamaican producers began remixing reggae songs without the vocals and adding effects to the instrumental tracks. The result was the birth of "dub," a reggae subgenre that relied on delay and reverb to create a washy, trippy vibe while heavily emphasizing the bass and drums. It was almost like they put reggae in a dryer in super-slow motion!

Producers like Lee "Scratch" Perry, King Tubby and Scientist were at the forefront, creating "B-sides" for popular tracks which took on lives of their own. Studio One, informally known as the "Jamaican Motown," was ground zero for early dub music. These tracks also created a trend which would resonate throughout every corner of the music industry by establishing the mixing engineers themselves as creative artists. Up until this point, engineers were expected to perform the mechanical tasks of recording, while producers made musical decisions to guide the process. The role of the producer/engineer as an artist is even more prevalent today with the evolution of recording technology, and it really began with these dub producers.

As these remixes gained popularity, musicians began looking for ways to replicate them live onstage. Artists like Augustus Pablo, Mad Professor and Burning Spear established themselves as icons, while bassist Robbie Shakespeare and drummer Sly Dunbar (known as Sly & Robbie) formed the most legendary and prolific rhythm section in dub, playing on hundreds of records as a duo and releasing several of their own.

Though it began in Jamaica, this music has spread throughout the world with contemporary artists like Rhythm & Sound, Mungo's Hi-Fi, Dub Pistols and Easy Star All-Stars blurring the lines between dub, electronic music, rock and pop [22a] [22b].

The Music

This groove is like a slow burn. The real challenge is getting the feel to be laid back and super-relaxed but not too messy. Notice that the quarter-note pulse is quite slow, so the metronome is clicking 8th notes to make it easier to lock in. Also note that the bass drum almost never plays on beat 1! This is a hallmark of this style of drumming and gives it that special dub/reggae flavor.

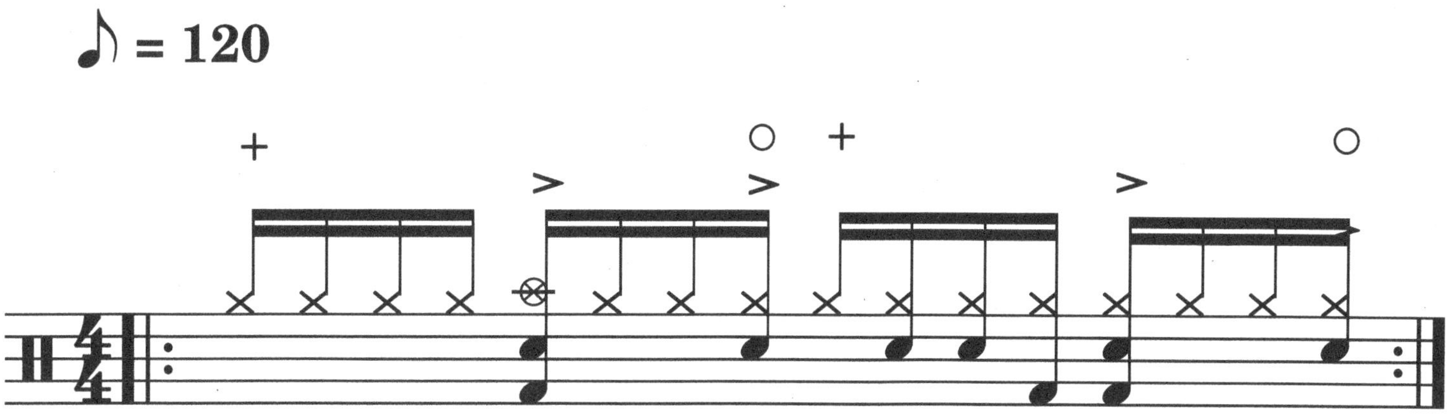

As you get more comfortable, you can explore variations using the hi-hat and snare. Open/close the hi-hat quickly and add some tom fills or carefully placed crashes to create new textures. These variations can be playful and loose as long as you stick to the basic premise of playing the snare on 2 and 4 and avoiding beat 1 with the bass drum.

Variation #1

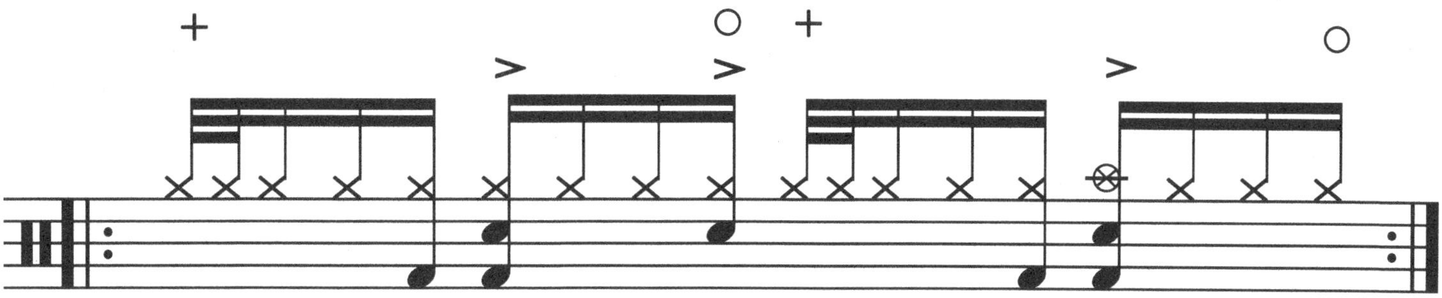

Variation #2

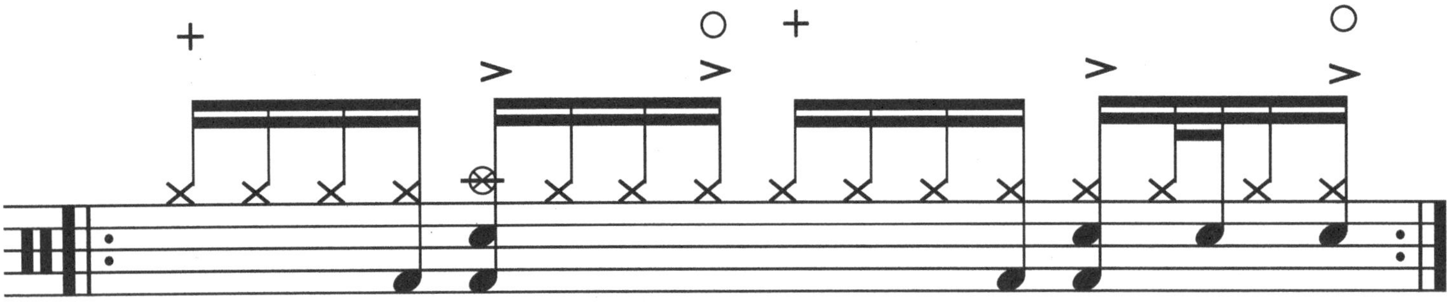

Variation #3

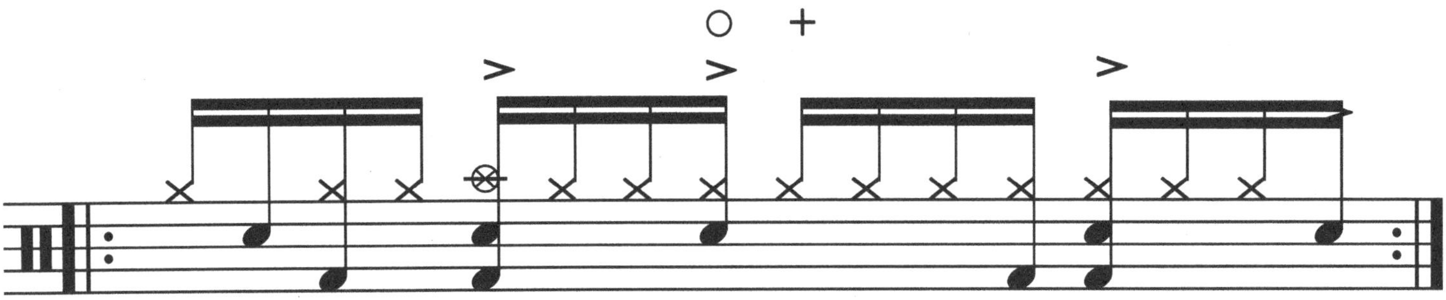

One thing I always try to remember when playing this style is that the space between the notes is almost as important as the notes themselves. If you check out my fills, I'll often become active towards the end of a measure and then wait to resolve the phrase until beat 2 of the next bar. Trippy! The bass player is doing something similar. His repeating line starts on the "and" of beat 1 and only hits the downbeat every other measure. The space we're creating in the rhythm section allows the other sounds to layer on top.

Fill #1

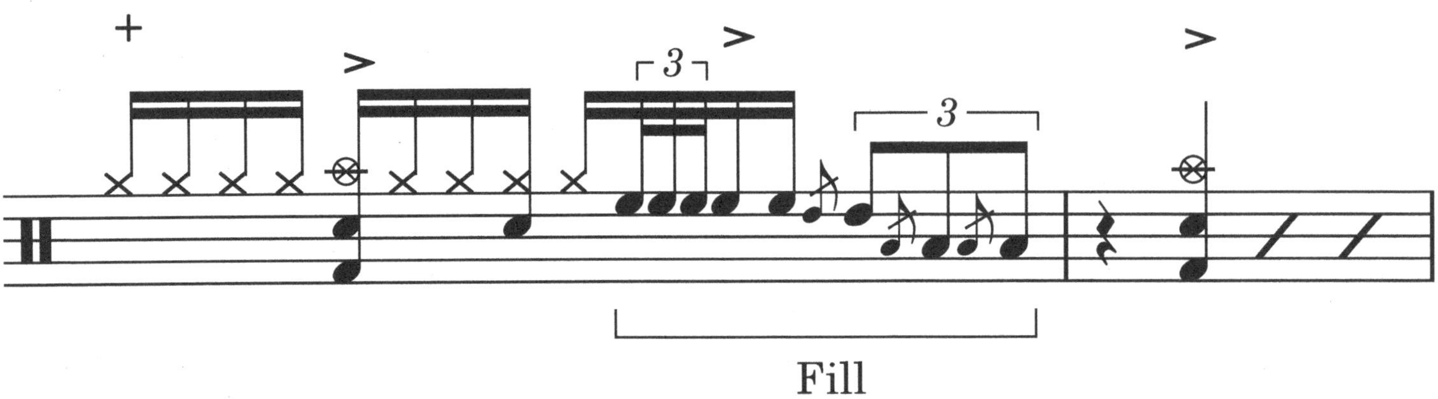

It's also important to stay mentally focused throughout the entire track and not add too much stuff because you're getting antsy or bored. Embrace the chill, get in the groove and cook it up nice and slow.

The Band

Dmitry Ishenko:

"Dub music was basically producers taking the rhythm section tracks and adding effects to them. Over the years, it became a thing where musicians would try to replicate that live. The bass is actually the melodic foundation of a reggae track. The drums and guitar are playing more of a rhythmic part using beats 2 and 4, but the bass is what is carrying the melody. I try to make it more 'dubby' by using an octave pedal and I do not play on beat one, that's the key. But I repeat my part constantly and try to be as laid back as possible. Sometimes we add 'drops' and it cuts out in the middle of a phrase...it's a very unexpected surprise."

Elias Meister:

"The guitar part on this is extremely simple in terms of playing backbeats with this dotted quarter/triplet-y delay which is not exact...that's also part of the style, because it used to be people with analog machines putting effects on there. It's not quantized, it's just very loose and then there's another track that adds the delay and feedback textures. There's a lot of space for the beat to just happen and also within the beat itself, but that kind of creates the magic of it. The low parts of the sound and the drums and bass are very pushing, so when they're not there for a moment, the space itself almost creates the feeling of a note. You feel that space a lot, so you can really play with it too."

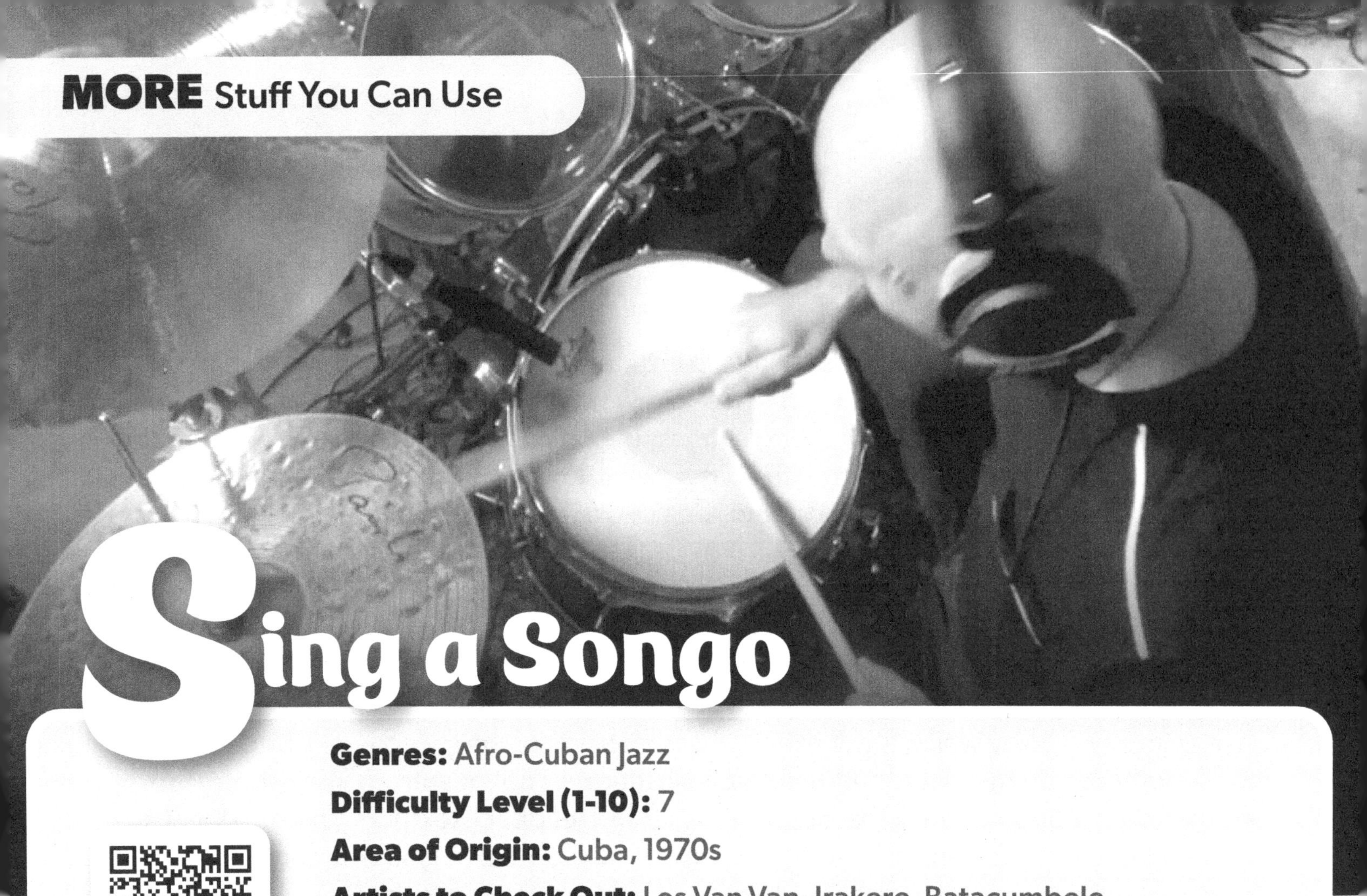

Sing a Songo

Genres: Afro-Cuban Jazz
Difficulty Level (1-10): 7
Area of Origin: Cuba, 1970s
Artists to Check Out: Los Van Van, Irakere, Batacumbele
Drummers to Check Out: José Luis "Changuito" Quintana, Ignacio Berroa, Horacio "El Negro" Hernandez, Dave Weckl, David Garibaldi, Walfredo Reyes Sr.

The History

The Cuban Revolution in 1959 brought about a widespread political, social and cultural reckoning for the island. Though the socialist regime exerted strong control over the music industry, many Cuban artists resisted and drew on global inspiration to expand and evolve. American R&B, jazz and British rock all gained a foothold in the '60s and '70s, deeply influencing traditional Cuban bands. One of the most important acts from this era was Los Van Van, a Cuban orchestra run by bassist Juan Formell. With José Luis "Changuito" Quintana on drums, they are widely recognized as the originators of the style called songo.

Changuito took traditional rhumba rhythms and adapted them for the drum set. He also made them funky and accessible to the younger audiences that Los Van Van were targeting. This was dance music at its core, but it also felt jazzy and featured trombones and other horns which weren't typically a part of classic lineups. By incorporating bongo, conga, cowbell and other hand-percussion parts into his patterns, Changuito even played a role in reshaping the composition of Cuban rhythm sections. He essentially took the entire percussion section and orchestrated it around the kit.

In the 1980s, bands like Chucho Valdes' group Irakere and Puerto Rican artists Batacumbele took these songo rhythms and expanded them even further. As artists around the world caught wind of this "funkifying" of the clavé, songo became a part of jazz and fusion music. Ignacio Berroa, Dave Weckl,

Horacio "El Negro" Hernandez, David Garibaldi and others incorporated it into their playing along with Timba, a later strain of Afro-Cuban funk which was its direct musical descendant [24a].

The Music

Afro-Cuban rhythms are some of my favorite grooves to play on the drum set. This jazzy songo is quite busy and syncopated, but it should still feel light and bouncy. There are a lot of texture options with the right hand. You can start on the cowbell (which I mount between my hi-hat and first rack tom) and switch to the closed hi-hat or ride cymbal bell for different sections. Notice that the bass drum on beat 3 is in parentheses. Try leaving it out sometimes to vary things up and create a little space. You can even do that with beat 1 too.

♩ = 120

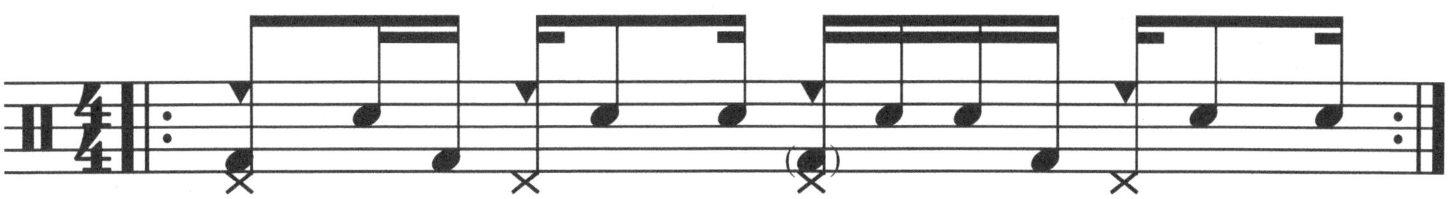

This groove should be driving and a little on top of the beat, but the trick is to let it breathe so it doesn't become too stiff. The quarter-note pulse is strong in your right hand, while the syncopation comes from the bass drum and snare. While I usually like to start working on patterns with just the feet, I think this one works best if you tackle it by playing the hands alone, then add the bass drum and hi-hat.

Variation #1

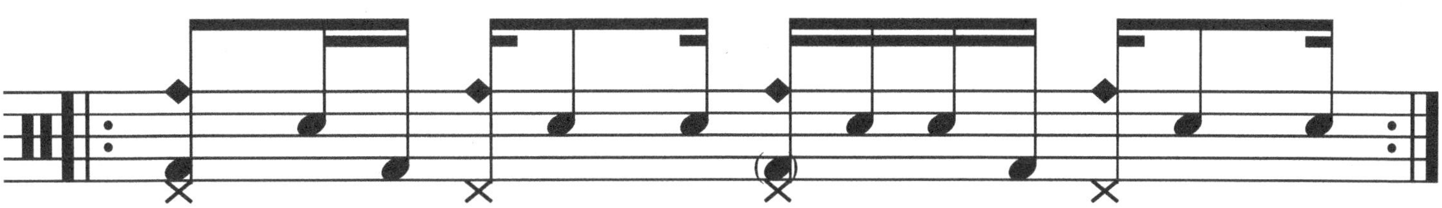

Variation #2

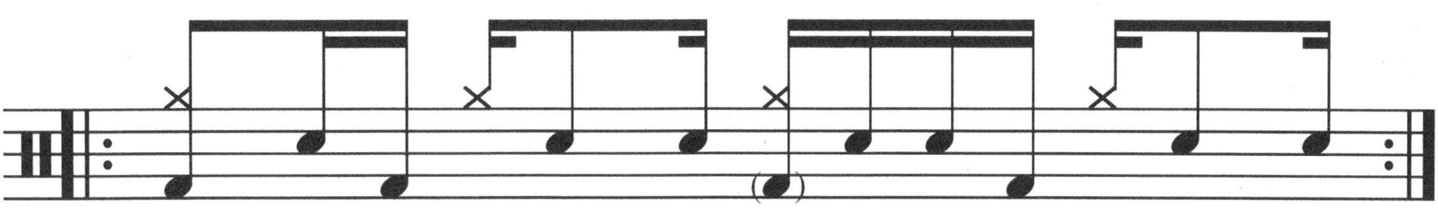

MORE Stuff You Can Use

Try to make your fills musically appropriate for this style by adding some thick double-handed tom/ snare phrases and mixing in a few crashes, almost as if you're mimicking timbales. Just make sure you come back to the pattern smoothly so you don't throw off the rest of the band, which is not easy at this tempo but very important.

Fill #1

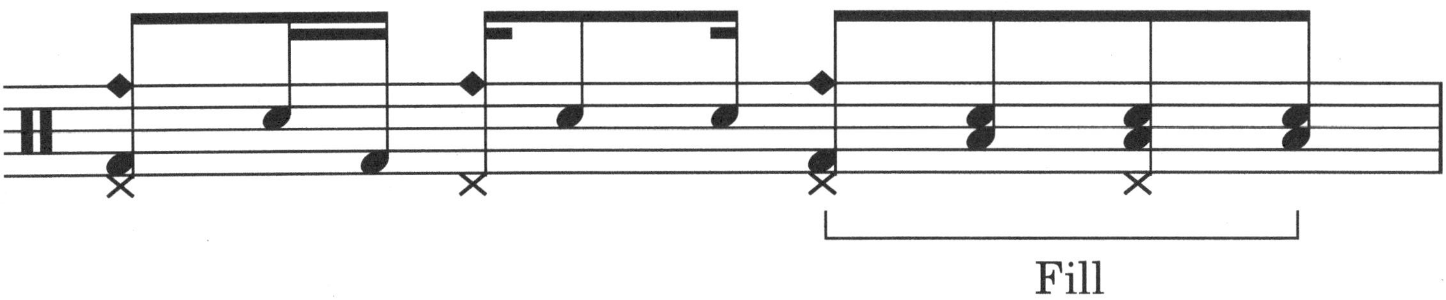

Fill #2

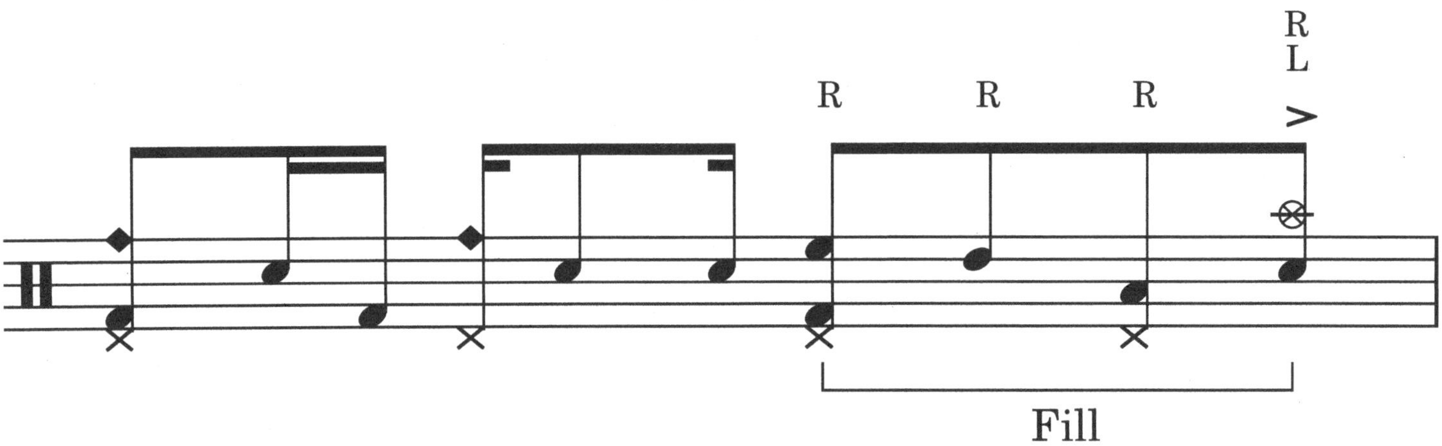

Fill #3

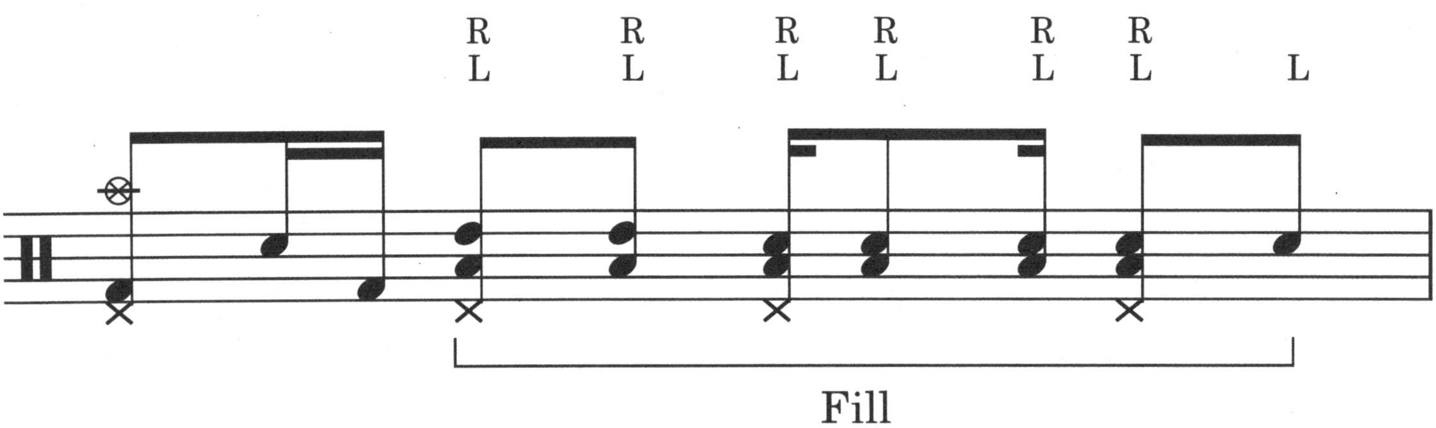

Fill #4

Fill #5

Once you get all the parts organized you'll start to hear how this pattern fits in with what everyone else is playing. The bass player is doing a tumbao-style syncopated pattern, while the guitar plays dynamic 16th-note strumming. This groove is busy and can feel frantic, so try to keep your cool and continue driving the beat forward.

MORE Stuff You Can Use

Here is the layout for the play-along track. The three sections are similar, but you can experiment with the texture changes as you move through the form.

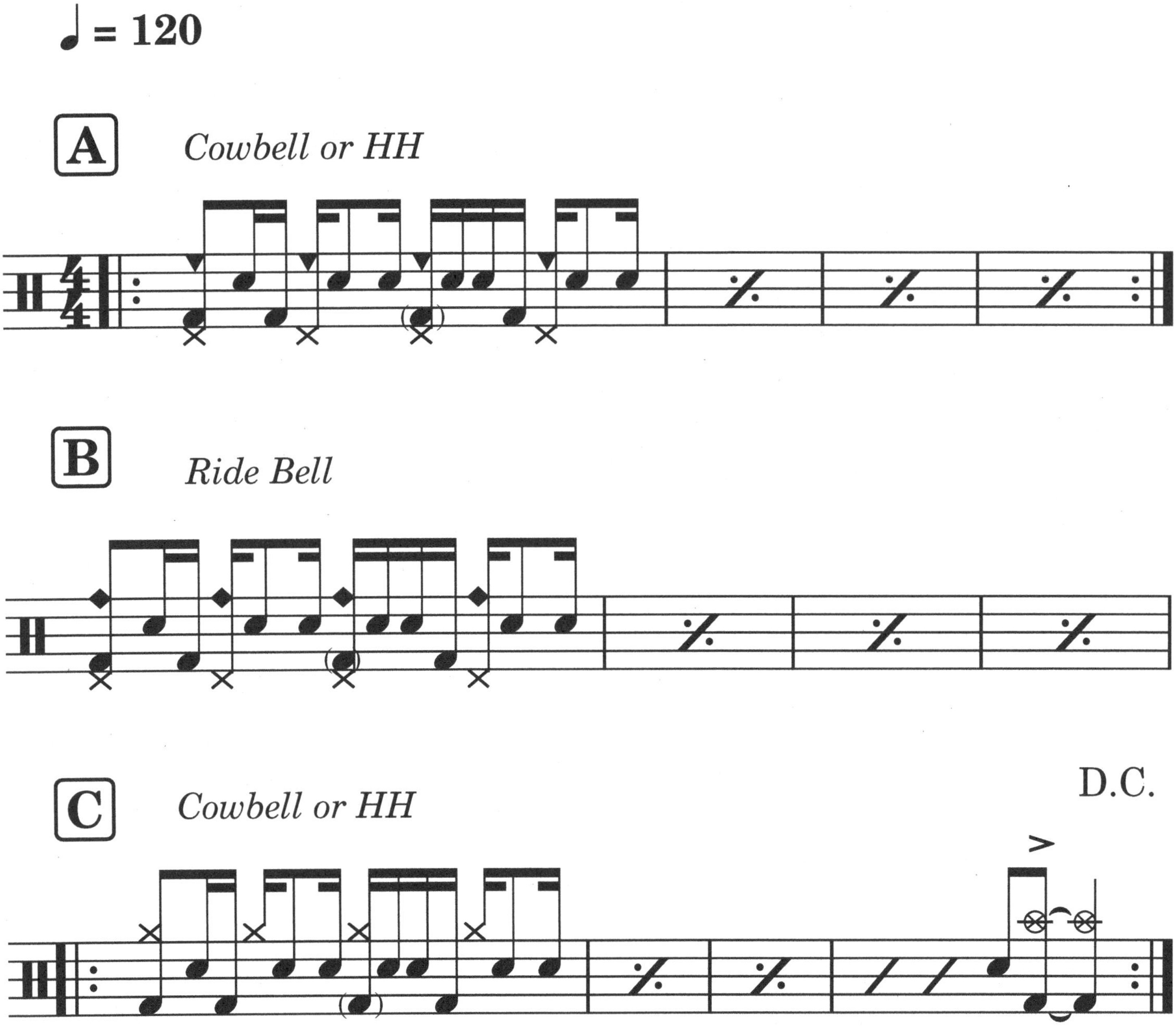

The Band

Dmitry Ishenko:

"It's a little bit busier than a classic salsa rhythm. I'm playing a tumbao-inspired bass line, but not totally that since in a tumbao you do not play the downbeats. But here, I'm landing on a downbeat every two or four bars just to indicate the next chord change. As far as the drums, I'm listening to a lot of the ride cymbal and the cowbell. I am also very much on top of the beat because that's the way a bass player plays salsa, kind of pushing ahead despite other elements. It's a very interlocking pattern and I'm almost trying to occasionally ignore everybody else and just play my own bass line on top of that, trusting that everything will resolve itself. It's ignoring while at the same time still hearing what's going on around me."

Elias Meister:

"The guitar is very prominent, kind of busy and very driving with the syncopated rhythm. I'm outlining the chords with some melody in there, but it's very much a part and there are slight variations in the rhythms. It's also super-busy and dense. I'm thinking about how this busy part I'm playing should sit within the bigger picture of the groove, not on top of it...like an interface thing. It should sit within the groove along with the drums, more like a percussion thing. If you imagine a bunch of people playing percussion and doing busy things, I'm one of them."

Ska-daddle

Genres: Ska

Difficulty Level (1-10): 5

Area of Origin: Jamaica, late 1950s

Artists to Check Out: The Skatalites, The Specials, The Mighty Mighty Bosstones, Reel Big Fish, The Bodysnatchers, The Selector, Toots and The Maytals

Drummers to Check Out: Lloyd Knibb, Philip "Fish" Fisher, Andrew Gonzales, Paul Douglas, Joe Sirois

The History

Jamaican ska music emerged in the late 1950s, with The Skatalites and innovative drummer Lloyd Knibb at the forefront. While this music drew from a wide range of influences such as African music, American jazz and R&B, it was truly unique in a number of ways. Ska rhythms emphasized the upbeats rather than the downbeats, with guitarists "skanking," bassists playing linear and melodic lines and drummers playing the bass drum on 2 and 4 with the snare or cross-stick. Knibb was the first drummer to put all these elements together, and his relaxed but driving feel deeply influenced generations of ska drummers. Early Skatalites songs "Guns of Navarone" and "Dynamite" showcased this early style which always also included a rollicking horn section.

As this music spread throughout the globe, a second wave of ska blossomed in England in late 1970s. This style became known as "two-tone," with bands like The Specials, Madness and The Selector combining traditional ska with heavier punk rock elements. This ska was edgier and angrier than the classic version, and it also featured more diverse groups like The Bodysnatchers, an all-female 7-piece two-tone band. Ska underwent yet another revival in the early '90s as American bands like The Toasters, Reel Big Fish and The Mighty Mighty Bosstones leaned in to this ska/punk fusion even more. This third wave, which was concentrated mostly in New York and Los Angeles, also featured wildly popular bands like Sublime and Fishbone with the incredible Philip "Fish" Fisher on drums.

The underlying groove in this music bore a strong resemblance to classic Jamaican ska, but with more distorted guitars and brash vocals. It also appealed to a new audience of younger fans, leading to a resurgence in popularity for classic bands like The Skatalites.

Stewart Copeland of The Police is also another important drummer is this genre. Despite not being in a traditional ska band, his use of upbeats, syncopated hi-hat articulations and fills that didn't end on the downbeat had deep roots in ska drumming. This innovative playing brought ska into a mainstream pop context and introduced it to many drummers around the world [23a] [23b].

The Music

This groove is all about being relaxed and consistent. That's easier said than done when you're backing a huge band with a horn section and there's tons of energy onstage. The bass drum plays quarter notes throughout while the cross-stick handles the backbeat. You'll notice that the bass player's line is quite active and serves as more of a counterpoint to the drums. The guitar is "skanking" on the upbeats while the horns layer on top, so it's important for the drums to hold things down during all this musical crosstalk.

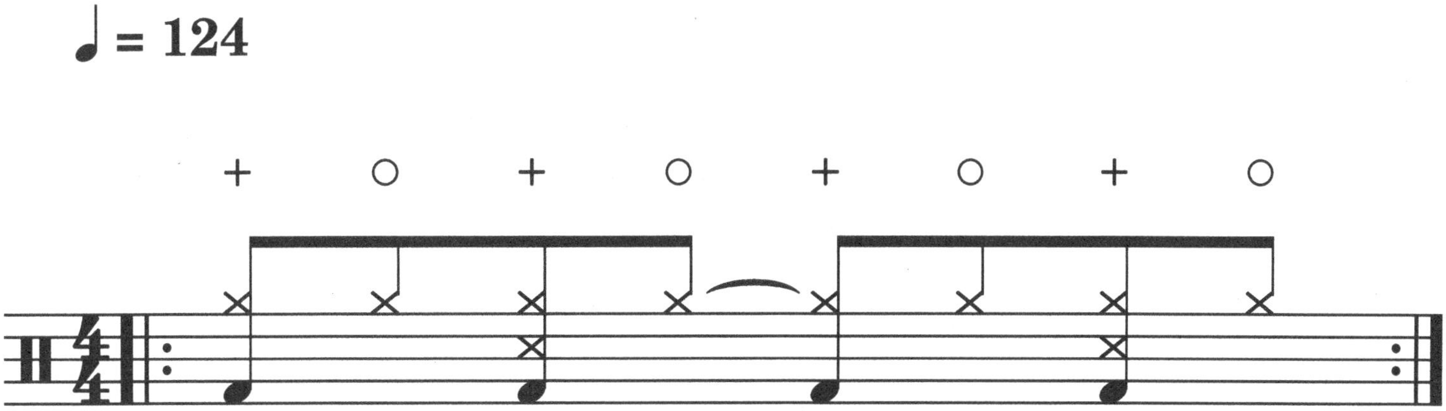

This is another groove where the concept of "station points" can make simple fills and variations more flavorful. I like resolving fills on the "and" of beat 4 and punctuating with the snare drum. It's like you're creating a quick moment of openness before contracting back into the cross-stick pattern. Add some extra accents on the "ands" of 2 or 4 for even more variety.

Variation #1

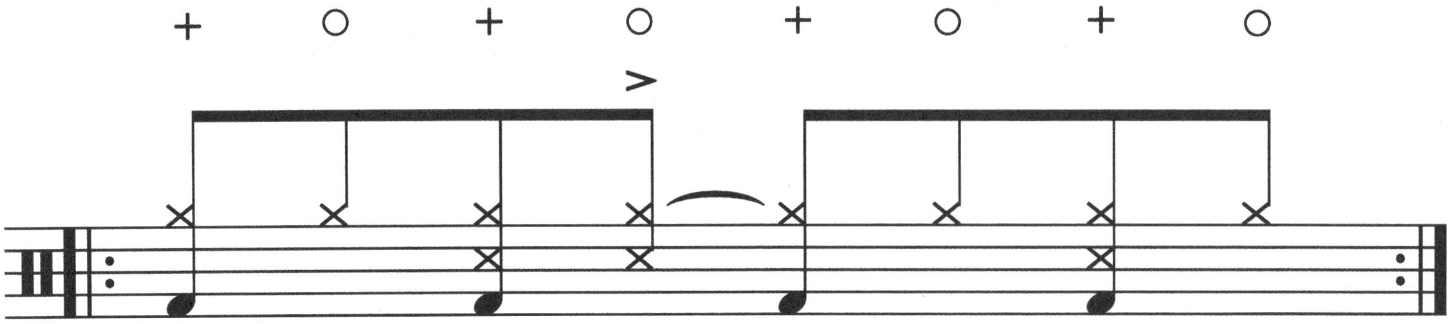

Variation #2

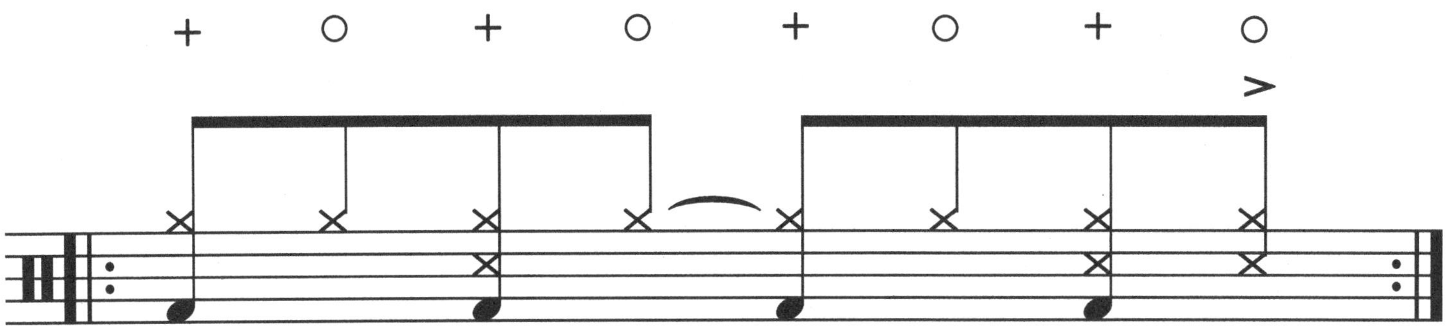

Variation #3

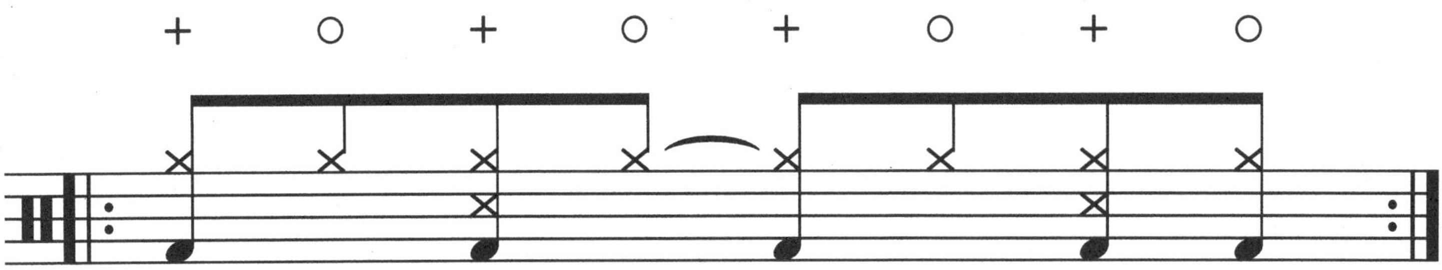

It's important to make sure you're getting the best possible cross-stick sound. If your stick isn't positioned in the right place on the hoop, it can sound too thin (2 or 3 inches over the edge usually does the trick with the stick reversed). Another important element of this groove is the opening of the hi-hat on the upbeats. Try lifting your toes inside your shoe to loosen the cymbals just enough to get that perfect tight sizzle. These may seem like minor bits of technique, but putting them all together can help you get an awesome overall sound. Use the concept of station points and experiment with ending your fills on the "and" of beat 4.

Fill #1

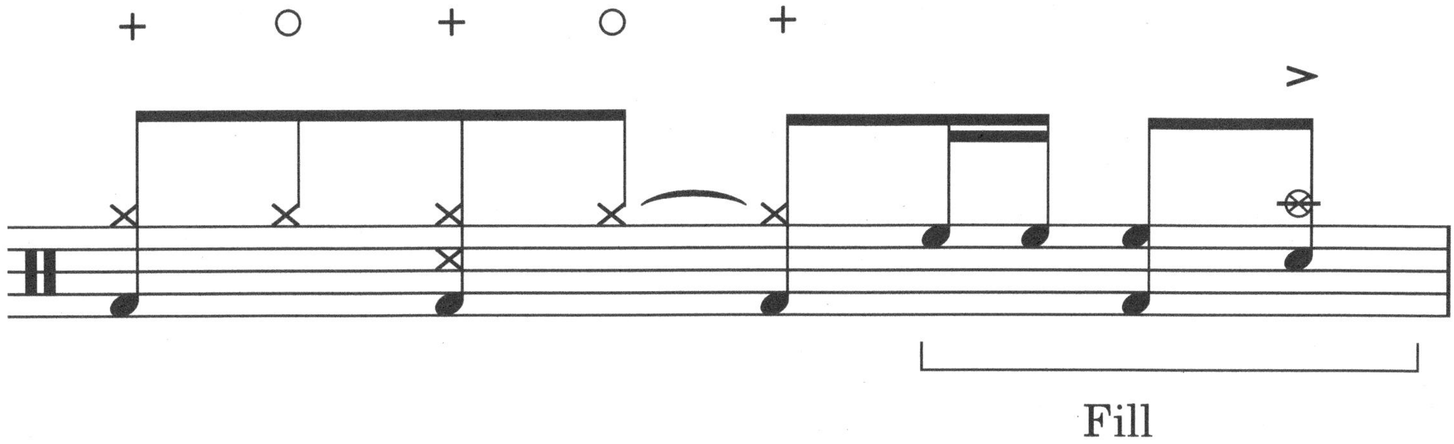

Fill #2

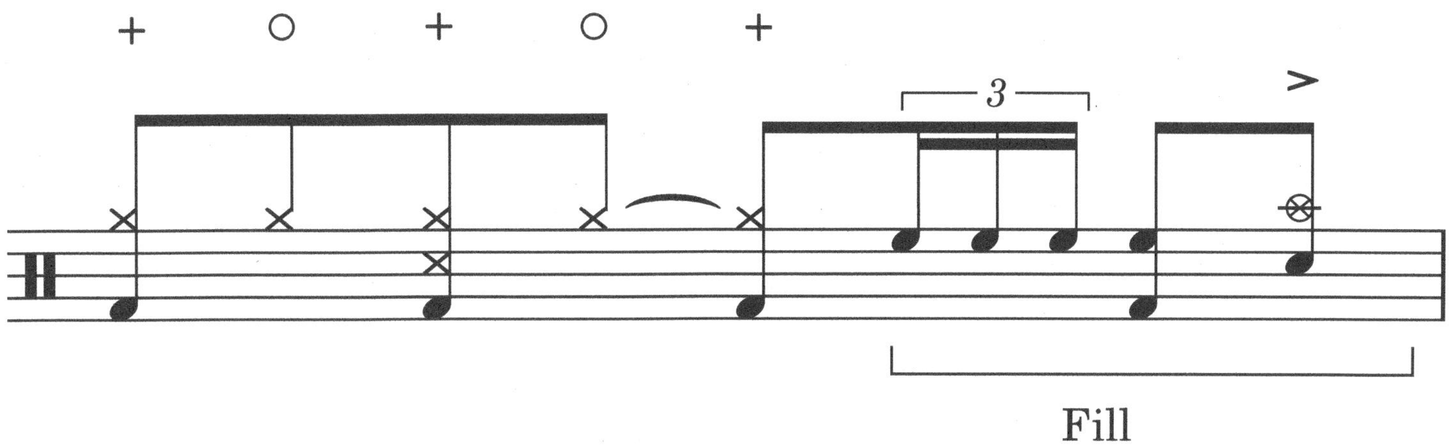

The drummers who are great at this style all have a good tone and feel. These concepts can seem really abstract at first, but they're just a result of good technique, good ears and attention to detail. So, buckle up, lay the groove down and enjoy the ride.

NB
TOP OF THE ROCK
PERCUSSIVE
ARTS
SOCIETY

The Band

Dmitry Ishenko:

"In ska music, what I'm doing on the bass is just playing a lot of 8th notes and usually arpeggiating the chord. So, the root, the third, the fifth...that's what I'm doing. But while I'm playing very lightly, I'm emphasizing beat one which is not the case with the other instruments. As a bass player, it's very important to listen to the bass drum in this particular groove. In a lot of Jamaican music like in reggae, ska and dub, the bass is almost kind of like the melody. The horns, guitars and keyboards are more like the support harmonic role."

Elias Meister:

"I'm feeling the upbeats pretty heavily on the guitar even though the rhythm section is marking the quarter notes clearly. I'm playing it light and super-dancey. It's very consistent in the way it evolves. The hi-hat part and the guitar are very much together, so it's important to lock that sound in. The way you open and close [the hi-hat] makes it very groovy. You want people to dance to this."

Wes Maples:

"The horn is kind of variable, going from a lead role to a support role which is pretty common in this music. We go from playing the main hook, which is very catchy and melodic to switching it up and playing more of a rhythm-section role where we're playing the upbeats (which in reggae and ska is known as the skank). We're harmonizing, getting some group hits together and accentuating rhythm parts which would be played by the keyboards and the guitar...we're reinforcing that. There's so much here. Even the bass line is very melodic with so many arpeggios. There's a lot of strong melodies throughout. So, even when you switch the horns to a rhythmic role, you're not lacking because the bass is arpeggiating strong melodic ideas."

Turf 'n Surf

Genres: Surf Rock

Difficulty Level (1-10): 4

Area of Origin: Southern California, early 1960s

Artists to Check Out: Dick Dale, The Ventures, The Surfaris, The Beach Boys, The Chantays, Jan and Dean

Drummers to Check Out: Steve Aschoff, Hal Blaine, Ron Wilson, Dennis Wilson

The History

As surf culture took over southern California in the early 1960s, a bold new style of rock music became its soundtrack. Surf rock featured reverb-drenched guitars which almost mimicked the sound of crashing waves. Early surf rock was mostly instrumental, with guitarist Dick Dale as a leading figure. Dale, who was actually a native Bostonian and Lebanese-American, fused Middle-Eastern scales with his signature spring reverb tone to become known as "King of The Surf Guitar [25a]." Fender actually built a specific reverb unit for Dale in 1961 after he blew up so many amplifiers in his quest for this innovative sound. Dale had so much success in southern California with his band the Del-Tones that he rarely toured, enjoying a late-career resurgence when his song "Misirlou" was featured in the opening of the Quentin Tarantino film *Pulp Fiction* (1994). Dale's longtime drummer Steve Aschoff played an important role in creating this signature sound.

Other bands like The Ventures ("Walk, Don't Run") and The Chantays ("Pipeline") also had instrumental surf hits, while The Surfaris wrote perhaps the most iconic drum feature since "Sing, Sing, Sing" with their classic "Wipeout," featuring drummer Ron Wilson. As the decade wore on, a second "wave" of vocal surf music emerged led by The Beach Boys and other groups. This music added lyrics that reflected the laid-back lifestyle of southern California, with hits like "Surfin' Safari" and "Surfin' U.S.A." gaining widespread popularity. The Beach Boys' Brian Wilson penned another hit for singers Jan and Dean called "Surf City" featuring legendary session drummer Hal Blaine (who played on a bunch of The Beach Boys' hits too). As the '60s wore on, surf rock's popularity faded with the British Invasion and arrival of bands like The Beatles. However, its lasting impact and later resurgence has reinforced its impact on the history of American popular music [(25b) (25c)].

The Music

A classic surf beat should be crisp and upbeat with tight articulation on the snare part, which is really the "melody" of this groove. Make sure to slightly accent the "and" of beat 2 to give it a nice shape, which also lines up with the bass.

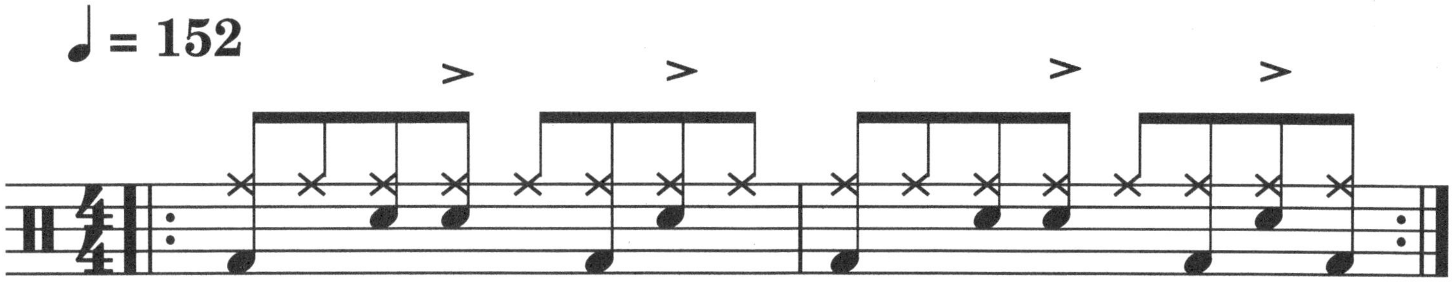

Variation #1

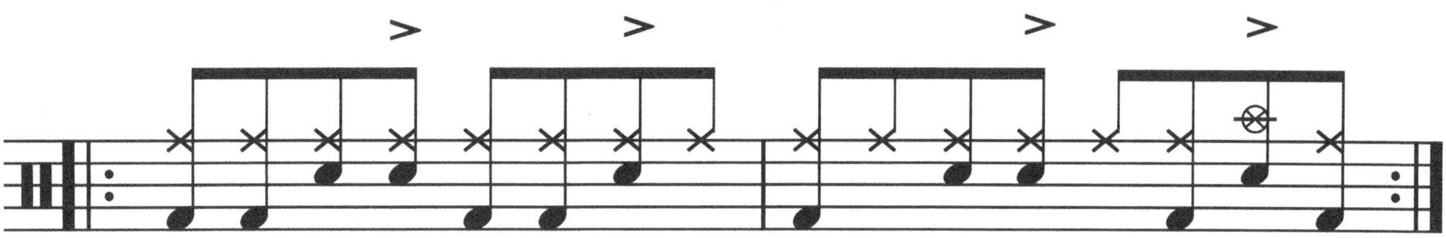

Fill #1

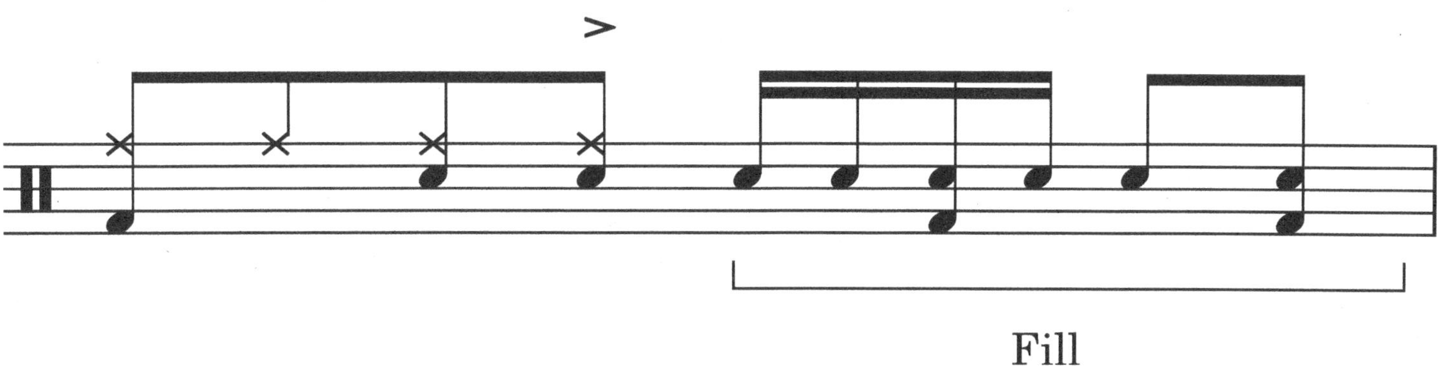

MORE Stuff You Can Use

You'll notice that the play-along track repeats a form that has 3 specific parts: an 8-bar A section, an 8-bar B section where the band changes their progression but you play the same thing, and then an 8-measure drum solo. While you'll want to hold down the groove over A and B, the solo section will give you a chance to explore some musical vocabulary in this style while the band plays hits.

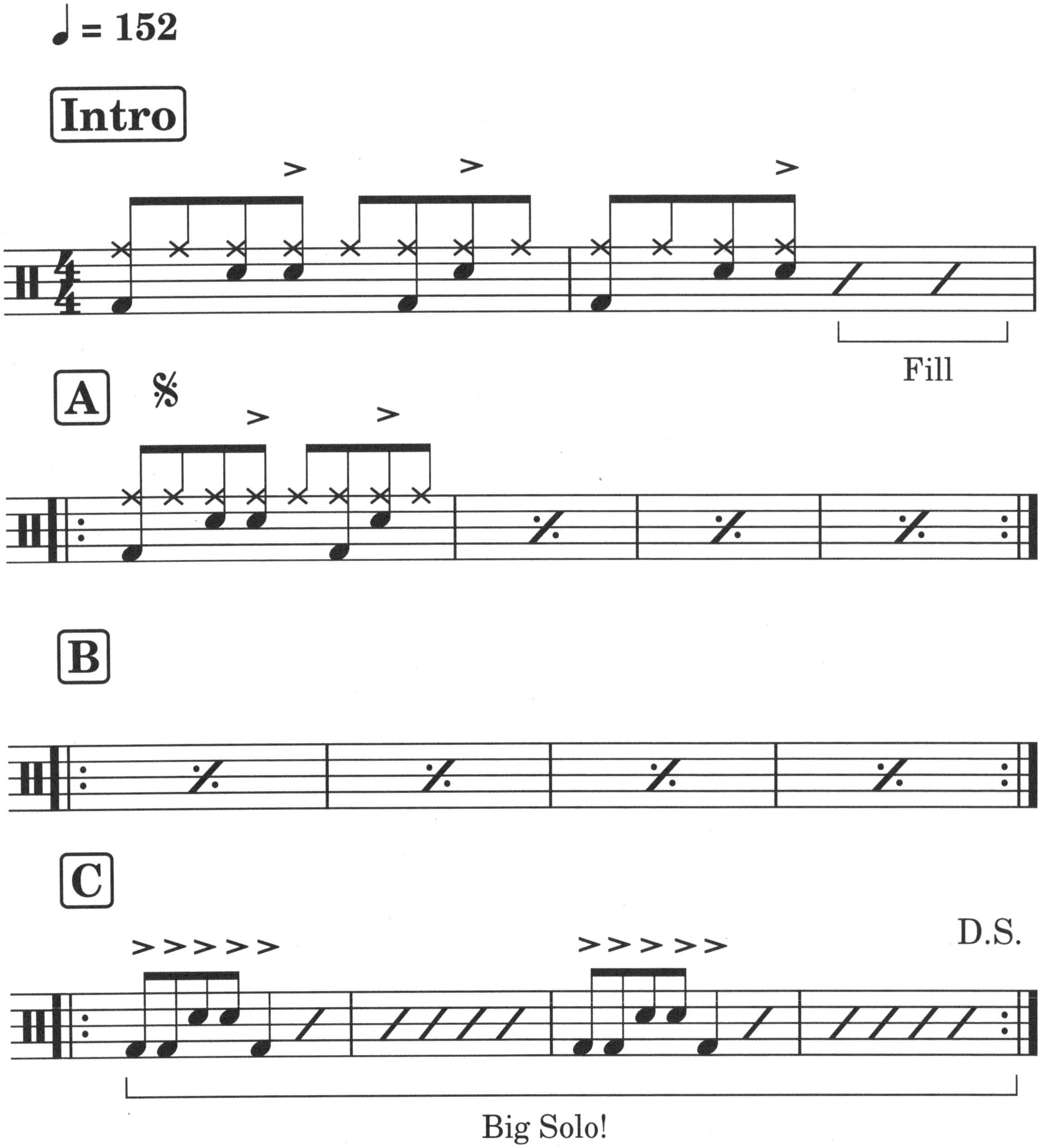

When I'm soloing, the main thing I'm thinking about is the melody of whatever song I'm playing. I actually try to sing it my head while I play. A lot of drummers get stuck repeating the same licks and basic ideas when they solo, and I think this is a great way to break through that barrier. You don't have to mimic the rhythm of the song's melody exactly, but those phrases can provide you with built-in ideas to start from. Trust me, this really works!

Once you wrap up the solo section each time, make sure to transition smoothly back into the pattern. I can't tell you how many times I've heard someone play an energetic and creative solo but lose their bearings and crash-land at the end getting back into the tune. It's important to always know where you are in the form and how long the solo is each time.

When you're grooving, stay on top of the beat and drive the band ahead. The bass and drums tend to keep things pretty simple in surf rock while the guitar plays over top. So, catch some waves and steer the band right in to shore!

The Band

Elias Meister:

"When I'm playing this kind of music, I'm thinking about having kind of a 'punk attitude' even though that's later music...just the way I'm approaching the guitar and hitting it kind of strong even though the sound is pretty clean with a lot of attitude. The guitar is definitely playing the melody but it's a very simple, repetitive thing with the 8th notes. I'm feeling more of the backbeats in this type of groove. It's very simple and kind of bluesy. It's very much about outlining the form and the rhythm that keeps repeating. So, even if you're soloing, you're not straying too far from that. You're not stretching it. You're not trying to add an element of surprise or anything like that. You want to play little embellishments on the rhythm that's already there."

Dmitry Ishenko:

"It's mostly an early '60s, straight-ahead rock and roll groove but the bass line is very specific. It's a dotted quarter note and then 8th notes tied over to give it a little bit of syncopation and flavor against the static 8th-note groove in the drums. I would say the rhythmic subdivisions are more of the 'duple' nature than triple. It's a lot of 16th notes or 8th notes. It's not triplet-y in any kind of way."

Ungrateful Dead

Genres: Jam Band

Difficulty Level (1-10): 4

Area of Origin: U.S.A., 1960s

Artists to Check Out: The Grateful Dead, The Allman Brothers, Widespread Panic, Phish, Dave Matthews Band, Max Creek, The String Cheese Incident, Aquarium Rescue Unit, Government Mule, The Spin Doctors, Blues Traveler, Soulive, Medeski Martin & Wood, Bela Fleck & The Flecktones, Garage A Trois, Joe Russo's Almost Dead, Lettuce, King Gizzard & the Lizard Wizard, Goose, Umphrey's McGee

Drummers to Check Out: John Fishman, Carter Beauford, Joe Russo, Aaron Comess, Bill Kreutzmann

The History

So...what exactly *is* a jam band? This is one of the hardest genres to clearly define since many of the musical elements we use to identify it are present in other styles too. Extended solos, harmonic and rhythmic odysseys and bold improvisations unbound by the conventions of pop are all features, however they only tell part of the story. Jam bands are really about the scene. Massive festivals, bootleg recordings, dancing, drugs and above all else, love and community...and it all started with one band.

As psychedelic rock became popular in the 1960s, The Grateful Dead emerged from Palo Alto, California with mystical front man Jerry Garcia leading the charge. Songwriter and rhythm guitarist Bob Weir was a creative force and the band had (gasp!) two drummers, Bill Kreutzmann and Mickey Hart. Unlike previous artists who discouraged audience members from taping live shows out of fear it would harm their album sales, The Dead actually set up a bootlegging section for fans. In the pre-internet era, these recordings were like gold to true Deadheads since you could only get them by being there or trading them. The songs themselves were merely a framework for unpredictable and thrilling musical journeys.

No two shows were alike and though they never had a number one hit, The Grateful Dead remain one of the most popular bands of all time.

The Allman Brothers were another influential force in the early jam band era, though it's debatable whether they were actually a jam band--or as guitarist Duane Allman puts it, "a band that jams" (you could haggle over this kind of thing for hours!). After Garcia's death in 1995, the scene enjoyed a massive resurgence with Phish at the forefront. Bands like Government Mule, Widespread Panic and Aquarium Rescue Unit (with guitar hero Jimmy Herring) also found devoted audiences as the festival scene exploded throughout the country. There were also musical offshoots which incorporated jam band elements and shared many of the same fans. Dave Matthews Band, The Spin Doctors (with the funky drumming of Aaron Comess) and Blues Traveler featured a more typical pop/rock song structure but with extended soloing. Medeski Martin & Wood, Soulive and banjo virtuoso Bela Fleck were instrumental acts with roots in jazz or bluegrass that also thrived in the jam band scene. The rich legacy of this music lives on today through artists like Umphrey's McGee, Goose, King Gizzard & The Lizard Wizard and The Dead themselves with John Mayer on guitar. Peace and love (and really long solos!) [26a].

The Music

Jam band drumming combines elements of jazz, rock and funk to create a loose and relaxed feel. The idea is to make the music conversational and interactive (that's the "jam" part). However, the "band" part is important too, so the first thing you'll need to do is get your groove locked in with the bass player.

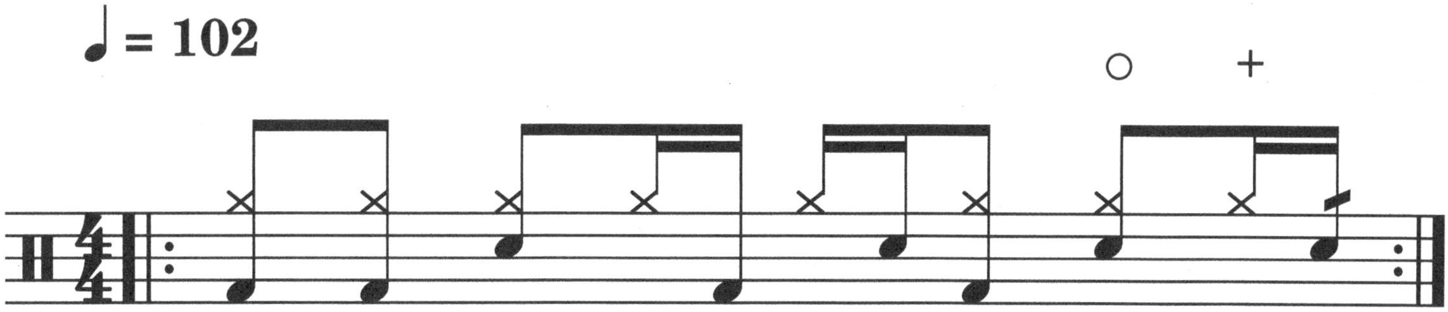

While the backbeat continues throughout the tune, there is tons of room to add snare and kick drum variations on the "e's" and "a's" of any beat you want. You can open the hi-hat, add crashes, fill at the end of 8-bar sections (or even in the middle) and just explore the musical space.

Variation #1

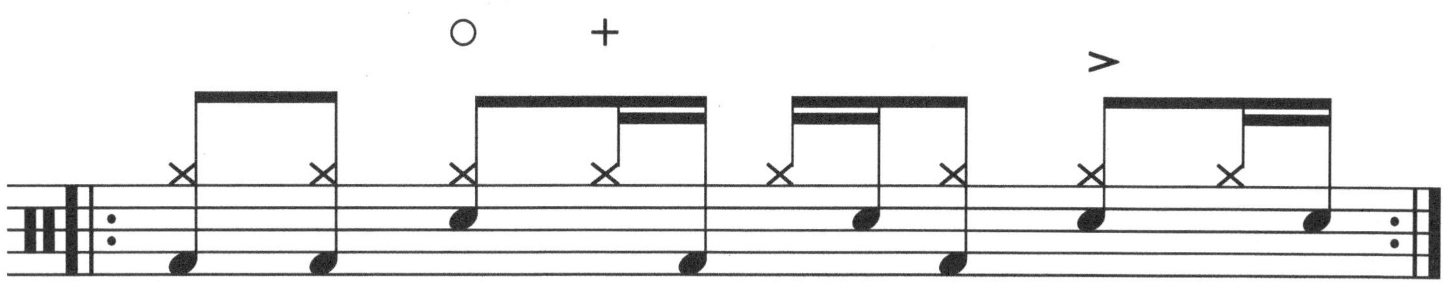

Variation #2

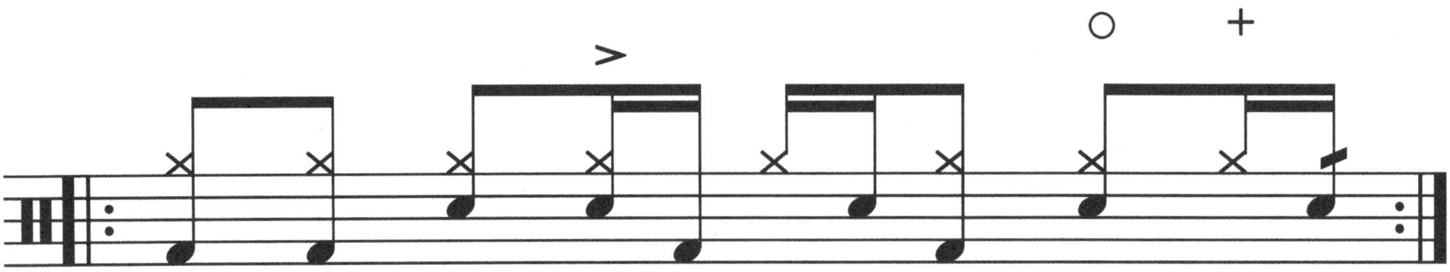

Variation #3

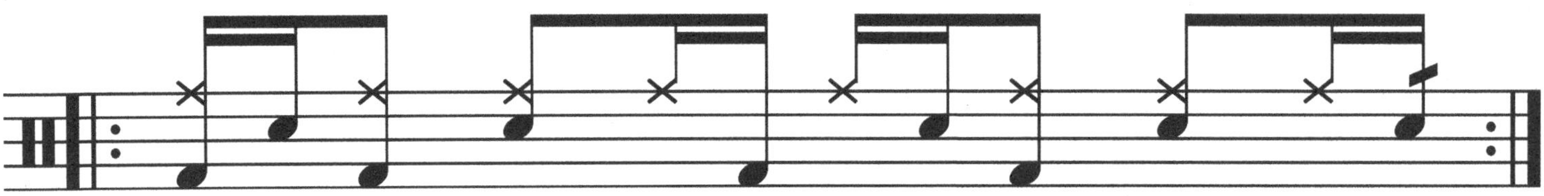

You can also change textures to build and contract since this music is all about peaks and valleys. Start on the hi-hat, move to the ride, add in the bell or get super-crashy. As long as you're listening and flowing with the rest of the band, the options are limitless. When I play this style, I try to build and develop phrases over a chunk of measures so it feels like we're actually *going* somewhere rather than just changing the pattern randomly. I think one of the biggest myths about jam band music is that it's just noodling. The best tunes in this style have strong musical intent, dynamic changes and a deep groove.

Variation #4

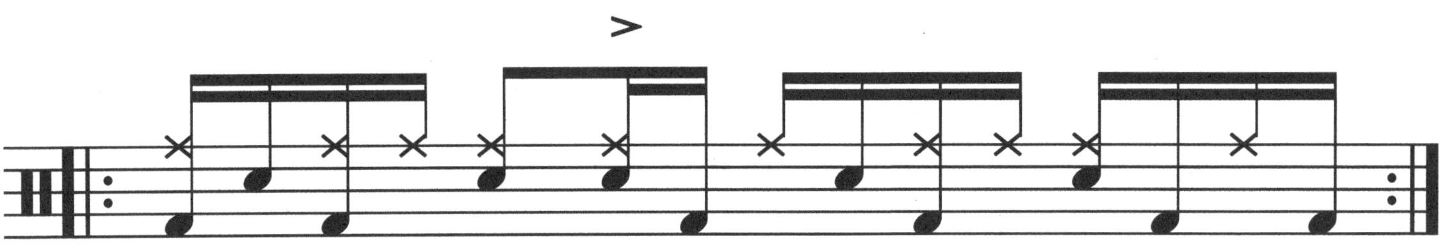

You'll notice the bass and guitar parts are quite busy and linear too. However, this is intentional and every note they're playing has a purpose. That's why it's so important to listen and interact. You don't necessarily have to "bite" and musically respond to every single idea you hear. Mimicking or parroting back a bass or guitar idea note-for-note is not necessarily the hippest musical choice. I try to be selective and use the drums to broadly push the music forward with layers of sound. This may seem abstract, but listening and responding is really the whole ballgame in jam band music. When you're creating ideas, it's important to use musical language that fits the style.

Fill #1

Fill #2

Fill #3

These tunes tend to stretch on for a long time, so it's important to avoid getting stuck in a rut where the music gets stagnant or boring. Don't be afraid to push the band in a new direction if you're feeling it. So, lay down the groove and let's jam out!

The Band

Dmitry Ishenko:

"Jam band music is a very American style. It's drawing on country, folk and blues all at once, but adding a certain looseness factor where things don't necessarily repeat like they do in a funk, soul or country track. The structure stays the same but the playing is constantly evolving and changing. I'm playing a continuously varying bass line which is almost like a counter-melody to the guitar and drums, but we're all in the same tempo and we're all kind of answering each other.

"One really cool thing about these kinds of bands is that they sometimes abandon their traditional musical roles. I could be playing the bass line, but I could be almost like a lead voice and so can the drums. It's like there's sometimes a reversal of roles, all flowing in and out organically. This is all about listening and feeling the pulse. But you definitely have to stay within the form of whatever song you're playing. It works as long as it evolves."

Elias Meister:

"The framework is simple and we're all propelling the groove in a very obvious way. There's no need to make it too obscure. You're laying on the blues vibes and it definitely has a playful feeling for me. I'm thinking about people dancing to this in a very happy way...and it's kind of loose and not too serious in a nice way. This is also a style where marking the sections creates a lot of clarity even if the part you're playing is kind of loose and not so mainstream. The marking of the sections really creates continuity in the music. You can change a little thing and it will change the whole part...just the feeling, the intensity of it or how busy it is. You can always play less and make it sparser."

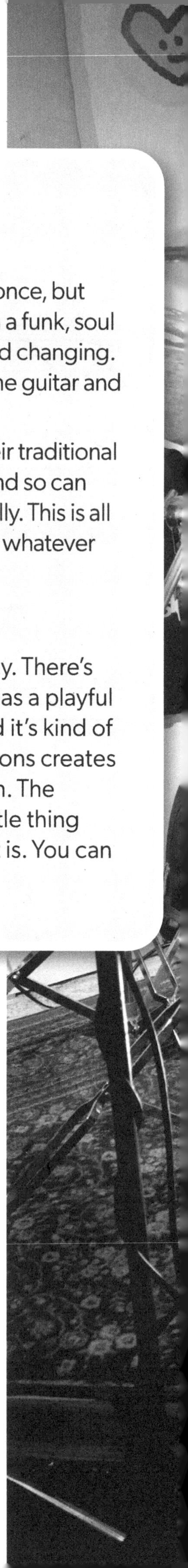

YAMAHA

Vintage Punk Junk

Genres: Punk Rock

Difficulty Level (1-10): 6

Area of Origin: England, New York City, 1970s

Artists to Check Out: The Ramones, The Sex Pistols, The Clash, Richard Hell and the Voidoids, The Damned, Bad Brains, Black Flag, Minor Threat, The Stooges, New York Dolls, The Sonics, MC5, Television, Circle Jerks, Dead Kennedys

Drummers to Check Out: Tommy Ramone, Marky Ramone, Topper Headon, Earl Hudson, Bill Stevenson, Rat Scabies

The History

The punk rock scene that emerged from New York in the mid-1970s was as much a cultural and social phenomenon as a musical style. The songs were fast, loud and totally in-your-face as artists thumbed their noses at the establishment and mustered a rallying cry for all those who felt left behind by mainstream society. Legendary rock club CBGB played a pivotal role in these early beginnings (sometimes called "proto-punk,") hosting acts like New York Dolls, Richard Hell and The Voidoids, Television and The Ramones, who became one of the most popular punk bands of all time. Drummer Tommy Ramone is widely credited with originating the frenetic drum pattern that became a defining characteristic of punk music. The Stooges, with tempestuous front man Iggy Pop were another important American band in these early days of punk.

As the decade wore on, punk rock made its way across the ocean, as British bands like The Sex Pistols, The Clash (with the incredible drumming of Topper Headon) and Buzzcocks led this second wave. British audiences also adopted the punk culture and style, as ripped jeans and tattered leather jackets became the unofficial uniform of punks everywhere. This non-conformity also extended to the way bands recorded their music, with many taping and self-producing albums. They didn't care that it was lo-fi or not up to traditional standards. That was the whole point!

At the same time British punk became popular, another strain emerged in California, as bands like Black Flag, Circle Jerks and Dead Kennedys pioneered hardcore punk. This style was even heavier-sounding and more visceral as punk rock began splintering into various subgenres in the '80s (pop-punk, post-punk, thrash metal, alternative rock). While the music itself has spread throughout the world and evolved over the years, one thing that endures today is its rebellious spirit and true punk attitude [27a].

The Music

For me, punk drumming is about one thing: stamina. Lots of drummers can play fast and loud. But can you do it consistently for the whole song without losing steam or becoming robotic and stiff? This music goes full-throttle from start to finish, so proper technique is a major key to getting across the finish line. It's important to use your wrists and avoid getting too arm-heavy. Keep your elbows down and try not to raise your shoulders even when you start to get tired. Once that happens, you're toast! There's a reason that punk songs are often just 2 minutes or less, however this play-along is 3 minutes and 30 seconds. If you can hold your technique throughout it and avoid getting locked up, you should be well-equipped to tackle a punk set with a live band.

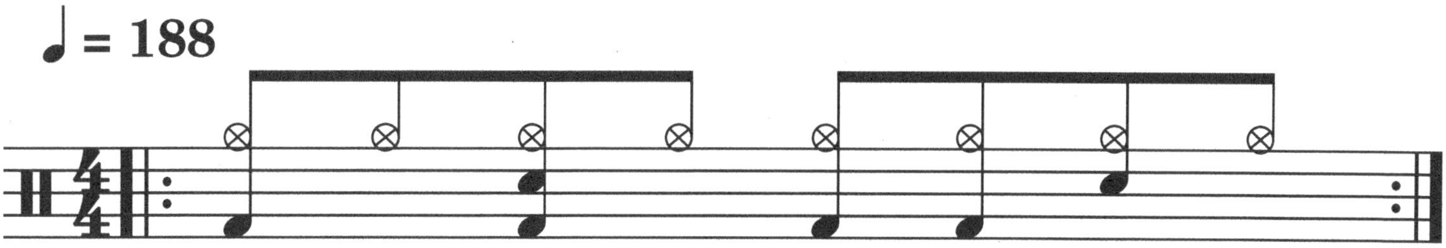

Stay as far on top of the beat as possible but try not to rush (also easier said than done). Keep the hi-hat super-loose to get that trashy texture. You can switch back and forth between quarter notes and 8th notes or move your right hand to the crash.

Variation #1

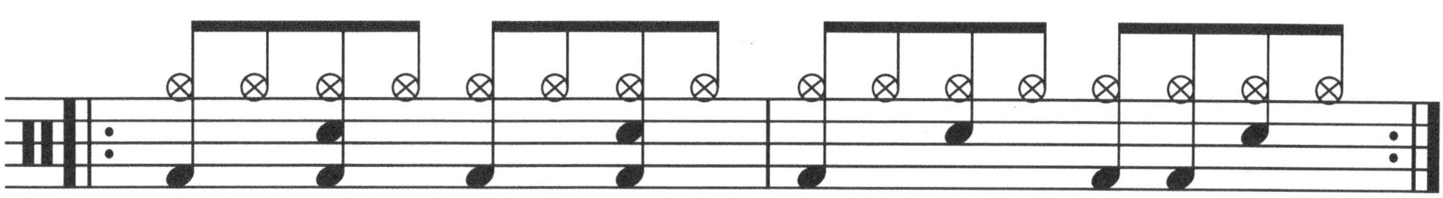

Variation #2

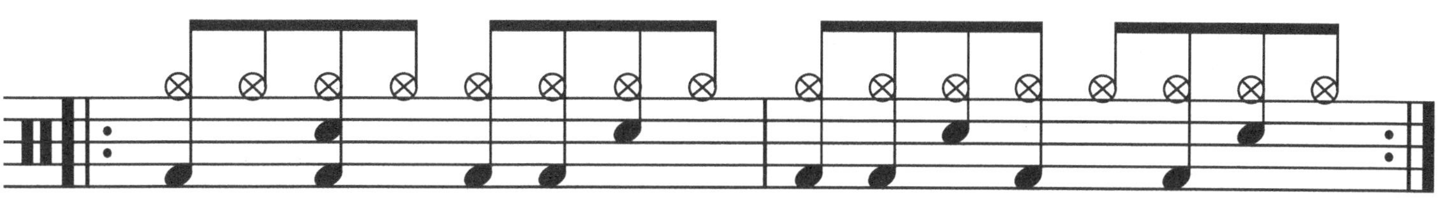

Variation #3

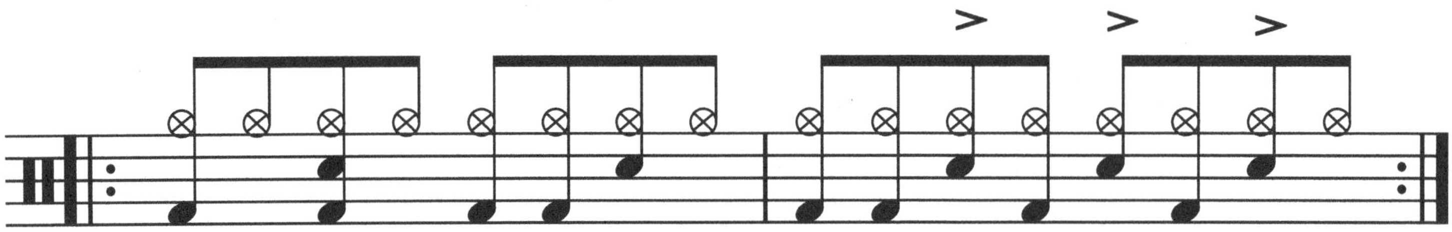

Variation #4

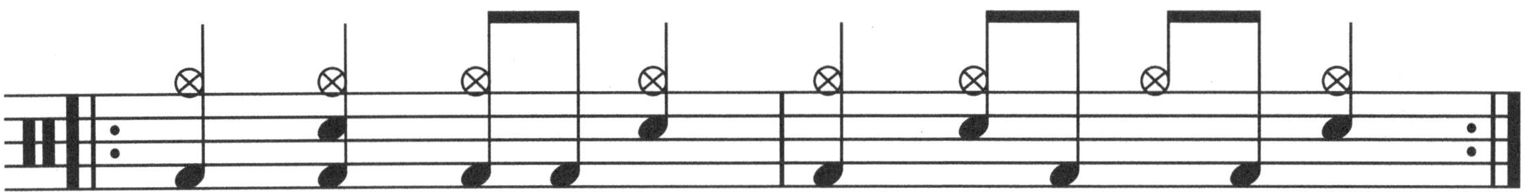

Variation #5

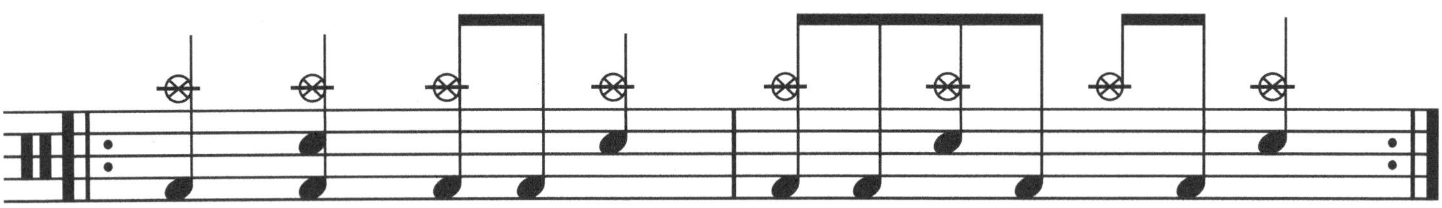

You can try adding some simple fills.

Fill #1

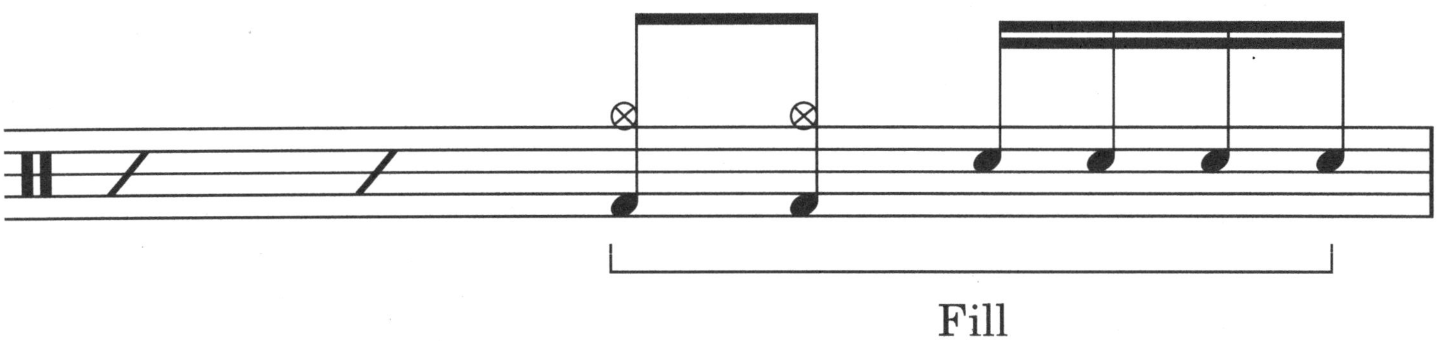

Fill #2

Fill #3

Since the tempo is so fast, this style of drumming tends to be looser and a little less precise than others. You'll also notice that the bass player and guitar player are just cranking out fast 8th notes and driving it forward. This music is aggressive and brash, so that's how you'll need to play if you want it to sound truly authentic. So, bring that punk energy and be relentless!

The Band

Dmitry Ishenko:

"My biggest respect to all the great punk musicians of past eras, because even though what they were doing was simple, you cannot take away the fact that they were staying with it intensity-wise and being consistent all the way through. For example, when I was recording this part it was almost tendonitis-inducing. There's a lot of repetition. You have to play these steady 8th notes at the same volume and you have to be on top of the beat and very aggressive. That is very physically draining, at least for the bass player. There are no breaks. It's almost like desperation.

"The last thing you ever want in this kind of groove is to run out of stream and slow down. That is a cardinal sin. If you feel like your hand is cramping up, start breathing really hard. That releases oxygen back into your body and all of a sudden, you uncramp. Trust me. Even in the quieter moments, from a rhythm section perspective, it has to be driving all the time."

Elias Meister:

"One thing I sometimes think about in this music is finding a moment to relax the energy just a little bit so you can go back up again. That gives it an arc of intensity. It's very difficult because the driving, loud attitude has to be there all the time...because it's punk music and you're thinking about people going crazy in a little club. There's no breaks and you're trying to shoot the intensity into outer space. It cannot stop. I'm trying to maintain a relaxed body even if we're exerting a lot of energy. That's a very good way to think about playing this kind of music, because you want to bring that intensity and really dig in, but you've got to maintain it for a while. So, you're trying to make yourself breathe easy and play strong. But it has to feel okay for your body."

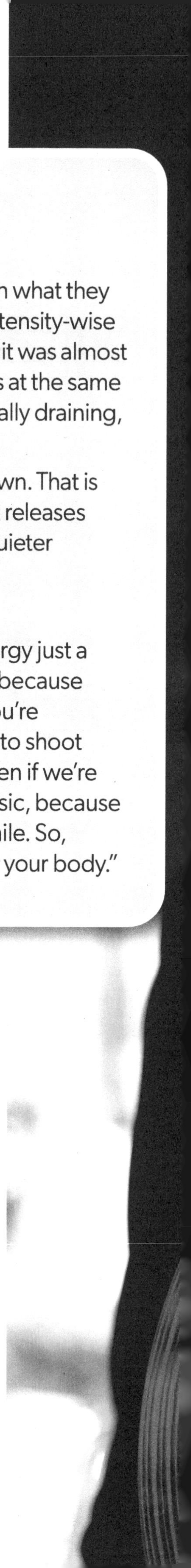

Wally's Funk

Genres: Funk, R&B, Jazz, Gospel

Difficulty Level (1-10): 5

Area of Origin: Boston, 1990s

Artists to Check Out: Sam Kininger Band, Lettuce, The A-Beez, Soulive, The Nth Power, Brian Thomas, James Calandrella

Drummers to Check Out: Charles Haynes, Nikki Glaspie, Louis Cato, Adam Deitch, Peter MacLean, John Blackwell, Mark Simmons, Deantoni Parks

The History

There's always that one special venue in every town that against all odds, survives for ages and becomes totally ingrained in the city's cultural DNA. It doesn't matter if it's a gritty rock club, a swanky blues spot or a tiny jazz bar. In Boston, that club is Wally's Jazz Café. Nestled amongst the brownstones and shops on Massachusetts Avenue near Berklee College of Music, this place has been around since 1947, moving across the street to its current location in 1978. Wally's began as the only African-American-owned jazz club in town and has served as a training ground for some of the city's most talented and ambitious young musicians. In the early days, that included Dizzy Gillespie, Charlie Parker, Billie Holiday and Roy Haynes (not a bad list!).

As the '90s rolled around, the club also began hosting funk nights. Musicians and sweaty fans packed this narrow 99-capacity room to hear everyone from The Roots' bassist Mark Kelley to Prince's late drummer John Blackwell. Wally's funk night wasn't just a jam session. It turned into an entire genre with a song list of "Wally's standards" with intricate arrangements and a distinct sound. Wally's funk *felt* different. It was on top of the beat, yet also behind. It was loud and rocking but also subtle. Along with bassists Kelley and later Aaron Bellamy, it was the drummers at Wally's that really made these grooves cook. Charles Haynes, who went on to play with everyone from Roy Hargrove to Patti LaBelle, was a creative force in the early 2000s. His pocket was deep and his creativity and spirit elevated everyone around him. Deantoni Parks (Andre 3000, Mars Volta) was another brilliant drummer who came out of the Wally's scene at this time, along with the unstoppable force of nature that was Nikki Glaspie. Still a student at Berklee when she began playing there, Glaspie went on to super-stardom after landing the gig with Beyoncé. She was later replaced by Louis Cato, who went on to become the bandleader on *Late Night with Stephen Colbert*. Going to Wally's funk night was like going to class and knowing you were hearing the future stars of tomorrow. I played there quite a bit myself and it was always a learning experience!

This music had a profound influence on anyone who squeezed themselves in-between those hallowed walls, whether they played or just listened. Today, Wally's funk night is still thriving with Bellamy and his wife, keyboard player Amy Bellamy at the helm. The reason is simple. The music is unique and inspiring, the players are top-notch and most of all, it's an awesome hang [28a] [28b]!

The Music

This groove should be super-tight and make people want to jump out of their seats and move. The 4-on-the-floor bass drum part is the driving force, along with the backbeat snare. But the real challenge is that it needs to be both on top of and behind the beat...wait, *what*? While the forward motion is strong, this groove needs to swing a little to settle into the pocket with the rest of the band. But it should be a tight swing. The way to achieve this is by adding "e's" and "a's" on the snare and bass drum that lay way behind the beat. The trick is keeping the bass drum and snare backbeat on top while these other notes are behind. Easier said than done, but super-hip if you can pull it off.

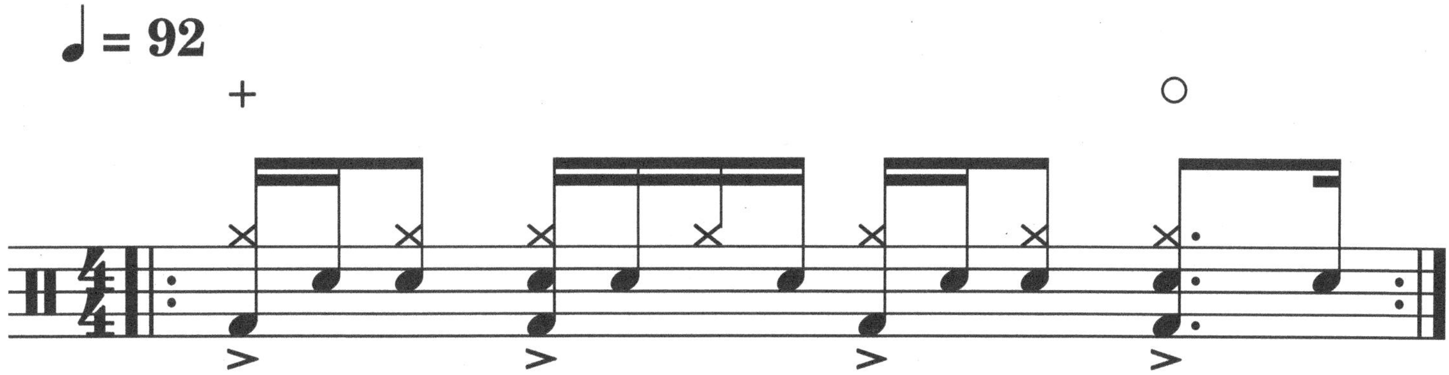

You can also open the hi-hat, mix in your left hand and add some crashes for more variation. Just keep everything focused and stay locked in the pocket.

Variation #1

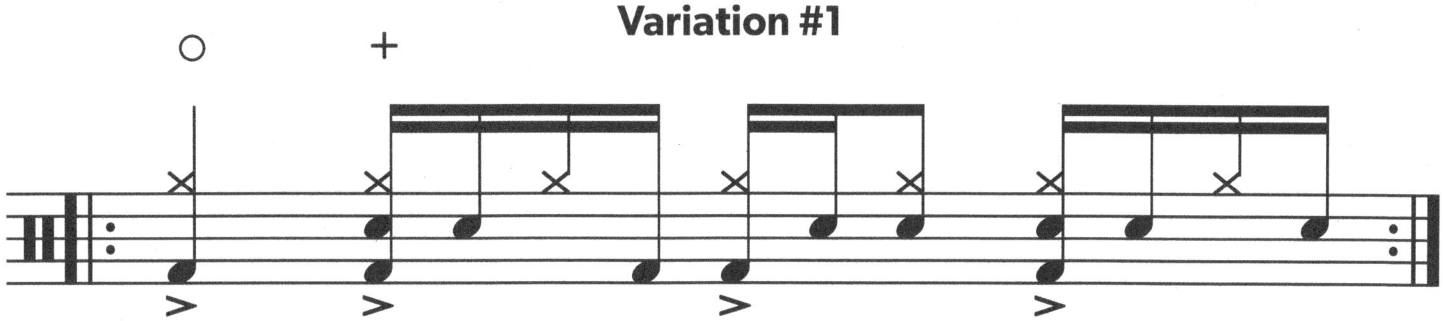

Variation #2

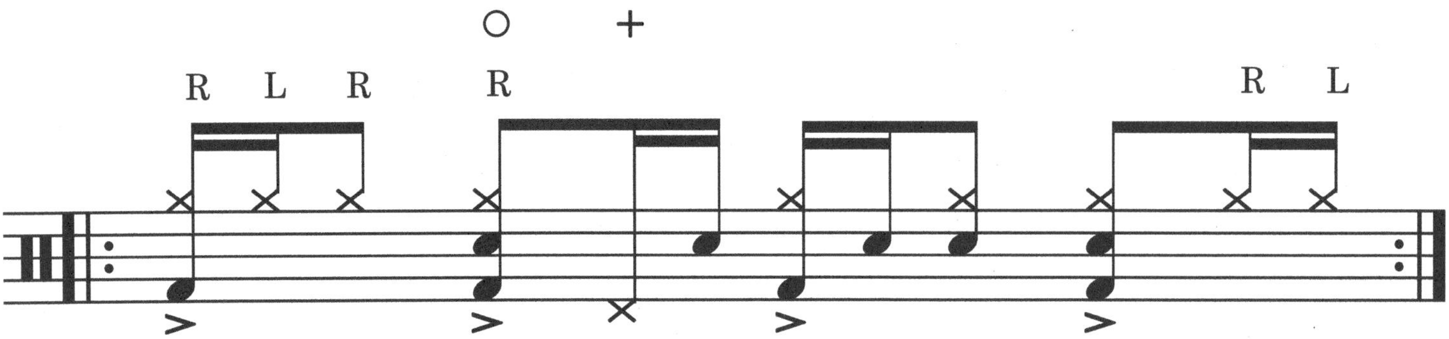

When you fill, it's important to use musical vocabulary that fits this style. I try to mix in the bass drum in interesting spots to break up runs of snare and toms. Even just substituting one bass drum note into a standard descending tom fill can give it a great melodic quality and make people go "whoa, what was that?".

Fill #1

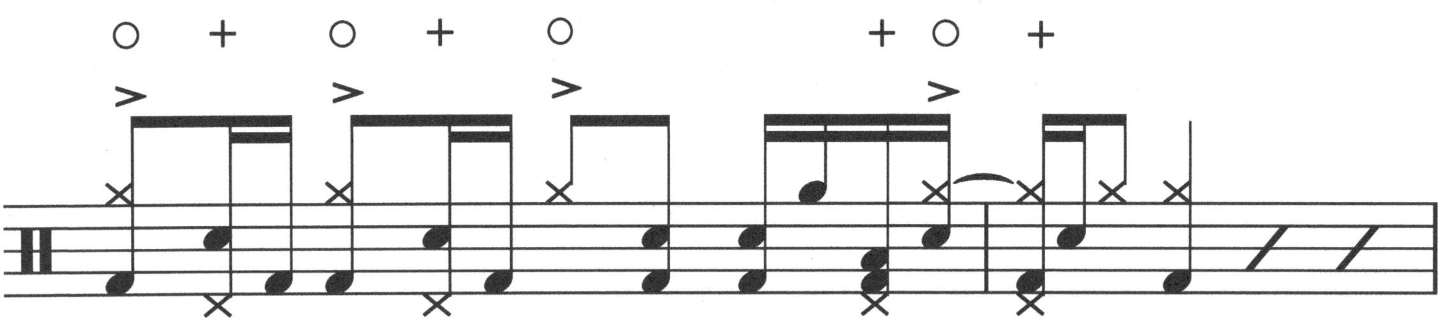

Fill #2

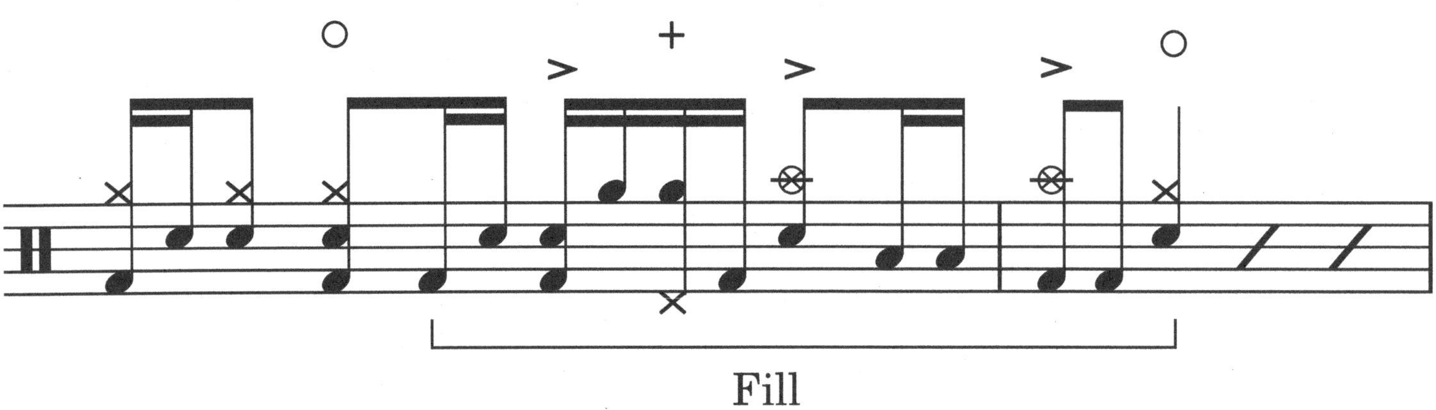

Fill #3

These embellishments are small on their own, but they can make your drumming so much more flavorful. Anything goes as long as that pocket stays tighter than a new pair of leather pants!

The Band

Dmitry Ishenko:

"The bass line in this Wally's funk type of groove is usually a two-bar phrase repeated over and over. It really comes out of the James Brown thing. In this track, I start in the low register and go up into the high register, so it's like a question-and-answer thing over the two bars. I'm really feeling the 'one' and listening a lot to the snare because that indicates the time feel. Out of all the components of the drum kit, the snare is really my guide. Of course, it's swung. This particular groove is swung 16th notes, so we're making sure to play them slightly laid back so they swing even harder. That's really what I'm thinking of. Charles Haynes, Mark Simmons, Deantoni Parks, Nikki Glaspie on Tuesday nights...that was the greatest."

Elias Meister:

"I'm thinking very much about the downbeats and locking in with the drums. That's the rhythm that enhances this almost like a percussion instrument, and you can have a slight variation in the end of the phrase after 8 bars. I'm playing constant 8th notes or 16th notes instead of a more syncopated thing...and then going back into it. The variation really happens with the register we're playing. It's very simple and groove-driven.

Wes Maples:

"I almost would describe it as 'sticky.' It's kind of short and punchy, but a little bit loose rhythmically. That kind of ambiguity is what makes it possible for the horns to be a little bit looser. That's what gives it a little more freedom and a little more funk...that ambiguity is nice in this context."

Welcome to the Jungle

Genres: Jungle Drum'n'Bass

Difficulty Level (1-10): 9

Area of Origin: England, 1990s

Artists to Check Out: Jojo Mayer's Nerve, Chase & Status, Pendulum, Roni Size (Reprazent), Squarepusher, KUDU

Drummers to Check Out: Jojo Mayer, KJ Sawka, Deantoni Parks, Andy Gangadeen, Mark Giuliana, Russell Holzman, Clive Deamer, Johnny Raab, Louis Cole

The History

It's rare to be able to trace the origins of an entire genre to one decades-old seven-second snippet of audio recording. But without the legendary "Amen break," live drum'n'bass would not exist. Recorded in 1969 by soul drummer George Coleman on The Winstons' song "Amen, Brother," the "Amen break" has become the most sampled clip in the history of drum programming. Fast-forward to England in the 1990s, where the rave scene spawned a generation of electronic musicians and producers deeply influenced by everything from reggae to classic soul. They chopped up beats like the "Amen break" to create a whole new style, which they called jungle (this is similar to how producers sliced up reggae grooves to create dub music in Jamaica). This style was raw and untamed, with drum'n'bass emerging later as a more refined outgrowth.

For drummers, this meant "reverse engineering" these highly technical programmed beats for live performance. This took an unbelievable level of technical skill and attention to detail. Though the lines between electronic/experimental music and jungle/drum'n'bass are often blurred, there are tons of incredible drummers performing and recording these jaw-dropping grooves. Swiss drummer Jojo Mayer is one of the most well-known masters of this style, performing with his live band Nerve, while Clive Deamer (known as the second drummer in Radiohead) is renowned for his drum'n'bass playing with jungle pioneer Roni Size. KJ Sawka slips effortlessly between drum'n'bass and rock with Australian band Pendulum, while Deantoni Parks defies the laws of gravity with Brooklyn-based band KUDU (seriously, check him out). Another important drummer in this style is Andy Gangadeen, who performs live with British electronic music legends Chase & Status.

What they all have in common is the musicality, creativity and technical facility to adapt to the music they're playing. Rather than seeing drum machines and programming as a threat to their livelihood, these drummers view them as tools for musical evolution. The more drummers are willing to break with traditional conventions and open themselves up to new ideas that integrate technology, the more they will be asked to join these situations onstage [29a]. Amen!

The Music

The biggest challenge in this type of drumming is staying loose and keeping a light touch. The moment you tense up and your technique breaks down, your goose is cooked! Even though this pattern is fast and furious, I try to think of the 16th notes in quarter-note groupings and almost trick my brain into feeling it's slower than it actually is.

Keep your shoulders down, your elbows relaxed and use your wrists and fingers. I like to play mostly on top of the hi-hat as opposed to "shouldering" it since this creates a cleaner, crisper articulation. It's almost as if you're emulating a drum machine. When I fill or play variations, I try to make them almost a little robotic. I mostly stick to the snare and mix in tight buzzes or quick open hi-hats for added flavor.

Variation #1

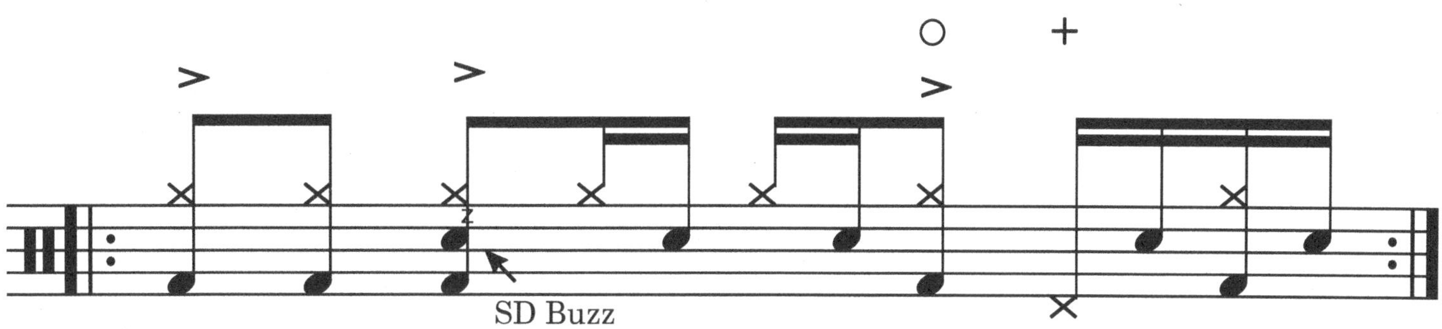

Variation #2

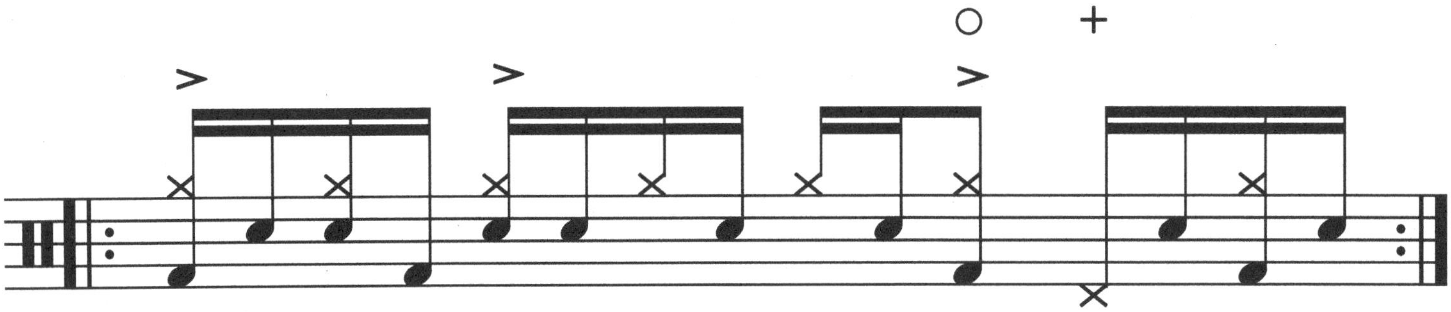

You can also switch to the ride, use the bell or add some crashes.

Variation #3

Variation #4

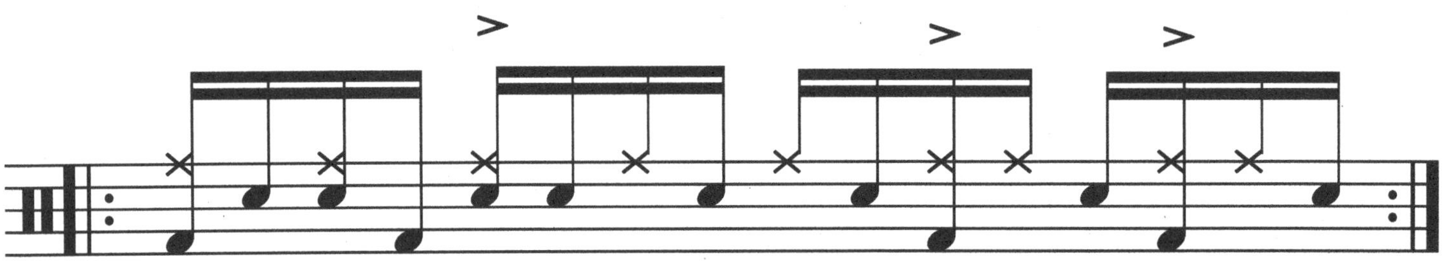

The drums and cymbals should be mostly dead-sounding with minimal decay. I like cymbals with an industrial or trashy vibe for this style, especially stacks. If you listen to the other instruments, they are far less active than the drums. The bass is playing long, drawn-out tones, while the guitar and synths add even more color. All the little notes you're playing act as the motor that propels this music forward.

Fill #1

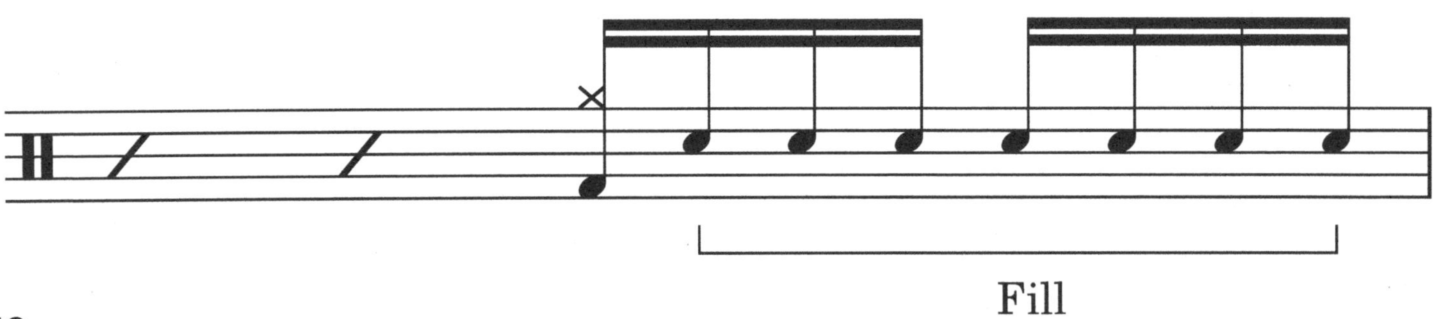

Fill #2

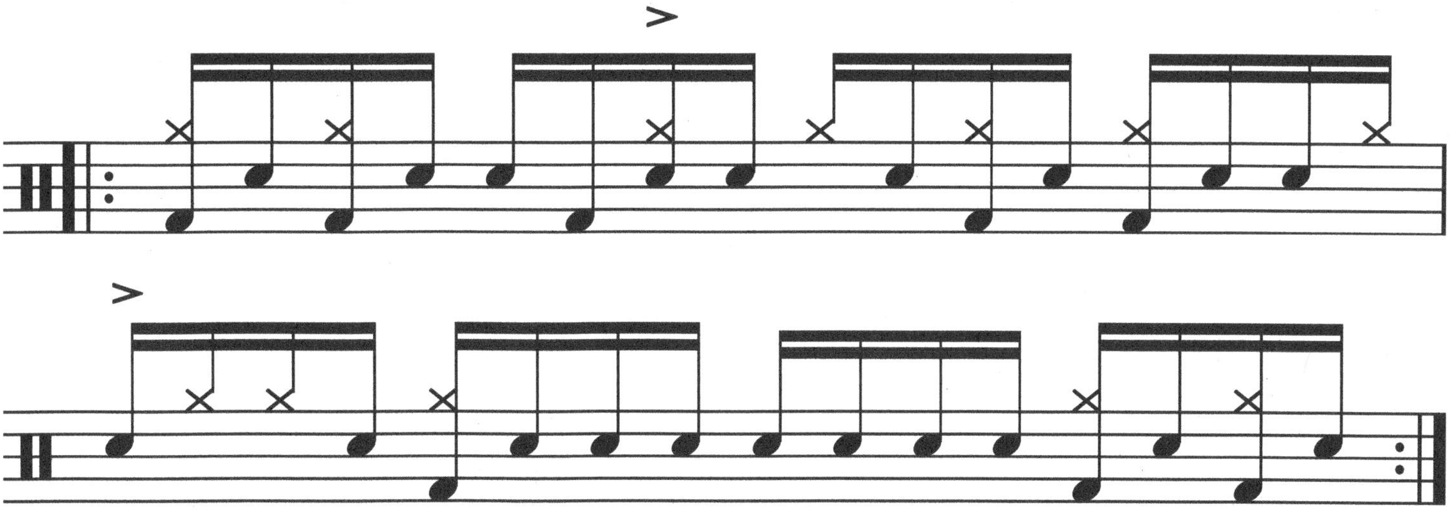

Though there's always room for embellishments and creativity, I try to keep the "meat and potatoes" kick/snare pattern in my head at all times. That way I can improvise within the framework of the music and react to the other musicians without getting too disconnected. This is one of the hardest styles of drumming to really master, but once you get going, it can be so much fun to play!

The Band

Dmitry Ishenko:

"It's almost like I'm replicating an electronic instrument on the bass. I'm using an octave pedal to try to sound like a bass synthesizer and playing the same thing over and over. Drum-wise, what I'm really listening for is that continuous 16th-note groove because it's constantly being played no matter what. It's important to bring [the intensity] up and down on the drums… busier, less busy, louder, softer. In this kind of static environment, I think it's vital for some dynamic variation, almost like a saxophone solo or something.

"I think an important thing to remember [on the drums] is not to repeat too many of your ideas in a row. It has to sound somewhat spontaneous. It doesn't stay. As soon as it goes into a pattern for too long, it becomes static and kind of loses the whole point. It's almost the opposite of a pop track where you have to be playing the same thing because that's the underlying vibe and things are built on top of that. But here, it's like the roles are flipped. You want to continue generating new ideas based on your old ideas so it goes up and down dynamically and texturally."

Elias Meister:

"We're leaving so much space for the drums. It's nice to find a good sound that can just kind of hang there. I'm really following the drums very closely because they're almost soloing. I'm playing the same hits over and over, but really trying to line them up in a cool way. It's very tight and then in the moment we go to the B section, we open it up. [That section] is a very simple part, just a different, longer sound which makes the drums sound different even though they keep going with a similar thing. It's a way for the drummer to play it almost like a solo vibe, but we're providing some context for it."

Xaxado of Your Smile

(Pronounced "sha-SHA-doo")

Genres: Brazilian Fusion, World Music

Difficulty Level (1-10): 6

Area of Origin: Brazil, late 1960s/early 1970s

Artists to Check Out: Azymuth, Airto Moreira, Banda Black Rio, Novos Baianos, Hermeto Pascoal

Drummers to Check Out: Airto Moreira, Milton Banana, Ramon Montagner, Edu Ribiero, Márcio Bahia, Vera Figueiredo, Isac Jamba, Duduka Da Fonseca, Kiko Freitas, Ivan Conti (Mamão)

The History

The cultural climate in 1960s Brazil mirrored that of many countries around the world. As global influences blurred the lines of traditional bossa nova and samba music, new styles began to emerge. American jazz and soul had a profound effect as Brazilian artists traveled to the United States, bringing rhythms from their native land. At the same time, jazz musicians like Stan Getz and Charlie Byrd began incorporating Brazilian music into their repertoire. As the 1970s rolled around, artists like Miles Davis and Weather Report brought about the era of jazz/fusion which also took on a heavy Brazilian influence. Drummers began adapting Brazilian rhythms for the drum set. This xaxado beat is a traditional dance groove from the northeastern region. It is pronounced "sha-SHAH-doo," hence the cheeky title ("The Shadow of Your Smile" is a classic Johnny Mandel tune). Other grooves to check out in this style include the baião, frevo, maracatu and coco.

Legendary drummer and percussionist Airto Moreira was at the forefront of this musical evolution as a founding member of seminal fusion bands Weather Report and Return to Forever. He also played on the 1980 George Duke album *A Brazilian Love Affair,* which was another important recording that blended fusion and Brazilian styles.

As American bands were incorporating these rhythms, artists in Brazil did the same with elements of fusion, jazz and rock. Groups like Azymuth (with Mamão on drums), Banda Black Rio and Novos Baianos became popular in this style, while composer and avant-garde multi-instrumentalist Hermeto Pascoal gained worldwide acclaim for his work on Davis' 1971 *Live-Evil* album. This cross-pollination continues today as drummers like Vera Figueiredo, Márcio Bahia, Isac Jamba and Ramon Montagner push the boundaries of how traditional Brazilian rhythms can be applied to modern music [(30a)].

The Music

This groove has a lot of hand motion between the hi-hat and snare, so if you can get that dialed in with the bass drum part, you'll be good to go! It's important to get locked in with the bass player, so start by working on just the kick and snare parts, then add the hi-hat. The syncopated kick/snare rhythm is the heartbeat of this groove and I try not to deviate from it too much.

This play-along has A and B sections, and while you play essentially the same thing for both, you can add some punchy tom fills to mark the transitions between them. I mostly keep a simple alternating sticking pattern, then orchestrate it around the kit to create nice melodic phrases. This groove is another example of how you can insert a single bass drum note in the middle of a standard fill to make it more angular and way hipper. Any variations or embellishments you add should have the main groove in mind. I like to throw in a few playful hi-hat phrases to give it some flavor. But be careful when you fill because it's really easy to get thrown off the pattern and there's not much time to recover if you do.

Variation #1

Variation #2

Fill #1

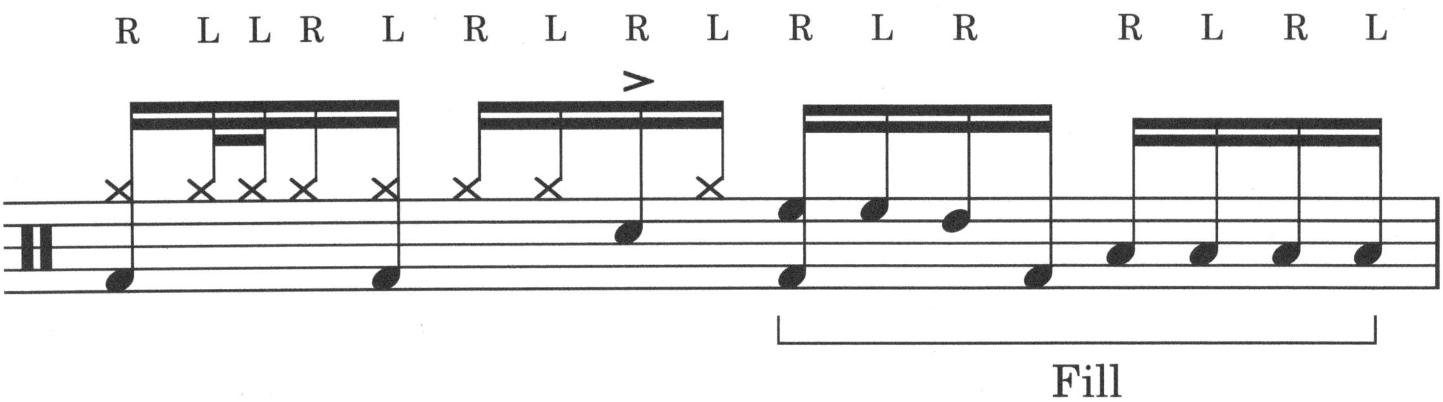

Fill #2

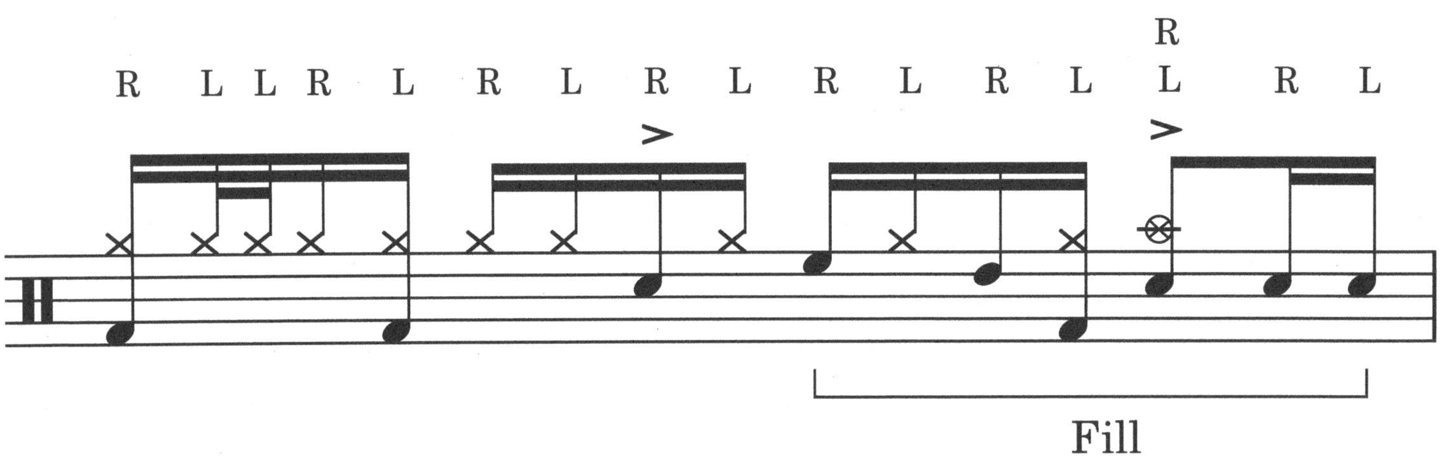

Fill #3

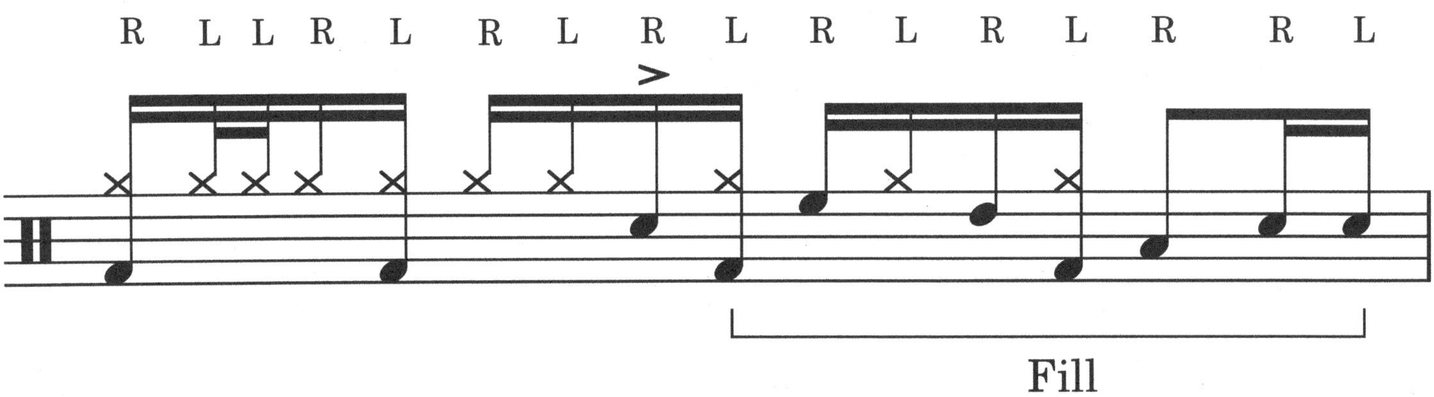

This groove is highly active already, so I try to use dynamics and articulation to create changes in the music instead of shredding all over the kit. The other musicians rely on the consistency of that kick/snare rhythm to layer their parts on top. If you pull that rug out from under them, the whole groove can crash and burn. So, lay that beat down and you'll keep 'em smiling!

The Band

Dmitry Ishenko:

"In my part, I make an emphasis on the second measure of that phrase. I emphasize it almost like a samba, but more stretched out. That gives it a certain gravity that makes it more akin to the original style. Just like a jazz soloist singing the melody of a song in their head while soloing, we are singing this clavé pattern. It's a rhythmic figure underpinning the pattern that we're hearing the whole time. You always have it in the back of your mind."

Elias Meister:

"I'm thinking about taking the main idea of this style and just going with it because it's a fairly open track with these long sections. I'm trying to lean into the groove and play melody parts that are reminiscent of this style. This is a tight but very playful thing, so we really want to line up the 16th notes that happen throughout with the drums and guitar. We're also adding these tiny variations. I'm thinking about people dancing to this kind of music. You want the groove to be really strong. I feel like we're building this tension in a very subtle way and then we release it into the next section. When you go into the next section, you want it to sit really well. That's the first and last thing you want to focus on, because if the groove is there, that's the most important thing. Anything else is just to keep it interesting, which is also nice and important. But the main thing is really to keep the groove going and flowing in a nice way."

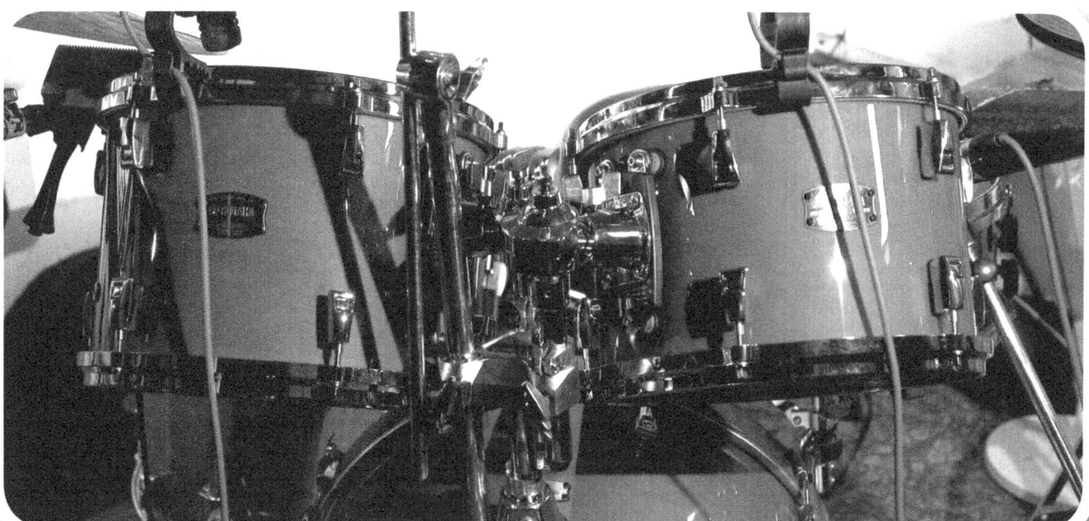

Your Big Pop Chops

Genres: Pop/Rock

Difficulty Level (1-10): 6

Area of Origin: England, U.S.A., 1980s

Artists to Check Out: Phil Collins, Peter Gabriel, Sting, Genesis, U2, Tears for Fears, Supertramp, Peter Frampton, Journey, Bryan Adams

Drummers to Check Out: Phil Collins, Manu Katché, Larry Mullen Jr., Chester Thompson, Jerry Marotta, Steve Smith

The History

Pop music underwent a dramatic evolution in the 1980s as technology created new avenues for musical invention. Synthesizers and digital recording techniques ruled the day, while music videos became an important visual accompaniment to artists' new releases. This was the era of "bigger" and "more!" Some artists focused on wearing outrageous outfits with even more outlandish hair and makeup, while others had a more refined presentation but added some of these elements of excess to the music itself. This meant heaping helpings of reverb, massive toms the size of oil drums and soaring vocals that made you feel as if you could touch the clouds themselves.

British pop/rock band Genesis was an important part of this era since it launched the solo careers of both Phil Collins and Peter Gabriel. Everyone knows the iconic tom fill in Collins' hit "In the Air Tonight" (1981), while Gabriel's 1986 album *So* practically redefined stadium rock by using new production techniques and a heavy reliance on world instruments. While Collins himself recorded drums on much of his own material (the great Chester Thompson from Genesis did many of the live shows), Gabriel used drummers Manu Katché and later Jerry Marotta to create cannon-like sounds amidst an impenetrable wall of percussion. Katché was an especially influential and underrated drummer in this era, as he also toured and recorded with Sting, playing on his hit albums *Nothing Like the Sun* (1987), *The Soul Cages* (1991) and *Brand New Day* (1999).

Journey also came to prominence in the early '80s, with Steve Smith on drums. Though they endured many personnel changes over the years, Smith's playing on the band's hit "Don't Stop Believin'" from the album *Escape* (1981) is one of the most important drum performances of this era (and one of the most poorly emulated by drummers trying to copy it!).

Another important band from this period was U2, with its dynamic front man Bono and soaring guitar sounds from the Edge. Larry Mullen Jr. held down the drum chair, playing on hits like "Where the Streets Have No Name" and "I Still Haven't Found What I'm Looking For" on their smash hit album *The Joshua Tree* (1987).

What these bands all had in common was a soaring pop/rock sound that made even the recordings feel like they took place in a stadium. While the '90s brought about big musical and cultural changes, this era of '80s pop/rock will always hold a special place in music history [31a] [31b].

The Music

Imagine you're playing in a stadium for thousands of people and the lights hit the kit just right. It's time for some massive, beefy toms and epic cymbal crashes! This groove has a thick texture and tons of hand movement, so it's best to practice them separately at first. While they play in unison most of the time, making sure you've got the descending movement correct can be a little tricky. This tom part is so dense and creates a strong melody, so it's important to try to internalize it. Try singing it in your head or out loud.

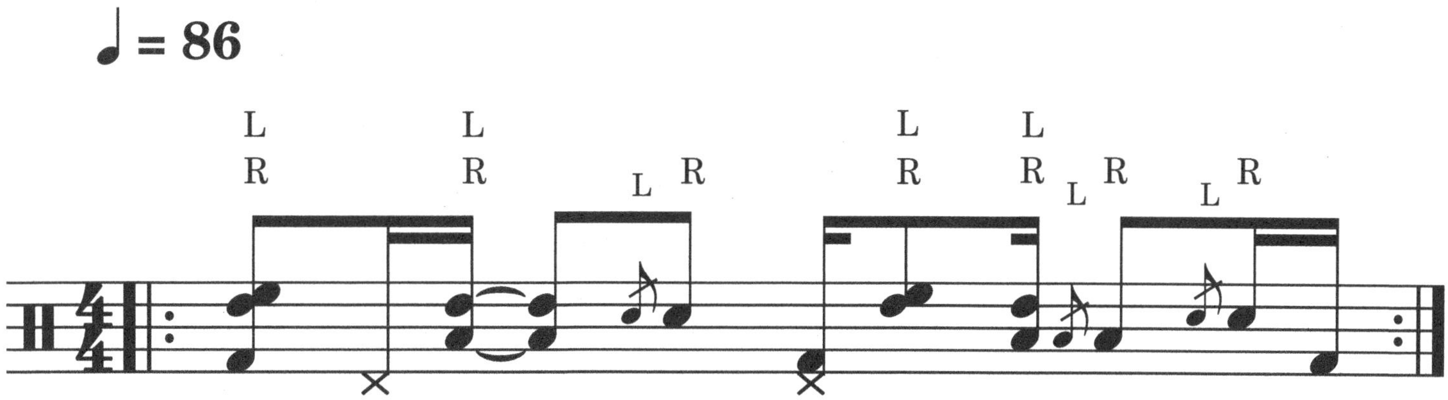

Right Hand

Left Hand

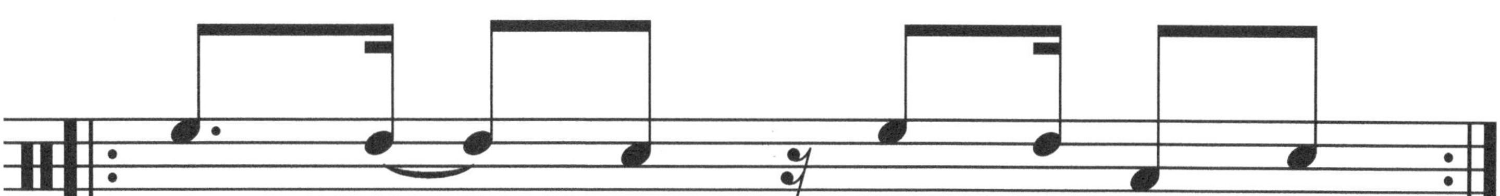

The bass drum part is super-simple, but it plays a big role in making everything feel solid and grounded. The hi-hat part is deceptively challenging and provides a nice bit of syncopation. Once you've got it all dialed in, try to focus on getting a great tone out of the drums. This groove has to be played with a purpose. Play into the toms and make the shells resonate. If you're too timid or just loosely floating around the kit, you won't get that beefy sound.

It's easy to get off track with this one, so I like to keep my fills simple and stick to the main groove. You can add extra tom notes and sprinkle in some crashes on the strong beats in unison with the bass player.

Variation #1

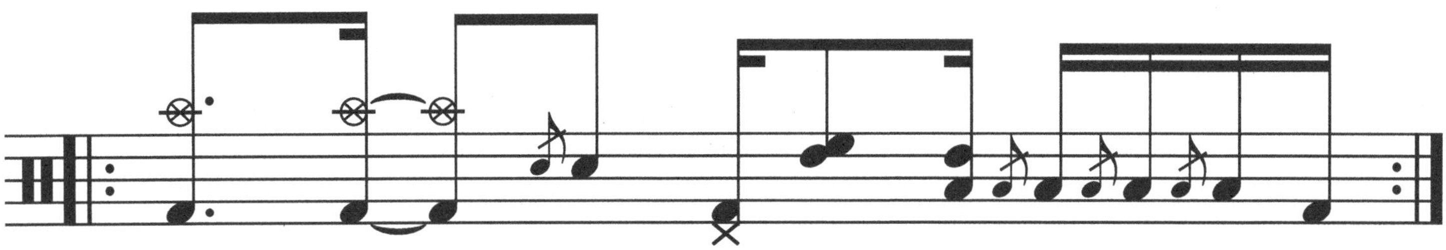

Fill #1

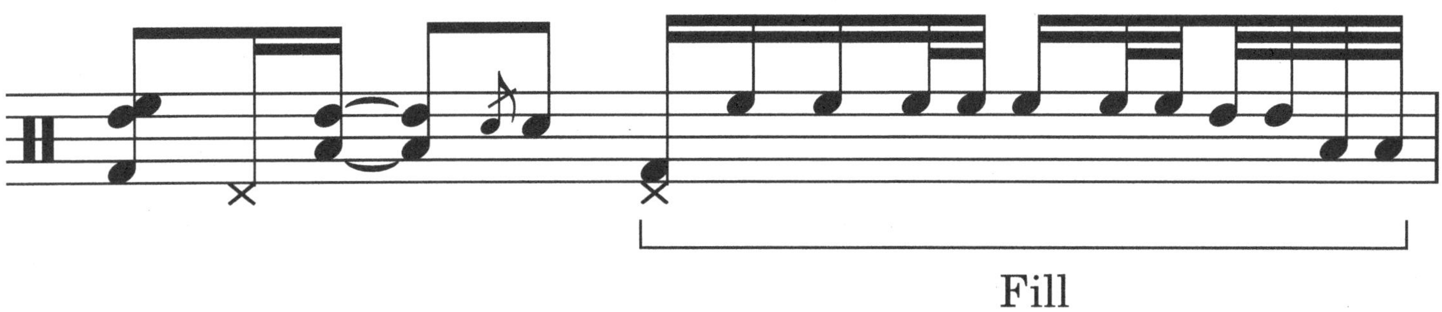

It's important for the drum part to lock in with that bass line, especially on beat 1, the "a" of 1 and the "and" of 2. The guitar sometimes plays this figure too. That rhythm section synergy is what really makes this one cook.

The Band

Dmitry Ishenko:

"I'm playing mostly whole notes and letting the drums do all the talking. I'm just making the chord change and adding an occasional fill-in note, that's about it. This groove is really all about the drums. The bass is just kind of a drone underneath. It's like world music, drum-active, but in a western pop sense."

Elias Meister:

"We're doing this dotted quarter-note rhythm together. That's very strong and we do not stray too much from it for the whole track. We're just changing the texture of the notes a little bit and really digging into that. We're thinking about how it would sound in a big arena where there's lots of room for it to reverberate. The sound should be big and deep. That's what we are going for. If you imagine how this kind of music was developed and what it was meant for, it makes a big difference in how you play it."

Zombie Apo-calypso

Genres: Calypso

Difficulty Level (1-10): 5

Area of Origin: Trinidad, Caribbean Islands, 1940s

Artists to Check Out: Lord Kitchener, Mighty Sparrow, Lord Blakie, The Mighty Shadow, Mighty Chalkdust, Calypso Rose, Black Stalin, Edwin Yearwood & Krosfyah

Drummers to Check Out: Ricardo "Cardo" Brewster (Mighty Sparrow), Book: *Fundamentals of Calypso Drumming* (Lennard Moses)

The History

Calypso originated in the Caribbean Island of Trinidad in the mid-19th century as a means of social and political expression for enslaved Africans. As the 20th century began, "calypsonians" (as they were called) like Lord Kitchener and Lord Invader gained popularity and began traveling the world to spread this music. This led to a global explosion in popularity in the post-World War II era, as American artists began recording classic calypso standards.

The Andrews Sisters had the first international calypso hit with Lord Invader's song "Rum and Coca-Cola" (1945), while singer Harry Belafonte became perhaps the single most important artist in the calypso explosion. His 1956 album *Calypso* introduced this style to a whole new audience, selling over 1 million copies worldwide the year it was released. The biggest hit on this album was Trinidadian folk song "Day-O (The Banana Boat Song)," earning Belafonte the nickname "King of Calypso" (which he was apparently uncomfortable with as a non-native).

As the popularity of this music spread worldwide, Trinidadian artists like Mighty Sparrow (with Cardo Brewster on drums), Lord Blakie and Calypso Rose saw a surge in popularity. Rose was an especially fascinating figure as the most prominent female calypsonian in a genre traditionally dominated by men. Her 1977 hit "Gimme More Tempo" has become a calypso classic. While most modern calypso bands have drum set players, steel pans are the leading percussion instrument in this style, with Trinidadian Ellie Mannette as an important figure (he was nicknamed "The Father of the Modern Steel Pan)."

As the 1970s rolled around, subgenres began to emerge, with soca being the most prominent. While it is similar to calypso, soca has elements of funk, rock and reggae, resulting in a heavier dancehall-type sound. Calypso and soca continue to enjoy worldwide popularity today as contemporary artists like Mighty Chalkdust, Machel Mantano and David Rudder spread the rich tradition of this music [32a].

The Music

A calypso groove has similar kick and snare rhythms to a soca, however there are some differences in vibe and style. Calypso tends to be a bit slower and has a lighter, looser feel than its funky Caribbean cousin. While calypso is an island dance groove, it's amazing how many genres of music use variations of this beat. I've been asked to play a calypso-style groove in everything from pop-rock recording sessions to jazz trios. This is definitely some Stuff You Can Use.

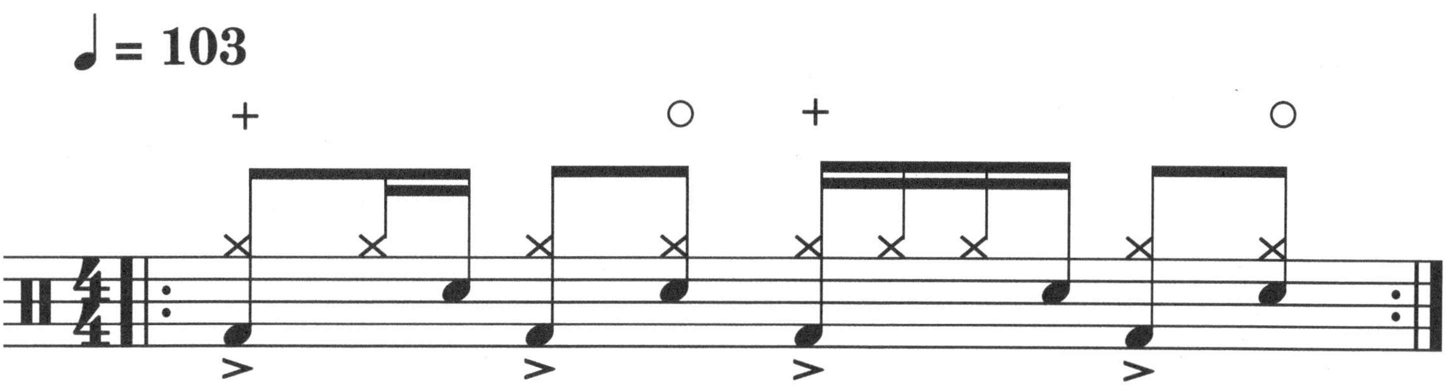

While a steady quarter-note bass drum is the heartbeat of this groove, the syncopated snare pattern is its most identifiable feature. When I hear that clavé (which is basically the "melody" of the groove), I immediately know it's a calypso! Keep that quarter note pumping on the bass drum and make sure the important notes of the snare pattern are there every time (the "a's" of beats 1 and 3, plus the "ands" of 2 and 4). You can use the hi-hat to create interesting variations with both your right hand and your foot. Lift your toes inside your shoe to slightly loosen the hi-hats on the upbeats and get that perfect tight sizzle.

Variation #1

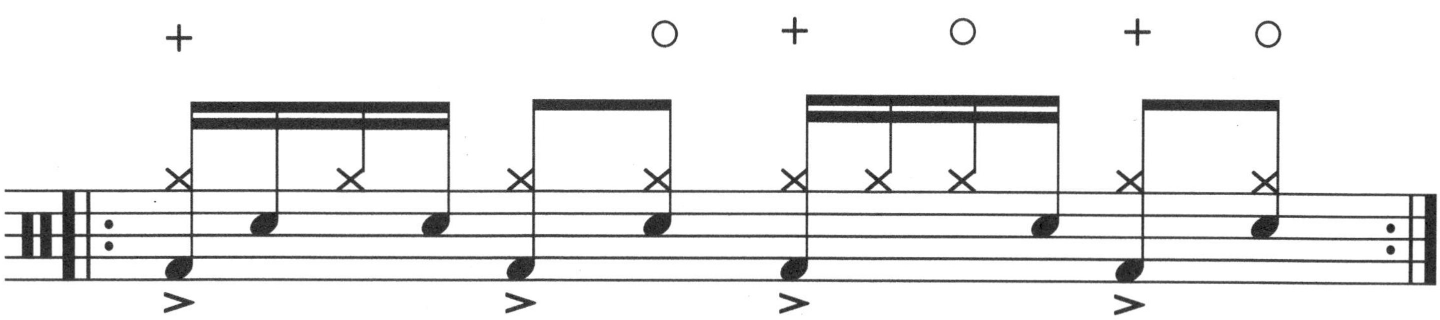

Variation #2

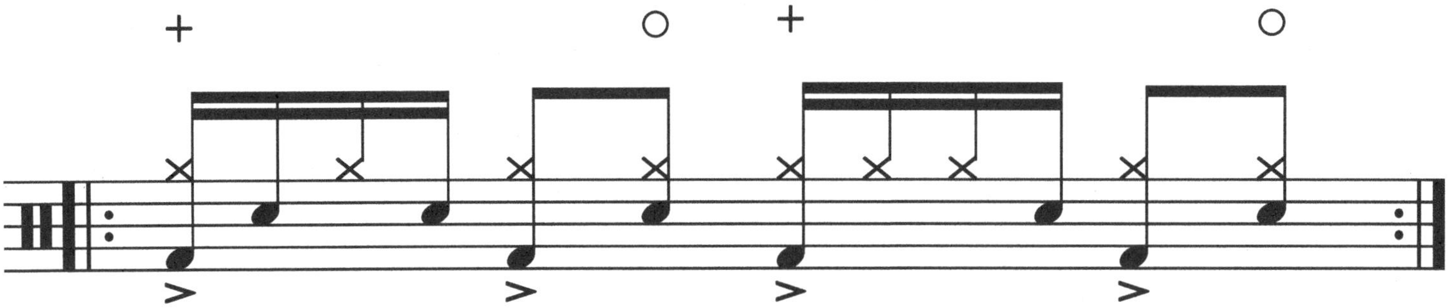

Variation #3

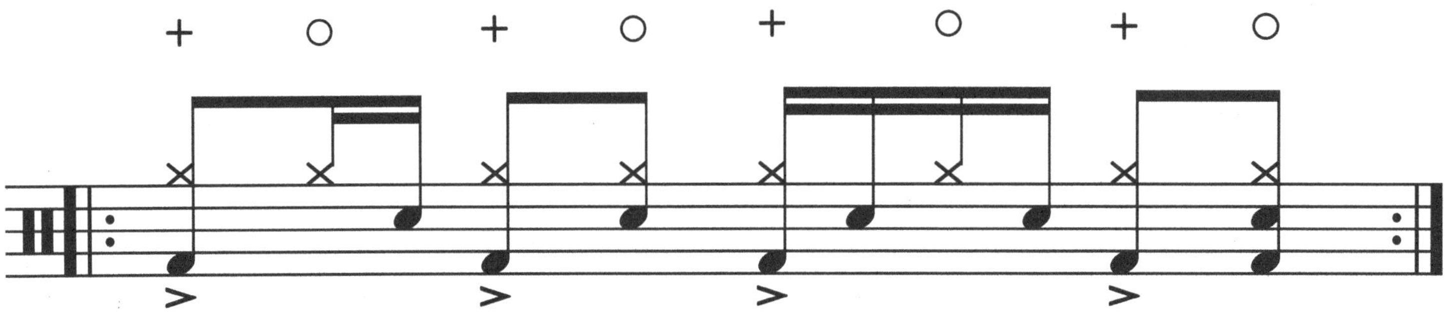

Switch to the ride and mix in the bell for more interesting texture changes that keep the main idea the same.

Variation #4

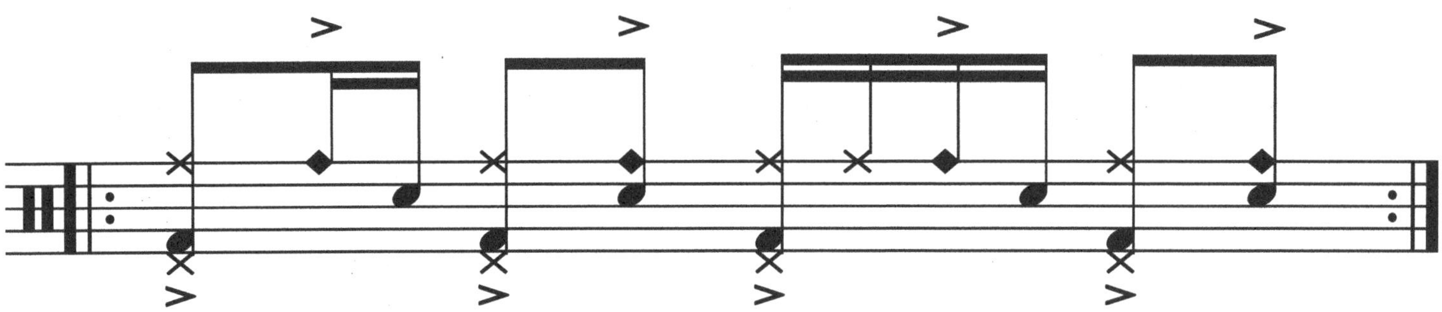

Any fills should always have the main groove in mind. I like to keep them short and punchy.

Fill #1

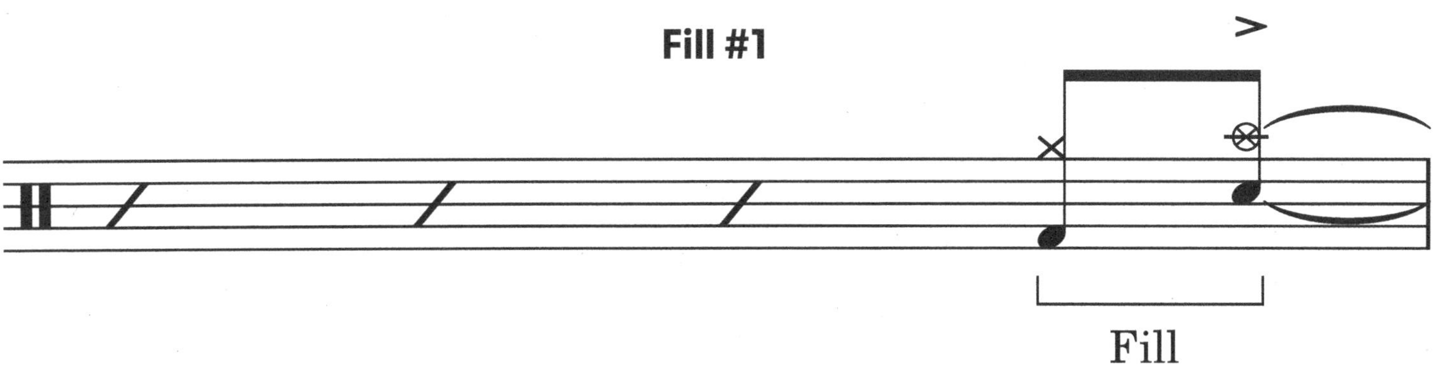

Fill #2

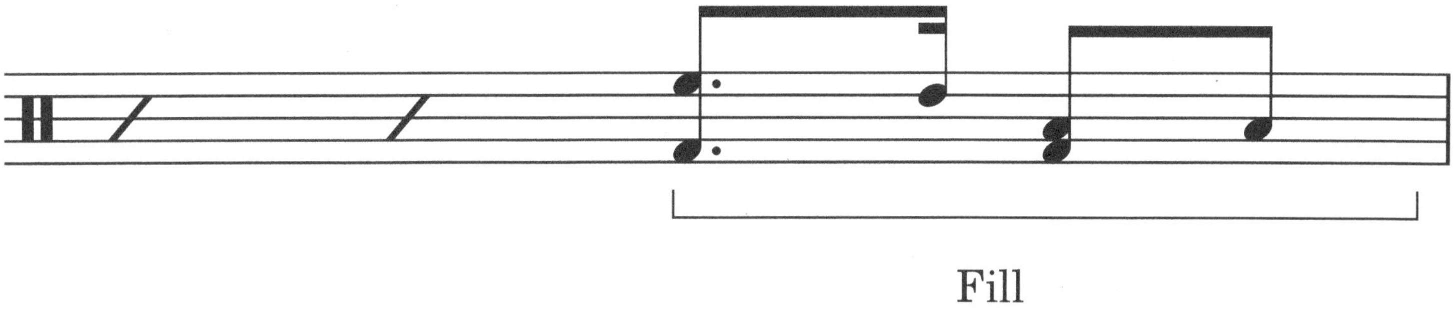

Fill #3

Much like many other styles in this book, the drummer's primary role in a calypso band is to keep people dancing their faces off from start to finish!

The Band

Dmitry Ishenko:

"I'm super-reliant on the drummer's pulse and the bass drum is a vital component of this groove for me. The bass is mostly doubling the snare drum melody and usually never plays on beat one. The bass line starts on the last 16th note of the first beat and is followed by two 8th notes. This particular tune is an 8-bar form, so on the 8th bar we all do a unison fill. That's the indicator that we're on to the next cycle.

"The steel pan in calypso and soca music is the 'loose element,' while the rhythm section is usually super-tight and on top of the beat driving the thing forward. That gives space for the steel pan to really stretch out backwards or forwards. That is really the lead instrument and it has a lot of flexibility. Overall, it's kind of like a machine as far as the rhythm section is concerned. We're just ploughing through, keeping a strong solid background for whoever's soloing. You always want to maintain a consistent groove for people to dance to."

Elias Meister:

"I'm trying to really stay with the groove and the main rhythm that's going on. I'm outlining the chords and it's a very repetitive part. I'm really digging into the groove with the drums. We're marking the different sections of the form and I'm playing the chords pretty straightforward with a simple rhythm. I'm more focused on downbeats in the first part of the measure, and then on the upbeats in the second half...it's not too much odd melodic material. The guitar and the bass are more in the background compared to the steel pan. You can add a little variation to the part, but in a very simple way."

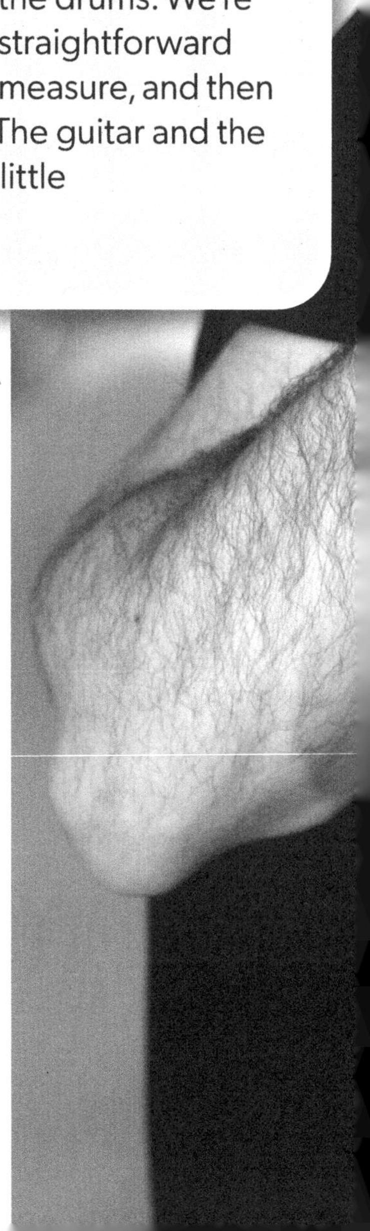

CALIFORNIA
Aero
WEST COAST

Glossary of Musical Slang

Atonal music doesn't have a "home base" in a particular key and uses all twelve notes of the chromatic scale.

Bashy drumming lacks proper control in trying to be loud and energetic.

B-Sides are on the back side of an LP where less important songs were placed. However, sometimes the B-Sides ended up being bigger hits than the tunes on the front.

Beat placement refers to where your groove sits relative to the metronome. Examples include on top of the beat (ahead), on the beat (dead center) and behind the beat.

The British Invasion began in 1964 when The Beatles came to America, spurring a wave of musical and cultural change. Other British bands like The Rolling Stones and The Kinks soon followed suit.

Check-in points are spots within the music when the drums, bass and other instruments come together to make sure they're in the same place, even if the music is complicated and everyone is playing different rhythms.

Clavé refers to a repeating rhythmic pattern that acts as a foundation for the music. Though is it most commonly associated with Latin music, it can occur in almost any style.

Crosstalk occurs when the musicians all play different rhythmic, melodic or harmonic patterns, creating a counterpoint similar to people talking over each other.

Displaced notes are shifted forwards or backwards on the beat to create syncopation.

Drops are rests or notes that have been removed within a groove, a concept commonly used by hip-hop producers to make monotonous beats more interesting and unpredictable over the course of a song. They often occur at the beginning or middle of a measure to make them more unexpected.

Duple refers to a rhythm that is subdivided into a factor of two, as opposed to triple meters which are multiples of three.

Feathering is a term from the early 20th-century Big Band era that refers to playing the bass drum lightly. The idea is to feel the resonance of the low note as much as audibly hearing it. Light as a feather.

The four-chord is an example of relative pitch. If a song is in the key of C major, the four-chord is F major, or the fourth note of the musical scale in that key. Drummers don't always need to know exactly what key a song is in, but being able to identify relative pitch in relation to the tonal center is extremely helpful, especially if you get lost!

Ghosting a note means playing it very quietly, as if it were a ghost creeping silently around your house in the middle of the night.

The grid is a term that recording engineers use to define how the music is organized relative to the metronome. Songs that were recorded with a click track are on the grid, while music played without a metronome is off it.

Hybrid grooves integrate hand percussion like shakers and tambourines with elements from the traditional drum set (snare, kick, hi-hat).

Lifts are rests or breaks in the music (i.e., stop playing). They are similar to drops but usually occur at the beginning or middle of a measure.

Motivic development is taking an idea and developing it slowly through variation. While Beethoven's 9th Symphony is perhaps the most famous example, every drummer should learn this concept to improve the musicality of their solos.

Musical language is the way we communicate ideas by playing. It includes the notes themselves and how they're organized, as well as the vibe and feeling behind them. Using the right musical language for the style you're playing will make it sound more authentic.

Odd-meter rhythms are time signatures where the number of beats-per-measure is not a multiple of 3 or 4. Common examples are 5/4 and 7/4.

Open forms are songs that do not have a predetermined number of measures or a repeating structure. They often rely on cues and musical communication to progress.

Overdrive refers to the gritty, crackly sound that guitar and bass players would get when they turned their amps up loudly in the 1960s, overdriving the capacity of the speakers. Today, there are effects pedals to create this sound without damaging the amp.

The pocket refers to the way a groove feels. Being "right in the pocket" is the highest compliment a drummer can receive.

Power chords include the first note (or root) and fifth note of the chord but lack the third, meaning they can be major or minor in tonality. Removing the third often makes these chords feel more direct and powerful, hence the name. They are most commonly used in rock and metal.

Programming is the concept of using music software and drum machines to create grooves, loops or other sounds.

The root note is the first musical pitch of a chord or key. All other melodic and harmonic elements are defined by their position relative to the root note.

The secret sauce is a small detail in your playing that makes a huge difference in how it sounds and feels. It can be a technical element like lifting your toes inside your shoe for that perfect hi-hat sizzle, or an interactive concept like marking the top of the form so the band stays together.

Skanking is what guitar players do in reggae or ska music, playing on the upbeats instead of the downbeats.

Slapback delay is a musical effect that gained popularity with guitar players in the 1950s. The short decay creates the feeling of quickly "slapping back" at the listener.

Station points is the concept of ending fills or musical phrases on beats other than the downbeat. Examples include beat four, the "and" of four or the "and" of beat one of the following measure. Occasionally using station points in both soloing and time playing will make your drumming way less square and predictable.

A street beat is a syncopated New Orleans groove most commonly associated with second-line parades.

Stuff You Can Use is not just collection of grooves. It's your whole drum sound and how you think about music and communicate with other musicians. It's knowing the history behind the music and using the correct musical language to create an authentic and unique sound in any style.

A two-beat groove has a heavy emphasis on beats 1 and 3 with the backbeat being less prominent.

Timbre is a term used to describe the musical character or tonal quality of a note or sound. Examples include bright, dark, muddy and mellow.

Tumbao is a syncopated rhythm played by the bass in Afro-Cuban music. It often does not include a note on beat one, as the last note of the previous measure is held over to create a feeling of forward motion.

A walk-up is a simple bass fill to connect two chords where the player actually ascends or "walks up" the musical scale.

Bibliography

1a) Staff, Cascade PBS. "The Genius of Fela Kuti and Afrobeat." *Cascade PBS,* August 2, 2025. https://www.cascadepbs.org/show/sound-field/episode/the-genius-of-fela-kuti-and-afrobeat-ygmjti/.

1b) PBS. "PBS Short Film Festival | Birth of Afrobeat | Season 2020," *PBS,* July 13, 2020. https://www.pbs.org/video/birth-of-afrobeat-ohrzo5/.

2a) Forrest, Ben. "Duško Gojković: The Trumpeter Who Used Jazz to Escape the Eastern Bloc." *Far Out Magazine,* October 18, 2024. https://faroutmagazine.co.uk/dusko-gojkovic-trumpeter-jazz-eastern-bloc/.

2b) Unciano, Richard. "Gankino, Kopanitsa & more in 11/16." *Folk Dance Scene,* July/August, 1991, p. 12. https://socalfolkdance.org/scene/scene_1991_07.pdf.

3a) Haskins, James. *The Cotton Club.* Hippocrene Books, 1994

3b) Zoro and Glass, Daniel. *The Commandments of Early Rhythm and Blues Drumming.* Alfred Music, 2008, p. 29.

3c) Moore, Stanton. *Take it to the Street: A Study in New Orleans Street Beats* and *Second-line Rhythms as Applied to Funk.* Carl Fischer Publishing, 2005, p. 56.

4a) Moore, Stanton. *Take it to the Street: A Study in New Orleans Street Beats* and *Second-line Rhythms as Applied to Funk.* Carl Fischer Publishing, 2005, p. 4.

4b) Vidacovich, Johnny and Riley, Herlin, Interviews by Thress, Dan. *New Orleans Jazz & Second Line Drumming.* Manhattan Music, 1995, p.12.

5a) Matos, Michaelangelo. "Electronic Dance Music | House, Techno & Trance." *Encyclopedia Britannica,* June 7, 2025. https://www.britannica.com/art/electronic-dance-music.

6a) PBS. "When Music Makes History," *PBS Short Video,* December 1, 2020. https://www.pbs.org/show/when-music-makes-history/.

6b) Zimmerman, Lee. *Americana Music: Voices, Visionaries, and Pioneers of an Honest Sound.* Texas A&M University Press, 2019, p.7.

7a) Edwards, Steve. "The Beginning of Fusion: Miles Davis Drew on Soul, Funk and Rock." *KNKX Public Radio,* January 3, 2025. https://www.knkx.org/jazz/the-beginning-of-fusion-miles-davis-drew-on-soul-funk-and-rock.

7b) Staff, Herbie Hancock Institute of Jazz. "Jazz in America: Free Jazz and Fusion." https://www.jazzinamerica.org/LessonPlan/8/7/213.

8a) Wartofsky, Alona. "Washington, D.C.'s Homegrown Funk: Go-Go Music." *Craftsmanship Magazine,* August 22, 2023. https://craftsmanship.net/washington-d-c-s-homegrown-funk-go-go-music/.

8b) Godfrey, Sarah. "The History of Go-Go: A 6-Step Guide to the Essentials - Washingtonian." *Washingtonian* (blog), June 17, 2021. https://www.washingtonian.com/2019/10/30/history-go-go-6-step-guide-the-essentials/#3gogos-backbone.

9a) Staff, MasterClass. "Learn About Klezmer Music: History, Style, and Musical Characteristics. *MasterClass,* September 29, 2021. https://www.masterclass.com/articles/learn-about-klezmer-music.

9b) Tamarkin, Jeff. "Who Are the Klezmatics?" *Purdue Convocations,* December 14, 2014. https://convocations.purdue.edu/who-are-the-klezmatics/.

9c) Rothman, Lily. "Rock Hashana: 10 Stars of the New Jewish Music." *TIME.com,* September 4, 2013. https://entertainment.time.com/2013/09/04/rock-hashana-10-stars-of-the-new-jewish-music/.

10a) Staff, Genrematic. "Arena Rock." *Genrematic,* August 22, 2023. https://genrematic.com/post/arenarock/.

11a) Shoemaker, Bill. "Jim Black: Opening the Filters." *JazzTimes,* May 1, 2024. https://jazztimes.com/features/profiles/jim-black-opening-the-filters/.

11b) Milkowski, Bill. "Before and After with Drummer Jim Black." *JazzTimes,* October 14, 2024. https://jazztimes.com/features/lists/before-after-with-drummer-jim-black/.

12a) Zoro and Glass, Daniel. *The Commandments of Early Rhythm and Blues Drumming.* Alfred Music, 2008, p. 36-41.

12b) Devi, Debra. "The Language of the Blues: SHUFFLE." *American Blues Scene,* July 8, 2016. https://www.americanbluesscene.com/2016/07/language-of-the-blues-shuffle/.

13a) Tooze, Sandra B. *Levon: From Down in the Delta to the Birth of The Band and Beyond.* Diversion Books, 2020, p. 148-149.

14a) Staff, *JazzTimes.* "The 10 Best Jazz Albums of the 1940s: Critics' Picks." *JazzTimes,* September 29, 2024. https://jazztimes.com/features/lists/the-10-best-jazz-albums-of-the-1940s-critics-picks/.

14b) Gennari, John. "Jazz in the Late 1940s: American Culture at Its Most Alluring." *The National WWII Museum | New Orleans,* September 14, 2021. https://www.nationalww2museum.org/war/articles/modern-jazz-late-1940s.

15a) Colligan, George. "Mike Clark: East Bay Funk." *All About Jazz,* September 25, 2013. https://www.allaboutjazz.com/mike-clark-east-bay-funk-mike-clark-by-george-colligan.

15b) Gilbert, Andrew. "Jazz Drummer Mike Clark Keeps 'bumping Into Funk' -and he's back in Bay Area." *The Mercury News,* February 2, 2017. https://www.mercurynews.com/2017/02/02/jazz-drummer-mike-clark-keeps-bumping-into-funk-and-hes-back-in-bay-area/.

16a) Woods, Bret D. "Industrial Music for Industrial People: The History and Development of an Underground Genre." *Florida State University Digital Research Repository,* 2007. http://purl.flvc.org/fsu/fd/FSU_migr_etd-0781.

16b) Hollingsworth, Ashley Perez. "Heart of Darkness: A Brief History of Chicago Industrial - Part One." *Newcity Music,* November 23, 2020. https://music.newcity.com/2020/11/20/heart-of-darkness-a-brief-history-of-chicago-industrial-part-one/.

17a) Petrusich, Amanda. "The Still-Burning Piano Genius of Professor Longhair." *The New Yorker,* May 10, 2018. https://www.newyorker.com/culture/culture-desk/the-still-burning-piano-genius-of-professor-longhair.

17b) Moore, Stanton. *Take it to the Street: A Study in New Orleans Street Beats* and *Second-line Rhythms as Applied to Funk.* Carl Fischer Publishing, 2005, p. 52.

18a) Myers, Madeline. "The History of Polka: From Europe to Northeast Ohio." *PBS Western Reserve* (blog), September 21, 2023. https://www.pbswesternreserve.org/blogs/luminus-stories-about-us/the-history-of-polka-from-europe-to-northeast-ohio/.

19a) Schaffner, Lauryn. "Who Really Invented the Power Ballad?" *Loudwire,* July 11, 2023. https://loudwire.com/who-really-invented-power-ballad/.

19b) Dominic, Serene. "Power Me, Ballad Me: The Power Ballad Timeline." *Detroit Metro Times,* June 11th, 2003. https://www.metrotimes.com/music/power-me-ballad-me-the-power-ballad-timeline-2176365.

20a) Questlove. "Interview: Red Bull Music Academy." Hosted by Monk One, Seattle, WA, 2005. https://www.redbullmusicacademy.com/lectures/questlove-phrenology-of-hip-hop.

MORE Stuff You Can Use

20b) Carmichael, Rodney. "Questlove Reflects on Changes in Culture and Music With His Book 'Hip-Hop Is History.'" *NPR,* May 29, 2024. https://www.npr.org/2024/05/28/nx-s1-4878583/questlove-reflects-on-changes-in-culture-and-music-with-his-book-hip-hop-is-history.

20c) Questlove. "Questlove: My Youth in 27 Records." *Vulture.com,* June 2013. https://www.vulture.com/2013/06/questlove-my-youth-in-27-records.html.

21a) Crary, Scott, director. *Kill Your Idols,* Palm Pictures. 2006, 75 minutes.

21b) Stella's Encounter. "A Brief History of No Wave," February 21, 2023. https://www.youtube.com/watch?v=TarCRjG88w8.

22a) Toop, David. *Ocean of Sound: Aether Talk, Ambient Sound and Imaginary Worlds.* Serpent's Tail Publishing, 1995. https://archive.org/details/oceanofsoundaeth0000toop/page/114/mode/2up.

22b) Degiorgio, Kirk. "The Roots of Dub." *Red Bull Music Academy Daily,* August 24, 2018. https://daily.redbullmusicacademy.com/2018/08/the-roots-of-dub.

23a) MDLBeast. "What is Ska Music." *MDLBeast.com* (blog), March 18, 2024. https://mdlbeast.com/xp-feed/music-industry/what-is-ska-music.

23b) Kauppila, Paul. "From Memphis to Kingston: An Investigation into the Origin of Jamaican Ska." *San Jose University Faculty and Staff Publications,* January 2006. https://scholarworks.sjsu.edu/cgi/viewcontent.cgi?article=1052&context=lib_pub.

24a) Staff, Timba.com. "The Roots of Timba Part 2 - The Songo Enigma." *Latin Pulse Music,* Retrieved August 3, 2025. https://www.timba.com/encyclopedia_pages/the-songo-enigma.

25a) Petrusich, Amanda. "Dick Dale, The Inventor of Surf Rock, was a Lebanese-American Kid from Boston." *The New Yorker,* March 18, 2019. https://www.newyorker.com/culture/postscript/dick-dale-the-inventor-of-surf-rock-was-a-lebanese-american-kid-from-boston.

25b) Staff, History-of-Rock.com. "Dick Dale and the Del-Tones." History-of-Rock.com, retrieved August 3, 2025. https://www.history-of-rock.com/dick_dale_and_the_deltones.htm.

25c) Jackson, Nate. "Dick Dale's Legend Lives on via Stories From the Past." *OC Weekly,* April 4, 2019. https://www.ocweekly.com/dick-dales-legend-lives-on-via-stories-from-the-past/.

26a) Piñeros, Benjamin. "Jam Bands: Where No Two Live Performances are the Same." *Tone Deaf,* July 16, 2021. https://tonedeaf.thebrag.com/history-of-jam-bands/list/check-out-ripple-by-the-grateful-dead/.

27a) Staff, Pitchfork. "Rip It to Shreds: A History of Punk and Style." *Pitchfork,* October 25, 2016. https://pitchfork.com/features/from-our-partners/9943-rip-it-to-shreds-a-history-of-punk-and-style/.

28a) Beuttler, Bill. "An Oral History of Wally's Café." *Boston Magazine,* August 16, 2023. https://www.bostonmagazine.com/arts-entertainment/2021/01/19/wallys-cafe-oral-history/.

28b) Hochschild, Rob. "Night School at Wally's." *Berklee Today,* Fall 2018. https://www.berklee.edu/berklee-today/fall-2018/night-school-wallys.

29a) Quinn, Steven. "Rumble in the Jungle: The Invisible History of Drum'n'Bass." Journal-article. *Transformations,* April 2002. http://www.transformationsjournal.org/wp-content/uploads/2017/01/Transformations03_Quinn.pdf.

30a) Staff, Oh! Jazz Magazine. "Brazilian Jazz: Irresistible Rhythm and Melodic Complexity." *Oh! Jazz Magazine,* retrieved August 3, 2025. https://www.ohjazz.tv/mag/jazz-appreciation-month-brazil-eng.

31a) Beviglia, Jim. "Behind the Album: 'So,' The Record That Transformed Peter Gabriel From Cult Status to Superstardom." *American Songwriter,* June 24, 2024. https://americansongwriter.com/behind-the-album-so-the-album-that-transformed-peter-gabriel-from-cult-status-to-superstardom/.

31b) Walthall, Catherine. "A Deeper Look at the Meaning Behind 'In the Air Tonight' by Phil Collins." *American Songwriter,* April 4, 2022.
https://americansongwriter.com/a-deeper-look-at-the-meaning-behind-in-the-air-tonight-by-phil-collins/.

32a) Ramm, Benjamin. "The Subversive Power of Calypso Music." *BBC.com,* October 11, 2017.
https://www.bbc.com/culture/article/20171010-the-surprising-politics-of-calypso.

Rob with Hudson Music Drum Editor Joe Bergamini

Track Listings

All tracks produced by Rob Mitzner and recorded @ C-Room Studio, Brooklyn, NY 2024-25

Afrobeat It
Wes Maples: tenor saxophone
Andrea Capozzoli: trumpet
Elias Meister: guitar
Dmitry Ishenko: bass
Rob Mitzner: drums, percussion
Music by Wes Maples, Elias Meister, Dmitry Ishenko & Rob Mitzner
Mixed by Charles Burst

Balkan Talkin'
Wes Maples: soprano saxophone
Elias Meister: guitar
Dmitry Ishenko: bass
Rob Mitzner: drums, percussion
Music by Elias Meister, Dmitry Ishenko & Rob Mitzner
Mixed by Charles Burst

Country Eggs 'n Jams
Elias Meister: guitar
Dmitry Ishenko: bass
Rob Mitzner: drums, percussion
Music by Elias Meister, Dmitry Ishenko & Rob Mitzner
Mixed by Charles Burst

Dr. John
Elias Meister: guitar
Dmitry Ishenko: bass
Rob Mitzner: drums, washboard, percussion
Music by Elias Meister, Dmitry Ishenko & Rob Mitzner
Mixed by Charles Burst

EDMnM's
Elias Meister: guitar, synthesizers
Dmitry Ishenko: synthesizers
Rob Mitzner: drums
Music by Elias Meister, Dmitry Ishenko & Rob Mitzner
Mixed by Charles Burst

Folky Dokey
Elias Meister: electric & acoustic guitars
Dmitry Ishenko: bass
Rob Mitzner: drums, percussion
Music by Elias Meister, Dmitry Ishenko & Rob Mitzner
Mixed by Charles Burst

Fusion Intrusion
Elias Meister: guitar
Dmitry Ishenko: bass
Rob Mitzner: drums, percussion
Music by Elias Meister, Dmitry Ishenko & Rob Mitzner
Mixed by Charles Burst

Go-Go Get It
Wes Maples: tenor saxophone
Andrea Capozzoli: trumpet
Elias Meister: guitar
Dmitry Ishenko: bass
Rob Mitzner: drums, percussion
Music by Wes Maples, Andrea Capozzoli, Elias Meister, Dmitry Ishenko & Rob Mitzner
Mixed by Charles Burst

Hava Nagila Monster
Wes Maples: soprano saxophone
Elias Meister: guitar
Dmitry Ishenko: bass
Rob Mitzner: drums, percussion
"Hangu from Podoloy" (Trad.)
Mixed by Charles Burst

I Heart The '80s
Elias Meister: guitar
Dmitry Ishenko: bass
Rob Mitzner: drums, percussion
Music by Elias Meister, Dmitry Ishenko & Rob Mitzner
Mixed by Charles Burst

Jim Black Attack
Elias Meister: guitar
Dmitry Ishenko: bass
Rob Mitzner: drums, percussion
Music by Elias Meister, Dmitry Ishenko & Rob Mitzner
Mixed by Charles Burst

Kerfuffle Shuffle
Wes Maples: tenor saxophone
Andrea Capozzoli: trumpet
Elias Meister: guitar
Dmitry Ishenko: bass
Rob Mitzner: drums, percussion
Music by Wes Maples, Elias Meister, Dmitry Ishenko & Rob Mitzner
Mixed by Charles Burst

Levon It Be
Elias Meister: guitar
Dmitry Ishenko: bass
Rob Mitzner: drums, percussion
Music by Elias Meister, Dmitry Ishenko & Rob Mitzner
Mixed by Charles Burst

Mambo Jambo
Elias Meister: guitar
Dmitry Ishenko: bass
Rob Mitzner: drums, percussion
Music by Elias Meister, Dmitry Ishenko & Rob Mitzner
Mixed by Charles Burst

Mike Clark Spark
Wes Maples: tenor saxophone
Elias Meister: guitar
Dmitry Ishenko: bass
Rob Mitzner: drums, percussion
Music by Wes Maples, Elias Meister, Dmitry Ishenko & Rob Mitzner
Mixed by Charles Burst

Nineties Nails
Elias Meister: guitar
Dmitry Ishenko: bass
Rob Mitzner: drums, electronics
Music by Elias Meister, Dmitry Ishenko & Rob Mitzner
Mixed by Charles Burst

Orleans Machines
Elias Meister: guitar
Dmitry Ishenko: bass
Rob Mitzner: drums, percussion
Music by Elias Meister, Dmitry Ishenko & Rob Mitzner
Mixed by Charles Burst

Polka Party
Wes Maples: soprano saxophone
Elias Meister: guitar
Dmitry Ishenko: bass
Rob Mitzner: drums, percussion
Music by Wes Maples, Elias Meister, Dmitry Ishenko & Rob Mitzner
Mixed by Charles Burst

Power Ballad Salad
Elias Meister: guitar
Lars Potteiger: organ
Dmitry Ishenko: bass
Rob Mitzner: drums
Music by Elias Meister, Dmitry Ishenko & Rob Mitzner
Mixed by Charles Burst

Questlove's Best Love
Wes Maples: tenor saxophone
Andrea Capozzoli: trumpet
Elias Meister: guitar
Dmitry Ishenko: bass
Rob Mitzner: drums, percussion
Music by Wes Maples, Elias Meister, Dmitry Ishenko & Rob Mitzner
Mixed by Charles Burst

Ride the No Wave
Elias Meister: guitar
Dmitry Ishenko: bass
Rob Mitzner: drums
Music by Elias Meister, Dmitry Ishenko & Rob Mitzner
Mixed by Charles Burst

Rub-a Dub Dub
Elias Meister: guitar
Dmitry Ishenko: bass, synthesizers
Rob Mitzner: drums
Music by Elias Meister, Dmitry Ishenko & Rob Mitzner
Mixed by Charles Burst

Sing a Songo
Elias Meister: guitar
Dmitry Ishenko: bass
Rob Mitzner: drums, percussion
Music by Elias Meister, Dmitry Ishenko & Rob Mitzner
Mixed by Charles Burst

Ska-daddle
Wes Maples: tenor saxophone
Andrea Capozzoli: trumpet
Elias Meister: guitar
Dmitry Ishenko: bass
Rob Mitzner: drums, percussion
Music by Wes Maples, Elias Meister, Dmitry Ishenko & Rob Mitzner
Mixed by Charles Burst

Turf 'n Surf
Elias Meister: guitar
Dmitry Ishenko: bass
Rob Mitzner: drums
Music by Elias Meister, Dmitry Ishenko & Rob Mitzner
Mixed by Charles Burst

Ungrateful Dead
Elias Meister: guitar
Dmitry Ishenko: bass
Rob Mitzner: drums, percussion
Music by Elias Meister, Dmitry Ishenko & Rob Mitzner
Mixed by Charles Burst

Vintage Punk Junk
Elias Meister: guitar
Dmitry Ishenko: bass
Rob Mitzner: drums
Music by Elias Meister, Dmitry Ishenko & Rob Mitzner
Mixed by Charles Burst

Wally's Funk
Wes Maples: tenor saxophone
Andrea Capozzoli: trumpet
Elias Meister: guitar
Dmitry Ishenko: bass
Rob Mitzner: drums, percussion
Music by Wes Maples, Elias Meister, Dmitry Ishenko & Rob Mitzner
Mixed by Charles Burst

Welcome to the Jungle
Elias Meister: guitar
Dmitry Ishenko: bass, synthesizers
Rob Mitzner: drums
Music by Elias Meister, Dmitry Ishenko & Rob Mitzner
Mixed by Charles Burst

Xaxado of Your Smile
Elias Meister: guitar
Dmitry Ishenko: bass
Rob Mitzner: drums, percussion
Music by Elias Meister, Dmitry Ishenko & Rob Mitzner
Mixed by Charles Burst

Your Big Pop Chops
Elias Meister: guitar
Dmitry Ishenko: bass, synthesizers
Rob Mitzner: drums
Music by Elias Meister, Dmitry Ishenko & Rob Mitzner
Mixed by Charles Burst

Zombie Apo-calypso
Elias Meister: guitar
Dmitry Ishenko: bass
Rob Mitzner: drums, steel pan, percussion
Music by Elias Meister, Dmitry Ishenko & Rob Mitzner
Mixed by Charles Burst

Rob with Bernard Purdie & Liberty DeVitto

Rob with David Garibaldi

Acknowledgements

As we reach the acknowledgements, I'd like to acknowledge something rather obvious. Writing an almost-200-page book (again) has been one of the hardest challenges of my life. A project of this enormous magnitude takes a whole team of people to push it over the finish line, and mine is the best in the business. In 2020, Hudson Music and Rob Wallis took a chance on an unknown author with a whole lot to say, and here we are five years later doing a sequel. I'm immensely grateful to him, my editor Joe Bergamini and the whole team at Hudson and Hal Leonard.

Then there's the band. I simply could not have created this book and the music that accompanies it without their expertise, musical knowledge and friendship. Dmitry Ishenko and I have worked together for over 20 years and everything I do is so much better when he's there. Elias Meister is a powerhouse guitarist and an incredible overall musician. It's been amazing to explore all this different music with these guys and realize that they can handle just about anything and make it sound authentic. We also had a pretty darn good time doing it. Wes Maples conjured up the horn parts on a bunch of tracks and his awesome playing and deep musical knowledge really took them to the next level. Andrea Capozzoli and Lars Potteiger are both longtime friends, and their killer playing is on these tracks too. I'm immensely grateful to all of them for their contributions.

I'm equally appreciative of my team behind the scenes. Ricky Hammerschmidt has designed both my books and made them look better than I ever could have imagined. He's a rock star. Charles Burst mixed all the music and he's a rock star too. He knows exactly how I want the drums to sound. Thomas Mester is one of the best photographers around and I'm lucky to have his beautiful pictures throughout this book.

I'm also privileged to have the support of the best drum companies in the world. I've never been the type who collects a ton of gear. I like instruments that sound great, get the job done and can take a lickin' and keep on tickin'. You know...Stuff You Can Use. Big thanks to Yamaha Drums (Greg Crane), Paiste Cymbals (Tim Shahady & Javier Caudillo), Remo (Roger Johnson), Vic Firth (Brian Stockard) and Low Boy Custom Beaters (Jeremy Brieske & Nate Babbs) for always making sure I have the best rig in the biz. These products make me feel inspired to play every single time I sit down behind the kit. I'd also like to thank Eric Leiderman, producer of *Late Night with Seth Meyers* for giving me a shot at the coolest gig on the planet and Dan Shinder of Drum Talk TV for believing in me and first introducing me to the folks at Hudson Music. The drum community is such a warm and supportive group. It's a privilege to work with these people and an even greater privilege to call many of them my friends.

Last but not least, I want to thank my family. Family is everything, and without their support this book wouldn't exist. My mom first suggested I take up the drums at age 12, and I can only wonder what was going through her head as she sat in Studio 8G at 30 Rock watching me play on NBC last year. I'd also like to thank my sister Jen, brother-in-law Greg and nieces Mia and Emma. I'm blessed to have the support of my extended family too. We lost my Uncle Chuck recently and I'm dedicating this book to him. Most of all, there's my partner Rebecca. I truly couldn't have done any of this without her.

So, I'd now like to acknowledge that acknowledgements are over and these are the most wonderful people in the world. Thank you, a million times over. As the great Dom Famularo would say, "onward and upward." So...**EVEN MORE STUFF YOU CAN USE???**

About the Author

Originally from the Washington D.C. area, New York-based drummer Rob Mitzner has recorded for Billboard Top-10 charting albums and films, recently appearing on NBC's *Late Night with Seth Meyers* as the guest drummer with the 8G Band. He is the author of the Amazon best-selling book *DRUMMING IN A BAND: STUFF YOU CAN USE* (Hudson Music) and his credits include over 80 albums across many genres.

His first drum teacher was Steve "Freelance" Larrance, who taught him that the drummer "drives the bus." After high school, he attended Brown University in Providence, RI, graduating with B.A. in Music and Political Science. While in college, he began studying with Bob Gullotti, who taught him the importance of melody on the drums. After graduating, he moved to Boston to begin a professional career, working with artists like Jerry Bergonzi, Bruce Gertz, Sam Kininger and Andrea Capozzoli. He then relocated to New York, where he gets to play a different style of music with an awesome band nearly every night.

This musical versatility has taken him around the world playing jazz, rock, pop, hip-hop, country and R&B, gracing stages from Lincoln Center to Caesar's Palace. He has been featured as a both a player and a writer in publications such as *DownBeat* magazine, *Modern Drummer* and Drumeo and proudly endorses Yamaha Drums, Paiste Cymbals, Vic Firth Sticks, Remo heads and Low Boy Custom Beaters.

He has served as a guest lecturer and clinician at NYU's Clive Davis Institute, The Percussive Arts Society (PASIC), Albright College and The Delaware Drum Show. When he's not performing or doing masterclasses, Rob runs C-Room Studio in Brooklyn where he records remote tracks for artists across the world, writes articles for music publications and drinks way too much coffee.